THE BEST
SPIRITUAL
WRITING
2001

THE BEST
SPIRITUAL
WRITING
2001

EDITED BY
PHILIP ZALESKI

INTRODUCTION BY
ANDRE DUBUS III

HarperSanFrancisco
A Division of HarperCollinsPublishers

THE BEST SPIRITUAL WRITING 2001. Copyright © 2001 by
HarperCollins Publishers, Inc. All rights reserved. Printed in the United States
of America. No part of this book may be used or reproduced in any manner
whatsoever without written permission except in the case of brief quotations
embodied in critical articles and reviews. For information address HarperCollins
Publishers, Inc., 10 East 53rd Street, New York, NY 10022.

HarperCollins books may be purchased for educational, business, or sales
promotional use. For information please write: Special Markets Department,
HarperCollins Publishers, Inc., 10 East 53rd Street, New York, NY 10022.

HarperCollins Web site: http://www.harpercollins.com

HarperCollins®, ▄®, and HarperSanFrancisco™ are trademarks
of HarperCollins Publishers Inc.

FIRST EDITION

Library of Congress Cataloging Card Number 98–12368
ISSN: 1525–5980

ISBN 0–06–251772–4

01 02 03 04 05 ❖RRD(H) 10 9 8 7 6 5 4 3 2 1

Contents

PHILIP ZALESKI

Preface

In early December 1968, a week before his death, something wonderful befell the monk and writer Thomas Merton. He had been on the road since September, passing through California, Alaska, Hawaii, and India on his way to an international monastic conference in Thailand. The barrage of strange impressions had taken their toll. Exhilarated, exhausted, torn between homesickness and wanderlust, his habitual round of mass and divine office, *lectio divina* and manual labor torn asunder, Merton was ready to be lifted to a new level of being. The opportunity came in the forests of Ceylon, as he stood before the three colossal Buddhas at the caves of Polonnaruwa:

> I am able to approach the Buddhas barefoot and undisturbed, my feet in wet grass, wet sand. Then the silence of the extraordinary faces. The great smiles. Huge and yet subtle. Filled with every possibility, questioning nothing, knowing everything, rejecting nothing.... Looking at these figures I was suddenly, almost forcibly, jerked clean out of the habitual, half-tied vision of things, and an inner clearness, clarity, as if exploding from the rocks themselves, became evident and obvious.

That a Catholic monk enjoyed this moment of insight in a Buddhist land has provoked considerable interest, even leading to speculation that Merton planned to renounce his vows and remain abroad, perhaps as a student of the Dalai Lama. But this seems improbable; Merton was entranced by many spiritual paths, from Islam to Zen, but he was an intensely devout Christian nonetheless, and Christians from St. Paul on have drawn inspiration from the iconography and practices of other faiths. More suggestive, I think, is his emphasis on the "silence" of the enormous statues. It is the first thing that he notices, and he returns to it again and again. The Buddhas of Polonnaruwa stand for a way of life that "needs nothing" and can therefore "afford to be silent, unnoticed, undiscovered." They have "seen through every question without trying to discredit anyone or anything—*without refutation*—without establishing some other argument. . . . For the doctrinaire," Merton adds, "such silence can be frightening."

Here, then, we have the paradox, which nipped at Merton's heels throughout his life, of a best-selling writer extolling the virtues of silence. What does it mean when a man pours out an ocean of poetry, essays, biography, autobiography, novels, journals, letters, and spiritual reflections yet seeks safe harbor in the land beyond words? What can we make of an author whose memoir is entitled, in its English edition, *Elected Silence?* We find a clue in *The Sign of Jonas* (1953), where Merton writes of the early disciples of Jesus that "the more they loved one another and loved God, the more they declared his Word. . . . That is the only possible reason for speaking—but it justifies speaking without end, as long as speech grows up from silence and brings your soul to silence once again."

This statement, I have come to believe, explains not only Thomas Merton's vocation but also that of all who shoulder the great task of spiritual writing. The spiritual writer has twin duties—one shared by all authors, the other a requirement of her special post: she must write well, and she must write truth. One learns the first through school, workshops, and thousands of hours of trial and error. But how to learn to write truth? Merton suggests that if this is our aim, our education must involve a periodic return to silence. The spiritual writer emerges from the silent world, the eternal spaces; for a while she plunges, pen in hand, into the noise and stench, heat and pain of creativity; and then she returns to silence. This silence cannot be compromised. Note that there is no synonym for silence. *Quiet* is not the same, neither is *stillness, peace, rest,* or *taciturnity.* Silence is an absolute; as such, it partakes of the nature of God. It is, not, however, to be understood as rejection of the world. Return to the Buddhas of Polonnaruwa: "the great smiles . . . filled with every possibility, questioning nothing, knowing everything, rejecting nothing." All art, all prayer, all good works manifest in some way the silence of which Merton speaks.

Merton here is making a demand so radical that to carry it out would turn the world of literature topsy-turvy. He proposes that the writer must be something more than a writer: he must be a saint, or at least a saint-in-the-making, for it is the saints who partake regularly of this silent world. Such a prescription, one imagines, will redden many an ear. Doesn't the poor wordsmith have enough to do, toiling all day in the fields of language, trimming a verb here, planting a pronoun there, praying all the while that he will produce a worthy harvest? And now must he be a holy man as well? Let's not flinch at the truth: Isn't the typical writer a heavy drinking, chain-smoking, promiscuous rebel? Isn't his proper habitat the garret (or the barstool) rather than the cloister? The evidence seems pretty damning. Paul Johnson, in a rather nasty book entitled *Intellectuals,* demonstrates vividly the moral and spiritual failures of a host of significant authors, including Rousseau, Shelley, Marx, Brecht, Hemingway, and Sartre. He makes a strong case for his final warning that "one of the principal lessons of our tragic century . . . is—beware intellectuals."

But perhaps it need not be this way. Merton proposes a different approach to the artistic life, born in hope instead of distrust, based upon a perception of the human being as a creature whose birthright includes heaven as well as earth. Every age has witnessed its share of men and women who exemplify this approach. Great artists of great integrity, like Ralph Waldo Emerson, Simone Weil, and John Henry Newman, come readily enough to mind, and there are a thousand more.

What qualities set these authors apart from their fellows? What gives their words the special dignity and beauty that mark the best spiritual writing? Rephrasing Merton, we might say that the best spiritual writers are entirely at home in both the world of words and the world of silence. Just as there exists a hierarchy of literary talents, gauged by one's sensitivity to language (Dante at the top, tin-eared hack at the bottom), so too is there a hierarchy of spiritual talents, gauged by one's sensitivity to this realm of silence. Of these two worlds, that of silence—or the sacred—takes precedence. It is hardly an accident that few of the founders of the world's major religions wrote anything at all. We have no letters from Jesus, no memoirs from Buddha. Muhammad gave us a book, but Islamic tradition tells us that the words were not his but dictated by the angel Gabriel. To be sure, Jesus' parables rank as great literature, for they instruct in delightful, surprising ways. They are brilliant miniatures. In them love and imagination meld into a perfect whole. But Jesus' parables conform to a standard that is not that of the academy; one cannot imagine Jesus winning a Pulitzer Prize. His parables have nothing in common with literary trends, with art for art's sake, with any accommodation to style at the expense of subject. We might say, laying aside all theological considerations, that the words of Jesus carry special force because they arise from the integrity of his life, the totality of his wisdom, and they speak directly to our souls.

This, then, may be the authentic task of the spiritual writer: to converse soul to soul, passing on what light she may possess. Her calling is to be a writer-at-work and a saint-in-the-making; her responsibility to point beyond writing to the spirit; her happiness to polish, in herself and in others, the triple gem of beauty, truth, and goodness. Those who undertake this great work enter largely uncharted territory, unknown to literary criticism and only provisionally mapped by those who have gone before. The sense of adventure is palpable; the possibilities for art are enormous.

As we begin to survey this unknown landscape, questions often ignored in the pursuit of beauty come to the fore: How does the artist balance art and morality? Must he worry about how his work affects his fellow humans? The earth? The heavens? To what extent is his creative activity a reflection of his being? This last is a prodigious puzzle. We know that art has its own laws, which seem distant from those of human psychology. Yet who can doubt that words that spring from one's mind and heart in some way mirror one's soul? Just as a child reflects her parents, so does art reflect its creator. The production of artists, writes Pope John Paul II in his 1998 *Letter to Artists,* "becomes a unique disclosure of their own being, of what they are and of how they are what they are."

As such, spiritual writing must be as wide and deep as its maker. There is no room here for a Pollyannaish approach to the genre, in which the only fit art is perky or do-goodish, a literary smile button. The spiritual writer expunges suffering from his work at his peril, for suffering is the greatest spiritual mystery, a path to wisdom and a mode of salvation. Indeed, any aesthetic bound by ideology—iconoclasm in the eighth-century Byzantine Empire or socialist realism during the heyday of international communism—will always be inimical to true art and true spirituality, for it denies the freedom of expression that the fundamental dignity of the human being entails.

At the same time, there's no need to dust off that hair shirt just yet. Being a good writer and being a good person (I am told on good authority) are a life's work, and one has to expect plenty of backsliding. A sense of humor remains essential. Accepting Merton's call to be saints-and-artists does signal, I think, that we need to detach ourselves from fashions and fads, that we should work with one eye on the earth and the other on heaven, that we must return regularly to silence. The more we dwell in this mysterious realm, source of all beauty, the more we will benefit. As the Polish poet Cyprian Norwid wrote, "Beauty is to enthuse us for work, and work is to raise us up." The more acquainted we grow with silence, the more our work will resound with that ineffable truth that all human beings need and seek. Perhaps Dostoyevsky was right when he wrote in *The Idiot* that "beauty will save the world."

As always, submissions are encouraged for future volumes of *The Best Spiritual Writing*. Please send writings to Philip Zaleski, 138 Elm Street, Smith College, Northampton, MA 01063. The best way for a periodical to submit material is to add *The Best Spiritual Writing* series, at the above address, to its complimentary subscription list.

Many people helped in the production of this volume. My thanks to John Loudon, Gideon Weil, Meg Lenihan, and the entire crew at HarperSanFrancisco; to Kim Witherspoon, David Forrer, and everyone at Witherspoon Associates; to Andre Dubus III; to all others who contributed in ways large and small; and, as always, to my most precious Carol, John, and Andy.

Introduction

Not long ago on an August afternoon, I found myself in a sea-side town on the West Coast. Its main street was on the water at the base of a steep rise dotted with brush, and on the ridge were large split-level houses cantilevered in the air, their concrete footings exposed in the eroding soil of the hillside. Down below, my family and two others on vacation with us were waiting for the ferry to take us farther north, but we were enjoying wandering through the shops on the beach selling everything from hand-tooled leather hats and vests to candles and playing cards and pastel paintings of the waterfront, which smelled of diesel fuel, dried seaweed, and the barnacle-thickened posts of the dock, its worn planks splattered with seagull droppings, the railings pitted with sand and sea salt.

The day was hot, and the doors and windows of the bars were open. We could hear the rock of their jukeboxes and stereo systems, could see the neon beer signs in the cool-looking darkness, but with seven children under the age of thirteen, this wasn't the place to refresh ourselves, so we ended up in an ice cream parlor on the water, ordered double and triple cones, then kept strolling with napkins in hand, stopping every few feet to wipe melting ice cream off the chins and fingers of all our kids. Up ahead was a bookstore, and I scooped up my two-year-old son and stepped inside.

In her essay "The Nature and Aim of Fiction," Flannery O'Connor writes, "The beginning of human knowledge is through the senses, and the fiction writer begins where human perception begins." Which is to say I didn't yet *know* I was in the wrong place, but I certainly began to *sense* it; first was the smell: this place didn't *smell* like a bookstore. Where was that beckoning scent of pine shelves and dust and slightly damp paper and the old-glue scent of hundreds of aging hardcovers? What I smelled instead was some kind of incense, a cross between ginger root and sage. On the sound system was chanting and the low tinkling of chimes. A woman sat behind the glass counter dressed in what looked like a Hindi sari, though she herself was blond, tan, and a severe-looking fifty. In the display case in front of her, laid out on black velvet, were polished stones and rocks in varying shades of white, pink, blue, and green, and on a small card beside them was written: *Spiritual Healers.* The woman and I nodded at each other, then she looked hard at the ice cream cone in my son's hand, at his messy chin and sticky little fingers. I smiled and told her I wouldn't let him touch anything, then took a few steps closer to the shelves full of books. But the words *Fiction* or *Poetry* were nowhere in sight, only *Healing, Psychotherapy, Transcendence, Self-Help,* and *Spiritual.* On the walls were posters of winged goddesses rising out of bears and deer, of rainbows and bright orbs whose fiery rays emanated outward and upward. I had, of course, stumbled into a *spiritual* bookshop, and I smiled and nodded at the lady behind the counter and got out of there as fast as I could.

I walked back down the sidewalk with my son, feeling vaguely reactionary and shallow, asking myself once again why all that transcendent language and imagery turned me off so much. But then I found another bookstore, one full of fiction and poetry, some Miles Davis playing, the man behind the counter in a T-shirt, smoking a cigarette and reading a fat hardcover with no dust jacket. This place even had that *smell* I'd been hoping for, and the back windows were open so you got the smell of the waterfront, too. I was low on cash and didn't buy anything, but when I left I felt revived in some higher part of myself.

Back at the dock, we waited for the ferry and watched the kids play and fight and play some more. I thought harder about the spiritual bookshop and why a place seemingly devoted to expanding one's consciousness left me so uninspired. Didn't I try to expand my own consciousness every time I sat down to write, which was daily? Wasn't I attempting some small act of transcendence every Sunday I attended church with my family? Or, for that matter, when I ran five or six miles along a country road? Or read a story to my children? Hadn't I, like so many of my generation, been worked on by the healers of the New Age with their totems and inner children and body work? Maybe I was just a low, sleepy animal too tied to the earthly and all of its fallen pleasures. Maybe I wasn't very "spiritual"!

Soon enough the ferry docked, and we climbed aboard, and I led the kids to the seats at the top. We got settled, and as the big boat pulled away, I looked out at the town on the water, the long double row of squat buildings beneath the high hill and the millionaire houses on the ridge. There was something resonant about that image, though I didn't know what it was until I saw the deep rain ruts in the hill's surface, the exposed footings of the house piers, which would one day fail, sending the fancy homes tumbling down to earth where the rest of us were. This was a completely material image, but it reminded me of all things that advertise themselves as spiritual and above the dirt and noise of Main Street, as if life is a staircase or mountain we ascend one level at a time and with patience and diligence and sacrifice achieve a higher state of being where all the answers lie. But there, in that image before me, was the rest of it, too: deny the earth and her gravity and hard rains and rutted soil, and she will pull you down. And it occurred to me that the form of spirituality I trust most comes directly from the sensual mess of life itself. Not above it or cut off from it, but *through* it.

It was an image that brought me this moment of insight, one that gave off a palpable sense of mystery my rational mind would probably never fully penetrate. It had given me an insight into what I was feeling and thinking, but it brought no real answers. I thought about the images in the spiritual bookshop I could no longer make out on shore, all those posters of rainbows and goddesses and golden suns on mountaintops and spirits rising out of animals. While many of them were probably derived from revered Native American stories and myths, so much life and resonance had been blanched out of them, their colors devoid of any undertones, almost gaudy, calling attention to themselves as loudly as a political slogan telling me what to think. And that's why they left me so cold; they had some sort of singular point to make about spiritual transcendence and how to do it, and when images are created solely to make points, their mystery is denied, their inherent truths reduced, their soul lost.

As a fiction writer, I've come to trust images and the stories within them implicitly. A few years ago, a woman in her seventies hired me to read her novel-in-progress and to give any suggestions for possible improvement. The opening scenes were wonderful; with precise, honest prose, she put me deeply into a textural landscape with her characters, all of whom felt three-dimensional and real to me. But fifty or so pages into the manuscript, things changed. While the prose itself was no less polished and self-assured, what the words were actually capturing no longer felt real or true; the characters had gone from being round to flat, and behind all these well-constructed paragraphs I could feel the author's presence as surely as one does the puppeteer behind the black velvet curtain of the puppet show. In over a dozen years of leading writing workshops, I had seen and felt this many times before (and I was not above making this mistake myself!). I suspected this gifted writer was no longer trying to find the story within her; instead, she had a point to make and was using her fiction to make it.

At our next meeting I told her how her characters were becoming one-dimensional. The women, instead of being complex, flawed human beings, were now being reduced to either total victims or complete superwomen. The men, too, were being painted as nothing but bullies or saints. There was no middle ground, no gray, no mystery. I asked her the same question I would try to have the courage to ask myself. Was she trying to say something in particular with this novel? She said yes, in fact, she was. By writing the life story of one woman in the twentieth century, her aim was to show just how harmful three thousand years of patriarchy had been to both sexes, especially women. This is certainly a noble and important intellectual goal, I told her. The problem was that her desire to illuminate such a theme, to transcend the concrete details of her characters' lives to make such a brightly burning point, was killing not only her characters but the soul of her story as well.

In his *Paris Review* interview, William Faulkner said, "The most important thing is insight, that is to be—curiosity—to wonder, to mull, and to muse why it is that man does what he does, and if you have that, then I don't think talent makes much difference, whether you've got it or not."

Blaise Pascal wrote, "Anything written to please the author is worthless."

I asked my writing student to try to let go of her desire to say anything in particular with her novel, to trust instead that there's more to her characters and their lives than only the oppression of patriarchy. And if she could not completely let go of her intent, then at least to put a Faulknerian question mark on it, to tell herself: I'm going to write this woman's story as fully and honestly as I can; *will* I end up saying something about patriarchy?

In his essay "The Magic Show," Tim O'Brien puts it this way:

> My general argument is that characterization is achieved not through a "pinning down" process but rather through a process that opens up and releases mysteries of the human spirit. The object is not to "solve" a character—to expose some hidden secret—but instead to deepen and enlarge the riddle itself. Too often, I believe, characterization fails precisely because it attempts to characterize. It narrows, it pins down, it explicates, it solves. . . . For me, at least, such solutions do not square with my sense of the immense complexity of man's spirit.

Some of the most intelligent and knowledgeable people I have had the pleasure of working with in the writing classroom have been psychologists, spiritual healers, members of the clergy, social workers of all kinds—"people workers," a friend of mine called himself and those devoted to helping other human beings. These hardworking, compassionate men and women had worked in prisons and nursing homes, halfway houses, group homes, psychiatric wards, and emergency rooms; they'd seen and heard about all the terrible and even wonderful things we can do to one another. So many of them came to me in their fifties and sixties, seemingly bursting with stories they had to tell. One would think it would simply be a matter of guiding them to their own abilities and letting them go. But, like most things in our lives, it wasn't that easy.

We all bring a host of our own personal demons and angels to the creative process, and any number of psychic obstacles can get in the way, but with those writers deeply versed in the study of human behavior, I began to notice a common stumbling block: they knew too much! All of their formidable clinical training and expertise had led them, consciously or otherwise, to the conclusion that they knew just what their characters' shadow lives were and, what's more, how to cure them of it and thereby earn that epiphanic and redemptive ending. The result tended to be flat characters, didactic prose, predictable story lines, and that same quality I'd seen in those posters at the spiritual bookshop—potentially rich images robbed of their essential complexity, their very truth.

In group discussions, we tried to get to the heart of the problem. Some, as is their right, saw no problem at all; these were psychologically sound and spiritually uplifting stories, and we were being too hard on them. I, and others, voiced the concern that maybe we weren't being hard enough. We made our case that because the writer already seemed to have all the answers, the humanity of the characters felt reduced and that these stories lacked a certain depth and texture from which no real spiritual uplifting was earned.

In *The Writing Life,* Annie Dillard reminds us,

> Giacometti's drawings and paintings show his bewilderment and persistence. If he had not acknowledged his bewilderment, he would not have persisted. A twentieth-century master of drawing, Rico Lebrun, taught that "the draftsman must aggress; only by persistent assault will the live image capitulate and give up its secret to an unrelenting line." Who but an artist fierce to know—not fierce to seem to know— would suppose that a live image possessed a secret?

Ultimately, it does not take much work to convince priests or psychologists that images possess secrets; our more difficult challenge was to try to convince some of them that their stories did not necessarily have to be redemptive or salvific in any way. Their job as writers was not to rescue or cure or fix or save their characters but simply to *paint* them as honestly and fully as possible with, as O'Connor wrote, "all those concrete details of life that make actual the mystery of our position on earth."

"Yes," one of the writers would say, "but what if you want to *transcend* those details? What if you want to be a *spiritual* writer?"

How, I wondered, had the word *spiritual* somehow been separated from the word *mystery?* But there it was again, the implied belief that spiritual means *above* everything, free of the smells and texture and unanswered questions of our lives, not through an act of transcendence but one seemingly of avoidance and escape.

It is revealing that books on spirituality and psychology are so often lumped together in the same sections of bookstores from coast to coast. On the one hand, this may be a positive development; how can the discipline of psychology continue to survive if it stays only in the realm of the nonmystical and seemingly ego centered? Yet so many of these works still promise their readers a treatment or cure for their particular set of "issues" or pathology or wounds. And perhaps this is why books on spirituality are placed alongside them. Both tend to be seen by publishers and booksellers and ultimately by readers as works that illuminate the path to transcendence. But without the pull of earth and its very soul, there can be no flight.

I think of a writer friend of mine, a Catholic priest and licensed social worker who works in the prison system. One of his duties there is to make the final decision on when a convicted sexual predator who has served his time is free to go. After all the other conditions for release have been met by the inmate, my friend insists on one more: the convicted sex offender must look him in the eye and describe his crimes in generous concrete and specific detail. Many of the inmates refuse, saying they're past all that now; they're "healed." Some even say they're too "spiritual" to do that. My friend then denies their parole. He tells them that only when they are able to go back through the heart of their violation against others, one honest, grounded detail at a time, will he begin to believe their claims of spiritual growth.

Again, we can go back to Flannery O'Connor:

The Manicheans separated spirit and matter. To them all material things were evil. They sought pure spirit and tried to approach the infinite without the mediation of matter. This is also pretty much the modern spirit, and for the sensibility infected with it, fiction is hard if not impossible to write because fiction is so very much an incarnational art. . . . The fact is that the materials of the fiction writer are the humblest. Fiction is about everything human and we are made out of dust, and if you scorn getting yourself dusty, then you shouldn't try to write fiction. It's not a grand enough job for you.

It is no accident that O'Connor, one of our grittiest and more sensual writers, is also constantly described as one of our most spiritual.

Great soul is found in art and all of its concrete, specific, and sensual particulars. And while I have been speaking here of fiction writing, it seems to me that no writing can approach the truly spiritual until it seeks to evoke the lowly terrain of the soul and the body that holds it. This is precisely what Philip Zaleski has been doing with this anthology since its inception in 1998 when he wrote in that first preface, "I take the best spiritual writing to be prose or poetry that addresses, in a manner both profound and beautiful, the workings of the soul."

The *soul*. That is what was missing for me in that spiritual bookshop on the West Coast that summer afternoon, yet there was plenty of it back out in the grit and noise and heat of the street and in that other bookstore, too, where, incidentally, I also saw copies of this very anthology. Now we have a new volume of poetry and prose that promises us a spiritual experience of some kind, and because these writers—the celebrated and not yet known—have not neglected the province of the soul, the very texture of our daily lives, I know we can fully expect our spirits to be truly nourished and illuminated here. As Lao Tzu instructed us, readers and writers alike: "Soften the light; become one with the dusty world."

THE BEST
SPIRITUAL
WRITING
2001

Secrets of the Confessional

from *The New York Times Magazine*

The first time I heard confession was a couple of weeks after my ordination in 1973, at St. Matthew's Cathedral in Washington, D.C., where John F. Kennedy's requiem Mass was celebrated. The penitent was a tourist who had wandered in almost by accident. "I was on my way to a McDonald's," he said, "but I saw the church and remembered Kennedy's funeral—then I noticed the little green light in the confessional, so I came in. I'm not really sure of what I want."

"Well," I replied, "I hope you don't want a Big Mac with french fries, because if so, you have made a great mistake."

He chuckled, then said: "Look, Father, it's been a long, long time. I'm going to tell you things you have never heard in confession before."

"That's not too difficult," I said. "This is my first confession. Anything you say will be a shock to me." He started to laugh, hard. Those in line fled to the other confession line.

I wasn't taking the occasion lightly. The mystical tradition speaks of something called giddiness before the sacred, a way of expressing the infinite disproportion between you and the mystery with which, somehow, you have become involved. I was simply feeling the infinite disproportion of it all.

Many think of confession as a frightening exposure of the deepest self. The confessor looks into the darkest regions of the human psyche, uncovering the most embarrassing secrets—not only what you have actually done, but also what you wanted to do. (Confessor: "Did you entertain impure thoughts?" Honest penitent: "No, Father, they entertained me.") And so, one does everything possible to seek refuge in euphemisms and abstractions and, above all, to avoid being heard by those waiting outside the confessional.

And yet my experience as a confessor has had nothing to do with hearing juicy secrets. Most penitents I have had repeat formulas that they learned in second grade and refer to their sins in formal categories. I have heard things like "I was unfaithful twenty-three times in deed, and about fifty times in thought." I remember a political exile telling me, "I have tortured prisoners." I thought, "At last, a new sin!" But what could I say to this man— tell him not to do it again? Suggest counseling? Then he really stunned me by asking, "Must I tell you exactly how many times?"

I have often heard confessions in very unlikely places, like subways and theaters. Once the captain of a plane approached me in midflight. Terrified, I asked him, "Do you know something that I don't know about this flight?" He assured me that nothing was wrong; he had simply gotten the urge. Yet what he said didn't seem urgent to me. Nor did those other on-the-spot confessions. I used to think that people who felt a burning need to confess minor infractions had no inner life—or that their outer life was either pretty dull or, as in my torturer penitent, frighteningly immoral. Similarly, I used to think that list-style confession was a sign of an underdeveloped or legalistic view of morality.

Eventually, those in charge changed the rite of confession. They added Scripture readings, encouraged a conversational style, and introduced "reconciliation rooms" that resembled a cheap psychologist's office. Priests studied "counseling" and learned to modulate their voices supportively. Confession became therapy, and a confessor unable to provoke a therapeutic experience was judged worthless. In truth, however, nothing in our vocation qualified us as therapists.

On the day of my ordination, my own mother, suitably proud, taught me that lesson. "I used to think priests knew everything," she told me. "Now I worry, because you are a priest and I know you don't know anything."

Since then I have come to know this: Confession is not therapy, nor is it moral accounting. At its best, it is the affirmation that the ultimate truth of our interior life is our absolute poverty, our radical dependence, our unquenchable thirst, our desperate need to be loved. As St. Augustine knew so well, confession is ultimately about praise.

Confessing even the most dramatic struggles, I have found, people reach for the simplest language, that of a child before a world too confusing to understand. Silent wonder is the most natural response to a revelation that surpasses all words, a beauty that is beyond images; if one must say anything at all, what better way than in a few words that, in their very formalism, protect the infinite majesty of this mystery? The language of the inner life is not the language of experts or of eloquent dramatists or of a mature and healthy self-acceptance. The language of the inner life is a serene silence, a deep hurt, a boundless desire, and, occasionally, a little laughter.

Night Eyes

from *Utne Reader*

Fifteen years ago, I was abducted—there is no other word for it—into the realm of the Dream. It occurred without precedent or preamble: One day I was going about my business, with its usual mix of high goals and low concerns; the next, I was cast away in a far country from which I've never quite returned. Before I knew that there are dreams and there are *dreams,* I treated them as most people do: as nocturnal reshufflings of the mental deck; as fantasy and wish fulfillment; as psychic leftovers, those emotional coffee grounds and crumpled-up impulses toward sex and violence ditched nightly down some inner Disposall.

But suddenly my dreams, usually hazy and easily dismissed, acquired a jolting, Technicolor realism. They gleamed with mysteries both opaque and insistent, their meaning tantalizingly beyond my grasp. In one, a maniac heralded as "the greatest mass murderer in the history of mankind" had "escaped from a cell" and was chasing me with an ax to decapitate me. In another, Death peered through my basement window, his gaunt face glowing like phosphorus beneath his hood, coolly casing the joint. Necks were a puzzling leitmotiv. Six long needles were stuck in my "neck-brain" by a circle of primitive tribesmen; a "World War II bullet" was lodged in my neck, and a kindly Chinese surgeon removed it; or I was crawling through a tunnel full of crumbling bones in a Mayan "necropolis." ("Neck-cropolis?" I asked myself, mindful of dreams' incorrigible punning, but I could make no further sense of it.)

I often went to my job as a magazine editor still enveloped in their creepy aura, determined to soldier on. But after one terrifying dream in which torturers hung an iron pot filled with red-hot coals beneath my chin, I couldn't ignore them any longer. I was sure that something inside me had gone drastically wrong. Each successive dream had spelled it out more explicitly until it glared down at me from a neon marquee: cancer.

I went to see a doctor and blurted out my fears, embarrassed that my only symptoms were a fistful of nightmares. After skeptically pressing and prodding my neck he informed me he felt nothing out of the ordinary. He suggested, not unsympathetically, that I was suffering from job-related stress, which was true enough. I awkwardly asked if there was an organ that might fit my dream's peculiar image of a "neck-brain." He suggested the thyroid gland and ordered a blood test, but my hormone levels were perfectly normal.

The nightmares continued. I badgered the doctor for a more complete workup, and this time, palpating my neck, he detected a hard lump—a thyroid nodule. A scan was ordered, revealing a dark suspicious mass that he assured me was almost certainly benign. Some weeks later, I felt a grim twinge of vindication when a needle biopsy confirmed what my dreams had hinted—it was a cancerous malignancy.

I took a sabbatical from my job. My days filled with a procession of friends, relatives, colleagues, and medical experts, each bearing conflicting advice, none willing to give my dreams their due. I could scarcely blame them. If I couldn't understand my bizarre visions, how could anyone else? But I felt doubly a pariah, self-exiled from an inner world I could not comprehend, yet regarded with suspicion by those who thought I was giving my dreams too much importance. I drove people to distraction trying to explain how *these* dreams were different—deeper, wider, higher, more *real*—but they didn't seem to know what I was talking about.

One evening before falling asleep, I scribbled, in some desperation, a formal request in the dream notebook I'd started to keep: *What is the direction of a cure?* That night, I had a startling vision: *Under the ground a white, snakelike worm is turning in upon itself in a perfect spiral. When its head reaches the center, blinding rays of light shoot out, and a voice solemnly intones: "You have been living on the outer shell of your being—the way out is the way in!"*

The image was as repulsive as a moldering grave ("The worms crawl in, the worms crawl out" goes the childhood singsong). I would come to understand much later that the worm was an ancient, archetypal image of the spiraling inner journey often framed as a kind of death and rebirth. But at the time, if I sought anything from my dreams, it was specifics: I wanted status reports on my illness, with symbols as clear as those on a TV weather map, not these mysterious hieroglyphs. My medical quest—finding the most accurate diagnosis, the best doctor, the ultimate cure—was tough enough. Now, when I was feeling that I needed to stay outwardly focused, my dreams were pulling me deeper within. In the weeks and months that followed, the conflict became ever more maddening. In the end, I chose surgery as much to still my dreams as to save my life.

The operation was more traumatic than I had anticipated. My cure left me wounded in body and spirit. I was unable and finally unwilling to step back on the merry-go-round of ambition. Driven by a journalist's curiosity and a need to feel less alone, I spent a decade interviewing hundreds of patients and doctors, plunging into the literatures of medicine and mythology, seeking new compass points for the healing process and a new map of my soul. I eventually wrote two books on the mind-body connection and found myself in a new career as a quasi–medical expert. But even after years of conscientious probing, I was haunted by a mystery.

What had been the source of the torrent of images that had threatened to submerge me even as I struggled for my life?

I had always been, in an unreflective way, a Freudian when it came to dream analysis. Dreams were elaborate concealments of the sex- and power-hungry id: Rip away the guise, and there, invariably, would be the glowering features of our instinctual being. According to Sigmund Freud's "sexual theory," which he championed over all other interpretive approaches, a dream, whether horrifying, ecstatic, or just plain baffling, had predictable mechanisms and symbols that could be deciphered.

Yet these dreams had made me feel utterly out of my depth. They had almost mystically anticipated events. (Had it been pure coincidence I'd dreamed that a Chinese surgeon took a "bullet" from my neck, and months later, a real Chinese surgeon—a Dr. Wang, the country's premier thyroid specialist and the spitting image of my dream doctor—had operated to remove my tumor?) They had galvanized me to act, almost against my will. What kind of dreams *were* these?

Most of us have had (or will have) at least one dream that stops us in our tracks. Such dreams tell us that we're not who we think we are. They reveal dimensions of experience beyond the everyday. They may shock us, console us, arouse us, or repulse us. Some are like parables, setting off a sharp detonation of insight; others are like gripping mystery tales, drawing us into the unknown; and still others are like mythic dramas or horror stories or even uproarious jokes. In our journey from childhood to old age, we may count them on one hand, yet they take their place alongside most memorable life events because they are so vivid and emblematic.

In the fifteen years since I began my exploration, modern researchers have begun using a host of terms—*impactful, transformative, transcendent*—to differentiate these big dreams from ordinary ones. In fact, as I had learned, many ancient cultures made the same distinction. I coined the term *healing dreams,* because they seem to have a singular intensity of purpose: to lead us to embrace our deepest contradictions—between flesh and spirit, self and other, shadow and light—in the name of wholeness. They very word for dream in Hebrew—*chalom*—derives from the verb "to be made healthy or strong." With remarkable consistency, healing dreams proclaim that we live on the merest outer shell of our potential and that the light we seek can be found in the darkness of a yet-unknown portion of our being.

I'd had what psychologists call "prodromal" dreams, which anticipate a medical problem not yet clinically detected. But our healing dreams extend far beyond matters of physical health; indeed, they are a distinct category of experience, with their own special character. Like drama, they often have unusually coherent narrative structures. Islamic dream texts refer to ordinary dreams as *azghas*—literally, "handfuls of dried grass and weeds," signifying a lack of arrangement. These differ from the more coherent messages of *ahkam,* "genuine inspirations from the Deity, warnings from a protecting power, or revelations of coming events." Storytelling in healing dreams tends to be more artful, containing a rich array of literary or cinematic devices—subplots, secondary characters, sudden reversals and surprise endings, flashbacks and flash-forwards, even voice-over narration and background music.

Healing dreams often involve a sense of the uncanny or paranormal. Within the dream, we may have special powers to telekinetically move objects; receive information as if via telepathy; levitate; transform ourselves into other creatures; visit heavens or hells. Dreamers report out-of-body experiences; actual events foreseen; talking with the departed; having a near-identical dream to that of a friend or loved one; and other strange synchronicities.

Such dreams can profoundly challenge our reigning models of reality. My firsthand experience with the precognitive power of dreams forced me to give serious thought to the mystical belief that time is an illusion. We may not be as purely earthbound as we think we are but beings of another sort, plying a sea of past, present, and future.

Most important, healing dreams, if we heed them, can be transformational—creating new attitudes toward ourselves and others, magnifying our spiritual understanding, deepening the feeling side of life, producing changes in careers and relationships, even affecting society itself. After a healing dream, one may never be the same again.

Before my illness, this interplay between the dream world and the real one was at odds with my understanding of how dreams worked. I remembered from my college psychology texts that there were various schools of dream interpretation, although they were seldom on speaking terms with one another. There were what might be called the symbolists, who took dream elements as representations of hidden meanings that could be decoded by a skilled interpreter. On the other hand were the phenomenologists, who said there was nothing hidden behind the curtain— dreams were dress rehearsals of new ways of being and doing, experiences that could in themselves lead to personal growth. And then there were physiological reductionists, who insisted dreams were mere neural discharges, "noisy signals sent up from the brain stem" that created random images. Dr. David Foulkes, a leading proponent of this now-resurgent viewpoint, has written, "The reason why dreamers can't understand what their dreams mean is that they don't mean anything." The dream, he has suggested, has no "message"; moreover, "if we persist in search for one, we're in the angel-counting business."

One of the great services rendered by Freud was his stalwart insistence that *all* dreams *were* meaningful. Severing dream interpretation from religious dogma, Freud attacked the lingering view that dreams with grotesque or "sinful" images were nonsense or worse. To the contrary, he said, the dreams we find most repellent are the very skeleton keys to self-revelation, and even a commonplace dream, passionately inspected, is a "royal road to the unconscious."

Freud enlisted Carl Jung, a brilliant young Swiss analyst, to help him dispel what he viewed as centuries of encrusted superstition. In one letter to his heir designate, Freud expressed his delight that they were setting out together to "conquer mythology," unaware that the obverse would soon come to pass. Jung had already begun to treat the dream less as a libidinal rebus than as a labyrinth leading to humanity's "collective unconscious." If Freud saw a snake as a phallic symbol, Jung was interested in its mythic heritage as a creature associated with wisdom and healing. And if Freud believed symbols were a dream's way of concealing the truth, Jung believed they were more an attempt to *reveal* it.

History has judged the founding work of both Freud and Jung to be a mix of brilliant insight and misconception, a legacy their successors still contend with. A therapist once remarked to me that it was a shame there were only these two lights to illuminate the vast region of dreams, but this is hardly true. The world's indigenous peoples possess a treasure trove of dream knowledge. The opinion endures among many Western psychiatrists that tribal peoples do not understand how to interpret their own dreams—indeed, naively believe them to be real occurrences. But non-Western cultures have long been aware of subtleties in dream life that the West has myopically missed.

In dreams, the psychoanalyst Erich Fromm once pronounced, "we are concerned exclusively with ourselves. . . . 'I am' is the only system to which thoughts and feelings refer." Yet the privatization of the dream remains a peculiarly Western practice. Dreams in many cultures—among the Plains Indians, for example—are a key component of social problem solving, with vital public and even political implications. The Zuni Indians of New Mexico have a custom of making public their "bad" dreams ("good" dreams, however, are sometimes withheld even from close relatives). Anthropologist Barbara Tedlock reports that dreams are of such integral importance to Mexico's Quiche Maya people that one out of four people is initiated as a "daykeeper," their term for a dream interpreter. An Australian Aborigine told me, "We tell our dreams to the group because different people have different gifts and might help understand it." It sounded to me like the informal dream-sharing groups that have sprung up in Western societies over the past several decades (until he added a comment I found intriguing: "We often meet each other while we're sleeping"). The psychoanalytic idea that one's dreams pertain solely to the intricacies of one's own personality is a viewpoint that indigenous peoples find almost laughable.

Jung made it a point to seek out Hopi Indian elders and African shamans to learn their opinions on the subject. Those conversations contributed to his conclusion that our minds contain not only our own personal unconscious but also a deeper stratum of universal motifs. How are the contents, which he called the storehouse of relics and memories of the past, transmitted from one generation to the next? Jung seems to suggest that such collective images are contained within what could be called a "nonmaterial sphere of awareness." For the past fifty years, researchers have used many labels to describe such a sphere, hoping to explain cognitive functions that shouldn't by rights exist: clairvoyant reality (Lawrence LeShan); nonlocality (David Bohm); one mind (Erwin Schrödinger); totality (Jung); mind-at-large (Aldous Huxley); morphogenetic fields (Rupert Sheldrake).

Whatever name or concept one applies, there is pure mystery in how healing dreams appear to draw upon unfamiliar myths and icons, "know" the archaic meanings of words, and even, seemingly, display images of the future or the thoughts of distant minds. While these almost occult elements should not overshadow the need for careful, humble psychological work—or for healthy skepticism—it is also no good hiding our heads in the sand, pretending such phenomena don't exist. Some would say that the healing dreams are simply presenting back, in exotic form, our own intelligence: We are talking to ourselves; where else would it come from? But I am persuaded that the tracks of something beyond the egocentric "I" are unmistakable.

It now seems clear to me that any dream theory I've heard is, if not wrong, at least radically incomplete. Any single interpretive strategy is inadequate. To expect conventional psychological theory to explain it all is akin to playing by the rules of checkers when the healing dream is playing four-dimensional chess.

We live in a practical era, one that stresses the productive usage of things. Yet healing dreams are not easily reduced to the utilitarian. Although they offer practical revelation, they have more in common with the realm of art, poetry, and music, where what you "do" with an experience is not the overriding issue. Such dreams open up a gap in the ordinary, allowing something new, and often indefinable, to enter our lives. We can work with our dreams, "unpack" them, analyze them, learn from them. But it is that residue of mystery that gives them enduring power, making them touchstones we return to again and again.

Many people wonder why they should bother with their dreams at all. A common answer is that they will help us with our lives, and this is certainly true. Even the most extraordinary dream, properly investigated, has much to say about bread-and-butter issues like work, love, and health. But the healing dream is less the promoter of our waking goals—material achievement, perfect romance, a modest niche in history—than an advocate-general for the soul, whose aims may lie athwart those of the ego. It is often uninterested in the self-enhancement stratagems we mistake for progress. "It's vulgarizing to say that we can use dreams as tools, like shovels," a dreamworker once told me. "It's more like the dream uses *you*."

But we're "used" only if we're willing to dwell for a time within a dream's ambiguities without resolving them. In some cases, we may not be meant to solve the mystery, at least not right away. Rather, *it* means to solve *us. Solve* comes from the Latin *solvere,* "to loosen, release, or free." It is the same root as in the word *solution*—one of whose meanings is the dissolving of individual ingredients into a greater whole. In dreams our narrow selfhood is loosened; the ego experiences itself as an element in something larger.

No interpretive task is more dicey, more fraught with peril and promise, than depending on dreams in crisis. We are being confronted with an ancient, urgent question: not merely What does the dream mean, but What does the dream *want?* Here, when our lives may be at stake, dreams persist in their symbolic utterance (though sometimes the dreams themselves get fed up with the bobbing and weaving of metaphor and opt for a gloves-off punch in the eye). Even more troubling, healing dreams may ultimately care as much, or more, for our spiritual growth as for our physical survival. In the case of illness, for instance, our only reasonable goal should be how to get better; but dreams seem to insist, over and over, that it is not enough to cure our physical maladies. *Become well for what purpose?* they inquire, sharply, persistently. *To what end?*

I've puzzled over my dreams, cherished them and run from them, and when I couldn't figure them out, saved them as one would save stray bolts in a junk drawer, wondering if they might someday prove valuable. But to take dreams seriously—enough to act on them, to live by them—is potentially subversive. Dreams smash down the barricades: They admit all, proscribe nothing, view life through a different moral aperture. They do not always flatter us. They are a mirror of human imperfection, held before the face of our most burnished ambitions. They may scare us: A nightmare is a concrescence of our most private terrors. But even a purely exhilarating dream, a flight to the heavens astride a winged horse, stirs a different sort of unease—a suspicion that we may harbor an unrealized greatness, a potential that, if we dared fulfill it, would bring an end to ordinary life.

These days, I try to listen to my dreams, even for critical decisions, though such a provisional reliance on phantasms may mark me for a fool. I can't help but see life in a binocular way, through night eyes as well as day sight, and this changes everything—my relationships to others, to myself, to reality in general. Some dreams, I think, *are* a form of reality. These don't seem "dreamy" in the normal sense, denoting things that are wispy and indistinct. To the contrary, they make the everyday seem cloudy, evanescent. The closer I look, the more my dreams seem to insist upon the same spiritual onus: *You must live truthfully. Right now. And always.*

In an era when everything is being mapped—every geographic feature from the highest heavens to the sea bottom, every physical object from distant supernovas to the last glinting speck of the human genome—dreams remain, by their very nature, terra incognita. They push at the edge of our limitations, urging us toward the wild, unbounded lands of the possible.

Sabbaths, 1999

from *The Hudson Review*

I

Can I see the buds that are swelling
in the woods on the slopes
on the far side of the valley? I can't,
of course, nor can I see
the twinleafs and anemones
that are blooming over there
bright-scattered above the dead
leaves. But the swelling buds
and little blossoms make
a new softness in the light
that is visible all the way to here.
The trees, the hills that were stark
in the old cold become now
tender, and the light changes.

II

It's hard to recognize
Amidst this multiplicity
With mortal eyes
Thy singular divinity.

III

I dream of a quiet man
who explains nothing and defends
nothing, but only knows
where the rarest wildflowers
are blooming, and who goes
where they are and stands still
and finds that he is smiling
and not by his own will.

IV

Once, it seems, your birthday
was only yours. Now I know
it is also mine. Who
then could have foreknown
—sixty-three years ago!—
that on that day, this year,
you and I, having begun
another garden, would sit down
with our children and with
our children's children, to eat
and be thankful? But this
is what we were born to do.

V

The spring woods hastening now
To overshadow him,
He's passing in to where
He can't see out. The woods

Is all around. It charms
Mere eyesight to believe
The nearest thing not trees
Is the sky, into which
The trees reach, opening
Their luminous new leaves.
Burdened only by
A weightless shawl of shade
The lighted leaves let fall,
He seems to move within
A form unpatterned to
His eye or mind, design
Betokened to his thought
By leafshapes tossed about.
Ways untranslatable
To human tongue or hand
Seem tangled here, and yet
Are brought to light, are brought
To life, and thought finds rest
Beneath a brightened tree
In which, unseen, a warbler
Feeds and sings. His song's
Small shapely melody
Comes down irregularly,
As all light's givings come.

VI

What a consolation it is, after
the explanations and the predictions
of further explanations still
to come, to return unpersuaded

to the woods, seeing again
the growth of the blessed trees
above all is a mystery.
A tree forms itself in answer
to its place and to the light.
Explain it how you will, the only
thing explainable will be
your explanation. There is
in the woods on a summer's
morning, birdsong all around
from guess where, nowhere
that rigid measure which predicts
only humankind's demise.

VII

Light and shadow, the leaves'
deep mosaic all astir—who
has found out the design?
And the birds, like leaves
that come and go, call down
from their altitudes, airs
all extremities and heights.

VIII

In Heaven the starry saints will wipe away
The tears forever from our eyes, but they
Must not erase the memory of our grief.
In bliss, even, there can be no relief
If we forget this place, shade-haunted, parched

Or flooded, dark or bright, where we have watched
The world always becoming what it is,
Splendor and woe surpassing happiness
Or sorrow, loss sweeping it like a floor.
This shadowed passage between door and door
Is half-lit by old words we've heard or read.
As the living recall the dead, the dead
Are joyless until they call back their lives:
Fallen like leaves, the husbands and the wives
In history's ignorant, bloody to-and-fro,
Eternally in love, and in time learning so.

IX

We travelers, walking to the sun, can't see
Ahead, but looking back the very light
That blinded us shows us the way we came,
Along which blessings now appear, risen
As if from sightlessness to sight, and we,
By blessing brightly lit, keep going toward
That blessed light that yet to us is dark.

X

Again I resume the long
lesson: how small a thing
can be pleasing, how little
in this hard world it takes
to satisfy the mind
and bring it to its rest.

Within the ongoing havoc
the woods this morning is
almost unnaturally still.
Through stalled air, unshadowed
light, a few leaves fall
of their own weight.

The sky
is gray. It begins in mist
almost at the ground
and rises forever. The trees
rise in silence almost
natural, but not quite,
almost eternal, but
not quite.

What more did I
think I wanted? Here is
what has always been.
Here is what will always
be. Even in me,
the Maker of all this
returns in rest, even
to the slightest of His works,
a yellow leaf slowly
falling, and is pleased.

XI

The difference is a polished
blade, edgewise to the eye.

On one side gleams the sun
of time, on the other
the never-fading light,
and so the tree that stands
full-leaved in broad day
and the darkness following
stands also in the eye
of Love and is never darkened.

The blade that divides these lights
mirrors both—is one.
Time and eternity
stand in the same day
which is now in time, and forever
now. How do we know?
We know. We know we know.
They only truly live
who are the comforted.

XII

The incarnate Word is with us,
is still speaking, is present
always, yet leaves no sign
but everything that is.

BEN BIRNBAUM

How to Pray: Reverence, Stories, and the Rebbe's Dream

from *Image*

About a third of the Babylonian Talmud is story—or "incidents" in the Talmud's unpretentious phrasing—and the death of Rav Eliezer on folio 28B of the tractate *Berachos* is one of the work's many formula incidents: familiar blossoms that brighten even the most severe juridical terrain. The narrative convention in this instance is this: a teacher is dying, and his students get to ask him one question before the curtain falls.

Rav Eliezer was no common teacher. Likely born early in the second half of the first century, he became one of the men who devised rabbinic Judaism following the destruction of the Jerusalem Temple in 70 C.E. and without whom Israel and its jealous god would long since have joined Egypt, Babylon, Assyria, and their jealous gods in the purgatory of museum blockbuster shows. And the men who stood by Eliezer's deathbed were clearly worthy of their master. For notwithstanding his condition, they ran one right up under his chin. "Teach us," they said, "the ways of this life so that we may be worthy of life in the World to Come"—which is to say they asked him how to gain eternal life. And Eliezer joined his final breaths to brace a suitably comprehensive answer: "Care for the honor of your colleagues; teach your children to shun rote memorization, and seat them on the knees of those who have studied with the sages. And when you pray," he concluded, *"da lifne me ata omdim"*—know before Whom you stand.

While it may seem uncharitable to criticize a dying man for not rounding on a tough pitch, respect for the Talmud's own relentless standards of discourse requires us to observe that Rav Eliezer's statement is a wobbly double down the line—prolix and not absolutely coherent (scholars still argue about the translation and import of the phrase here rendered as "rote memorization"). And as any moderately experienced student of Talmud would know, Rav Eliezer's final teaching does seem but a pallid echo of the bracing assertion found in the tractate *Avoth* that the world exists for the sake of three things and three things only: charity, study of Torah, and prayer.

Eliezer's last sentence taken alone, however—his declaration regarding prayer—is another matter, a blast so pure, long, and true that it has withstood the caviling of eighteen centuries' worth of rabbinic color commentators and stands today as the definition of a definition of Jewish prayer, linked to the subject the way "All Gaul is divided into three parts" is linked to Latin or as Atlanta used to be linked to air travel in the South back when Delta was king of the regulated skies: "You can go to heaven or hell, but you gotta go through Atlanta," they said. Likewise, you can go anywhere you like in the consideration of Jewish prayer, but first you need to make your way through "Know before Whom you stand."

Know: prayer is neither delirium nor reflex; it calls for an attentive intellect, what the rabbis called *kavannah*—intentionality. There is no accidental prayer.

Know before Whom: Whom, not what. Prayer is personal. The God of the Habiru is not an abstraction, is not nature, fate, or time decked out in a white beard. "An 'I' does not pray to an 'It,'" Abraham Joshua Heschel wrote in a twentieth-century color commentary on Eliezer's final words.

Know before Whom you stand. Prayer does not take you into your self or out of our world. It is not a transcendental meditation.

The relaxation response is not its goal. Nor is prayer oratory. Rather, prayer places you in proximal, eyes-front relationship with the Creator. And so the Hebrew word for liturgical prayer is *tefilah,* an invocation of God as judge.

But the Talmud is merely the glorious Talmud. It is not Judaism; it is not the lives of men and women, lived in the valleys and on the flats—holy ground that is nonetheless ground.

One day about sixteen hundred or so years after Rav Eliezer did his best to answer the last question he ever heard, a Russian Chassidic rabbi known as Shneur Zalman of Ladi was praying alongside his son and, turning to the boy, asked what bit of scripture he was using to focus his prayers. The child answered that he was meditating on the phrase "Whatsoever is lofty shall bow down before Thee." Then he asked his father the same question: "With what are you praying?" The rabbi answered, "With the floor and with the bench."

In Brooklyn, New York, in the early 1950s, I learned to pray as most of us learn to pray: with the floor and with the bench, or in my case with the sheet linoleum and the gunmetal folding chairs in the Young Israel Synagogue of New Lots and East New York, a brick shoebox with painted-glass casement windows that stood at the corner of Hegeman Street and Sheffield Avenue, shouldered by a dry cleaner's and by a long row of squat apartment buildings that we called brownstones when brownstone was not yet an evocation of a lost urban Elysium but simply a word that described a stone so modest and common that it had no real name.

The Young Israel of New Lots and East New York was a devoutly Orthodox congregation, and the world it supported was suffused with prayer: morning, afternoon, and evening worship; blessings before drinking Coke or eating cookies (and they were not the same blessing); blessings after each meal and when putting on new clothes and after burying the dead. There were prayers to be said prior to an airplane flight, prayers of thanksgiving to be said upon landing safely, and dense kabbalic prayers on newsprint certificates that had to be taped to the headboards of cribs to ward off the demons and imps who joyed at murdering infants in their sleep.

We recited prayers as we climbed into bed and prayers as we groped for the off switch on the alarm clock; prayers when catching sight of a Jewish sage or a gentile sage (as with Coke and cookies, different blessings). There was even an extraordinary requirement to offer a prayer of thanks for bad fortune as for good. And each Friday evening at the Sabbath eve meal in every house I knew, fathers placed hands upon the bowed heads of their children and prayed aloud in Hebrew: "The Lord bless you and guard you. The Lord shine His face upon you and be gracious to you. The Lord turn His face toward you and give you peace"—a prayer and a gesture of benediction torn dripping from the pages of the Torah, as old as love and fear.

We families who were attached to the Young Israel of New Lots and East New York lived in a whirlwind of invocation, praise, thanks, blessing, petition, song and Psalm. But we also lived in rows of attached houses in a clotted and crowded place, a place where the Rav Eliezer's injunction to "know before Whom you stand" in prayer had to compete for attention with the injunction of the baby's croup, the injunction of the worn clutch on the DeSoto, the injunction of the willful teenager, the injunction of the twenty sales you needed to make before dusk if you were to earn the commission you were already sorry you'd taken in advance. And so, while prayer was frequent, it was frequently words—words spoken with an eye on the clock, with an ear attuned to the telephone or the cough from the upstairs bedroom or the spear point of anxiety lodged in the heart.

And I was a boy educated to be pious and learned. I knew very early Rav Eliezer's instructions for gaining the World to Come. I knew Maimonides' extraordinary ruling a millennium later that a man who has returned from a journey may abstain from worship for as long as three days, until he regains the degree of concentration that prayer requires. I knew the story of the Chassidic master Levi Yitzchok of Berdichev, who refused to enter a certain synagogue, saying there was no room for him in the building, so cluttered was it with words spoken without love or fear that had not risen to the Upper World but lay strewn in heaps on the floor like common trash.

And I, knowing these things, knowing what God expected of us, how could I make sense of the mumbled words, the tossed-off readings, the careless petitions, the hurried mumblings that so often passed for prayer and worship in the Young Israel of New Lots and East New York and on the streets and in the houses nearby? How could I reconcile God's demands and the demands of Brooklyn? Was it possible that the World to Come was a domain set up only for saints or those who lived in Manhattan between 57th and 96th—people who had nothing to worry about and so could pray with proper *kavannah?* Was it possible that just about everyone I knew and even loved would never make it into God's eternal care?

And then I read the story of the rebbe's dream. This happened when I was eleven or twelve years old, on a Sabbath afternoon in the Young Israel *shul,* in the parched hiatus between the late-afternoon service and the evening service that concluded the Sabbath. Bored, waiting for the Sabbath to bleed away into the week so I could again listen to the radio or spend my allowance, I picked up a children's magazine that was lying on a folding chair in the sanctuary.

I don't remember what the magazine was called, but I remember it as the Orthodox Jewish analog to *My Weekly Reader*. Distributed to students in yeshiva elementary schools, it offered stories from scripture and Talmud, Torah puzzlers, photos of grinning boys in black yarmulkes who had memorized 100 or 500 *mishnaim*, and profiles of heroes from Abraham to Hank Greenberg. And the back cover was always a cartoon story, and that's where I turned first and where I found "The Rebbe's Dream." And here it is as I remember it.

Once in a village in eastern Europe, there lived a rebbe known for the quality of his prayer. From every side people would come to hear, to be inspired, to watch this man climb the ladder of prayer from *kavannah*—intentionality—to *d'vekut*—the loving consciousness of God—to *hitpashtut ha-gashmiyut*, the highest rung of prayer, when the soul falls away from the body and enters the Upper World and God's immediate presence.

And one night the rebbe had a dream. In the dream an angel came to him and said, "If you would learn to pray properly, you must go study with Rav Naftali of Berzhitz." The rebbe was a pious and humble man, and so the very next morning he set out for Berzhitz, which turned out to be an isolated hamlet in the Carpathian Mountains in eastern Galicia. After a week of travel he found himself in the village synagogue, and there he waited until the local Jews assembled for evening prayer, and he asked who among them was Rav Naftali. They replied that there was no Rav Naftali in the village. He said that he'd been told on good authority that there was a Rav Naftali in Berzhitz and had in fact traveled a long way to speak with him. "Distinguished sage," one man then said, "someone's played a cruel joke on you for which God will surely take revenge. There is no Rav Naftali here, and the only Naftali at all is Naftali the woodsman who lives up in the hills and is no rav for certain but a *proste Yid*"—a coarse Jew—"not the kind you would care to know." And all the other men nodded.

The rebbe was deeply disappointed and decided to leave Berzhitz the next morning. But that night, asleep on a bench in the synagogue, he again dreamed that the angel came and said, "If you would learn to pray properly, you must go study with Rav Naftali of Berzhitz." When the rebbe awoke he decided that before he went home he would go to see this Naftali the woodsman. Perhaps the other villagers were mistaken about the man, he thought. Perhaps he was in fact a *lamed-vovnik,* one of the thirty-six hidden saints whose identity is known only to God and for whose sake alone the world is each moment spared the destruction it deserves.

And so he walked most of the morning on a rutted road through the forest until he came to a clearing where there stood a log-walled cabin and a horse shed. And he knocked on the door and a woman admitted him. "I'm a traveler seeking a place to rest," the rebbe said. The day happened to be a Friday, and so the woman invited him to stay for the holy Sabbath, and the rebbe sat in a corner of the house and studied from a book of Torah he'd brought with him.

Shortly before sunset, the rebbe heard the sound of a horse and wagon. A few minutes later a short, big-bellied man with a dark tangled beard entered. He stood an ax in a corner of the room, washed his hands and face in a bucket of water, and immediately began to mumble the prayers of greeting for the Sabbath. The rebbe was not impressed with the looks of his host or with his hurried prayers, but he joined him in worship, and then the two men sat down at the table to eat the Sabbath eve meal.

Together they said the blessing over the wine, and the rebbe took a few sips from his cup while Naftali drained his cup and immediately filled it again. Then came the blessing over bread. The rebbe ate a slice of challah, and Naftali ate half a loaf. Then Naftali's wife brought out a baked carp and served the rebbe a slice. Naftali ate the rest of the fish to the bones. The woman brought a pot of chicken soup to the table, then a dish of boiled chicken and turnips, then a fruit compote of apples and berries. Naftali ate prodigiously of each course, all the while drinking glasses of wine and hot tea.

And then, after he had quickly recited the blessing after meals, Naftali stood up, wished his guest a good night, and went off to sleep. In a minute the small cabin echoed with the sound of his snoring.

The next day, at the Sabbath dinner and then later at the third Sabbath meal, Naftali's wife brought heaps of food to the table, and Naftali ate like a dozen men, devouring every heap that was placed before him.

Saturday night arrived, and the rebbe was ready to leave, to go home, convinced he had misunderstood his dream. And so he said farewell to his hosts and thanked them for their hospitality. "Learned rabbi," Naftali then said, "so you don't go away thinking the worst of me, allow me to tell you a story. All my life I've had a great appetite for food, and that has been a blessing, giving me the strength to earn my living. And then one day a few years ago, I was alone in the forest when bandits attacked me. They were going to take my wagon and tools and kill me. And so I prayed to our Creator, saying, 'I have no learning, I have no pious habits—all I have is an appetite. But if You give me the strength I need today, for the rest of my life when I eat on Your holy Sabbath, I will eat for You, only for You.'"

The rebbe returned to his own village. He lived many more years. And when people told him how impressive and uplifting his prayers were, he was sometimes heard to reply, "Whatever I know about prayer is as dust compared to the knowledge of my master, Rav Naftali of Berzhitz."

That is the story of the rebbe's dream that I read many years ago in cartoon form in the dull hour between *minchah* and *maariv* in the Young Israel of New Lots and East New York. And when I had finished reading, I knew that what I had read was as true as Rav Eliezer's deathbed instructions or Maimonides' ruling or Levi Yitzchok's judgment. I knew I had read a story that could change your life if you weren't careful, or maybe if you were careful.

My guess is that if Rav Eliezer had been hanging around the Young Israel Synagogue of New Lots and East New York that afternoon, reading over my shoulder, he would probably have reached a similar conclusion about the power of the story of the rebbe's dream and been none too happy about it.

A member of the most unfortunate generation of Abraham's seed prior to 1939, Eliezer grew up at the edge of a chasm that split history. On the far side, the centuries-old order of ritual animal sacrifice by a caste of priests in a Temple on a particular hill in a particular kingdom in a particular land promised through God's covenant to the people of Israel. On the near side, silence and devastation. "From the day the Temple was destroyed, a wall of iron set itself between Israel and her father in heaven," Rav Elazar ben Pedat declared in one of the most frightening sentences in the Talmud.

Attempts to jump the chasm (or break through ben Pedat's iron wall) were plentiful, dramatic, desperate, and, in nearly all instances, doomed: a series of schisms, asceticisms, revolutions, and bloody martyrdoms. And in the midst of these convulsions came the response formed by Rav Eliezer and his colleagues (along with Christianity the only response to the Temple's destruction that has prevailed into our time). It was a response that through Mishnah and Talmud, through custom and law, rebuilt the faith of Judah on this side of the chasm as rabbinic Judaism: a faith made for a people in literal and figurative exile, "a pilgrim tribe," in the words of George Steiner, "housed not in place but in time," and worshiping a God also in exile, whose place was nowhere and everywhere, whose face was invisible and always manifest.

And the core of that rabbinic inspiration was the substitution of word for blood, of poetry for the knife, of the Young Israel Synagogue of New Lots and East New York for Jerusalem—of orderly, communal, regularized prayer for orderly, communal, regularized animal sacrifice. And so, these rabbis declared, just as sacrifice in the Temple had brought forgiveness of sin, so now did prayer. Just as sacrifice in the Temple had been a principal obligation on religious festivals, so now was prayer. As sacrifice had been the means by which one expressed gratitude for a harvest, for a child, for escape from danger, so now was prayer.

Berachos, the tractate of Talmud most concerned with prayer, not only contains hundreds of detailed instructions for liturgy and worship but is replete with signposts that direct people's attention to the Torah-endorsed link between the lost world of temple and the new world of synagogue. Rav Hiyya bar Abba, for example, speaking on folio 14B–15A in the name of his teacher Rav Yochanan, describes how a man should begin his day: "Scripture," he declares, "considers all who relieve themselves, wash their hands, put on phylacteries, and recite the *keryat shema* and pray to be like those who build an altar and sacrifice upon it." Thus did Rav Eliezer and his fellow rabbis try to connect present and past.

But even the noblest bridge admits the chasm. With all due respect to Rav Yochanan, the Temple priest's ablutions are not Everyman's morning piss. In her erudite history of rabbinic prayer, *To Worship God Properly,* Rabbi Ruth Langer nails the radical implications of Rav Eliezer and company's invention this way: "When prayer became incumbent on all the people, not simply upon the priests in Jerusalem, then all the people became equally responsible for contact with God."

That's not a bridge; it's a new explosion. And like other theological explosions—the Reformation, for one good example—it could well have resulted in a shattered core and a score of diminished and localized shards, some perhaps dedicated to gluttony or sexual ritual or dismaying forms of sacrifice as the way to please or placate God.

Da lifne me ata omdim: "And when you pray, know before Whom you stand." If one listens with a particular kind of care, Rav Eliezer's final words can sound like a desperate cry for order.

By coincidence (a condition that, like tragedy, is ineluctably joined to Jewish history), Chassidism, the eighteenth-century revivalist movement that produced the story of the rebbe's dream, was also a theological explosion, another response to yet another discontinuity in Jewish history. The crack first appeared in 1648, when an unprecedentedly murderous pogrom destroyed 300 Jewish settlements in the Ukraine. As in the first century, the unimagined tragedy led to millennial hysteria and a brace of messianic pretenders, two of whom failed dismally, publicly, and shamefully, in the aftermath of which an exhausted Judaism fell into a clinical depression, a stupor of sadness, anxiety, guilt, and obsessive regard for religious regulation.

Led by a set of charismatic rural religious leaders—not all of whom were rabbis—Chassidism took root in the backwater villages of western Galicia. Theologically, it placed heart above mind, man above text, loving-kindness above learning—seeking to reconnect Judaism with a God who had placed His people on earth so they might rejoice in His blessings.

As regards prayer in particular, Chassidism became infamous for flouting rabbinic regulations: for praying too late and too early; for praying too loud and too fondly; for dancing and singing in the midst of liturgy; for concluding the morning prayer with a whiskey toast to the day's remembered martyrs. It was said of Rav Chayim of Tzanz, for example, that he would stand for hours in prayer—not speaking the liturgy, but ecstatically repeating: "I mean nothing but You, nothing but You alone; nothing but You, nothing but You alone."

And there was Rav Moshe of Kobrin, who in reciting the preamble to just about every Jewish blessing—"Blessed art thou, Lord our God"—cried out "blessed" with such fervor that he had to sit and rest before he could continue with "art thou"; and the Koznitzer Maggid, who would dance on a table during worship; and the dark-visioned Kotzker rebbe who once chastised a man who complained that his heart ached when work kept him from praying at the prescribed hour: "How do you know that God doesn't prefer your heartache to your prayers?"

How, indeed, does one know what God prefers? Once when I was a boy in the Young Israel Synagogue of New Lots and East New York, late on a Sabbath morning, the men were preparing to return the Torah scroll to the ark after the reading so we could finish the service and go home to eat the Sabbath dinner. A man came forward from his seat and picked up the Torah from the reading table and would not let it go, would not let the service continue. A short, balding man in a navy blue suit, he put his arms around the Torah and his cheek against its silk covering, as one would hug a child in need of comforting. All activity stopped. The white cotton curtains that closed off the women's section of the *shul* parted, and the women and girls stared. Several men—leaders of the *shul*—went up to the man who had seized the Torah. They whispered to him, and he whispered in reply without raising his eyes to look at them. From where I stood I could see sweat on the man's high pale brow. And then the word passed from row to row and chair to chair: the man who held the Torah had that week been diagnosed with terminal cancer.

Nothing could be done. But he knew, as we did, that no harm could come to a person who held the Torah. Of course he knew, as did we, of the thousands of martyrs over the years who were killed while embracing the Torah, even, in some cases, while in the Torah's embrace, wrapped in the scroll by the murderers. But that was a mystery and old news. In the Young Israel of New Lots and East New York, Torah was life and this was today. And so the man held the Torah and would not let it go.

No one would take the sacred scroll from him under these circumstances, and besides it was unseemly to wrestle over a Torah. And if it fell to the ground, a general fast would be required.

I don't remember how the episode ended, but I remember it did not last long. I imagine he grew tired: a Torah scroll—roll upon roll of parchment, line upon line of God's word—is heavy in several ways.

At the time, I saw what this man did as an extraordinary act of prayer and supplication—the most extraordinary I'd ever seen. But was it prayer, or was it the reverse of prayer, an act of irreverence, of selfishness?

From the perspective of those who must build and maintain the stage on which prayers of every sort can play themselves out, the question is not easily answered. As Rav Eliezer knew, and as the rabbis who denounced Chassidism and in some cases excommunicated its leaders knew, if each member of the congregation dances on the table, if each roars the first words of the liturgy and falls to the floor or kidnaps the sacred scroll or decides that heartache or a quart of pickled herring with onions will do as a substitute, it won't be long before prayer faces man and not God, before the stage collapses under the weight of self-indulgence. On the other hand, if there can be no daring or originality or creativity in prayer, then no human being will mount that stage except out of a sense of duty—and certainly no imaginative human being will want to see what happens there, which means that prayer and religious observance will attract none but the reverential—which is a very different crowd from the reverent.

I happen to be of that generation of Abraham's seed whose members carry the names of those who died in the Shoah. Binyahmin Rand was my murdered great-grandfather. Likewise, my brother Akiva is named for Binyahmin's son. But Jewish history being the aforementioned tangle of coincidence and tragedy, Akiva also happens to be the name of Rav Eliezer's most eminent student, who, as it happens, is also known for the words he spoke in answer to his own students' final question.

In this case, the teacher was being flayed alive by the Romans, his flesh torn from the bone with metal combs. The students' question: How can you stand in silence while undergoing this torture? And like Eliezer, Akiva replied well enough that his words are remembered. "All my life," he said, "I've wondered how I would be able to fulfill the commandment of loving God with all my heart and soul and life." Great-Uncle Akiva's end was not so efficacious. After witnessing the first murderous assault on his village's Jews, Akiva survived the war as a partisan, went to the new state of Israel as a refugee, married, fathered two children, and one day sat in a warm bath and cut open his wrists.

My brother Akiva was born only thirteen months after I came into the world, and as I was from the go raised to be learned and pious, he took the other available option and raised himself to be a lout—quick-tempered, quick-fisted, stubborn, angry, and unlearned. And then, when I was nineteen and he was eighteen, we changed places—or more accurately, I determined to become a lout, which allowed him to become learned and pious.

Thirty years or so later, Akiva is the dean of a yeshiva in Yiddish Jerusalem, has thirteen children and a dozen grandchildren, and wears a long black beard and a black hat. I am an editor and writer at an American Jesuit university, have three children, no grandchildren, no beard, and own no hat that Akiva would consider worthy of a grown man's head.

For nearly two decades, Akiva and I had almost no contact, but now we meet every year or two when business brings him to the States, and we talk gingerly about the remaining things we have in common: family and Torah.

When Akiva visited Boston two years ago, I had begun to think about prayer and reverence, and so, over a breakfast of lox and eggs at a kosher deli, I asked how he understood Samuel II, chapters five and six, a text obsessed with reverence before God.

It's the story of David, newly made king, and how he goes with his army to bring the ark of the covenant to his new capital of Jerusalem. Relinquished by the Philistines after it caused them plague, the ark had since been stored in the home of Avinadav. And with the help of Uzuh and Achyo, two sons of Avinadav, David begins carting it home. (The English translation I use is from Judaica Press, tin-eared but simply accurate.) "And they came to Goren-Nachon, and Uzuh put forth [his hand] to the ark of God, and grasped hold of it, for the oxen swayed it. And the anger of the Lord was kindled against Uzuh, and God struck him down there" because only a Temple priest may touch his flesh to the ark.

Angry at God and fearful, David abandons the ark on the spot, returning to claim it three months later only after hearing that the man (a Gittite, no less) who had taken the ark into his house had since been blessed by God. And so David the brilliant opportunist brings the ark to Jerusalem "with joy. . . . And David danced with all his might before the Lord; and David was girded with a linen ephod"—which is to say, a short shift, which is to say that in the course of dancing with all his might before the Lord and all the people who lived in his city, the king of Israel exposed himself.

And Michal, David's first and much-neglected wife and daughter of his old rival, Saul, looks out at the procession and sees "the king David hopping and dancing before the Lord; and she loathed him in her heart." Later, after appropriate pomp and sacrifice, David heads home, where Michal greets him with: "How honored was today the king of Israel, who exposed himself today in the eyes of the handmaids of his servants, as would expose himself one of the idlers." This seems fair and sharp instruction from a born princess to her husband, the randy former shepherd, but it is also an act against God's anointed, as David scornfully makes plain. "And David said unto Michal, 'Before the Lord who chose me above your father, and above all his house, to appoint me prince over the people of the Lord, over Israel; therefore I have made merry before the Lord. . . .' And Michal the daughter of Saul had no child until the day of her death." End of chapter and verse.

What makes the text difficult, I told Akiva, is that here we have Uzuh, who lays a hand on the ark so as to keep it from falling to the ground—he gets zapped for all his good intentions. We have Michal, the princess and queen, for pointing out correctly to her husband that leaping up and down in a short ephod in a public place was behavior ill suited to royalty—she is cursed with barrenness. And then we have David, who for exposing himself before the ark and before all the people—no consequences.

The centuries have of course left us with plenty of rabbinic exegesis, most of it overheated. Some commentators, for example, have tried to sacramentalize David's behavior by saying that his ephod was not really a common ephod but the jeweled ephod worn by the Temple priest. Others have tried to explain God's extraordinary anger against the well-meaning if dim-witted Uzuh by developing a midrash that discovers four serious sins in Uzuh's one act of touching the ark. The inventive details do not bear repeating. Regarding Michal, another midrash says that she wasn't really cursed but had angered David sufficiently that he never again went to bed with her. But Akiva didn't try to pass off any of this on me. Instead he offered the following.

It's easy, Akiva said (the words he has always used when explaining something he understands and I don't). Uzuh, he said, was struck down not simply because he reached out to steady the ark, but because he did so simply to steady the ark, like a clerk filing a folder, like a librarian shelving a book—without awe or love. And Michal was punished not because she chastised the king, but because she did so "loath[ing] him in her heart" and not out of concern for God or the kingdom or the people. And as for David, he was forgiven because what he did—while inappropriate, demeaning, embarrassing, and certainly unsuited to royalty—he did "with all his might before God," which is to say, with selfless devotion. That's what Akiva told me.

And so, while eating lox and eggs, did my learned brother elucidate the difficult text and, though he didn't know it, at the same time provide an answer to the question of how Rav Eliezer and Naftali the woodsman and King David and the men and women of the Young Israel of New Lots and East New York might all be worthy of eternal life. "With all your might before God" will do it every time—will make a prayer of eating, of dancing, of singing, of kidnapping the Torah, even of an offering of mumbled words.

And here I could stop, standing foursquare on the Torah and my learned brother's midrash. Unlike my brother, however, I'm a modern. I can't feel comfortable except if I rest on vexatious ambiguity, the rough mattress I'm used to. And so a final story that returns me to the Young Israel of New Lots and East New York—the place where I received the chilling intimation, while reading the story of the rebbe's dream, that law and midrash were insufficient, that creation was in final analysis too spirited or opaque or enigmatic or obdurate to submit itself to any study except that conducted by a blind heart.

The story is about prayer and the Chassidic tradition of drinking a postworship *l'Chayim* each morning in memory of the day's listed martyrs. But more important, it is about the handful of men who made up the Young Israel's first minyan of the day, who prayed earliest and fastest and got on with it and who blessed me for a time by taking me into their odd company, allowing a milky-skinned boy of thirteen to be counted as a man each dawn at the sacred corner of Hegeman and Sheffield.

Tradesmen and shopkeepers, widowers who smelled of the camphor chips in their dresser drawers, men who were too angry or restless to lie next to their wives all night, they rose before dawn and made their way through the darkness to the corner of Hegeman and Sheffield, where they stood beside their gunmetal chairs below the Eternal Fluorescent buzzing behind its shield of painted glass, before the ark decorated with an emblem of guardian angels yawning like they'd been up all night arguing. And the moment the clock showed sunrise and they could count ten men, they began.

Never since have I heard such fast prayers, like a torrent sweeping the gutters, slaking the wilderness at the corner of Sheffield and Hegeman, the *umens* leaping like startled trout. Maybe it was twenty minutes to the finish—thirty on Monday and Thursday when we had to read Torah—and then we rushed to the long table below the bookshelves at the back of the sanctuary.

And one of the men took the Seagram's from the secret ark behind Maimon's commentary on the *Mishnah,* while another brought a tray of shot glasses, heavy as bad news, from the caterer's kitchen, and together we took into our bellies the first

golden happiness of the day, crying out a "L'Chayim"—To life!—
in memory of some saint we did not know but whose death on
this date was somewhere recorded, we believed. "For," as I wrote
in a poem published a few years ago:

> . . . the world was old
> and men died each hour,
> some of them saints or martyrs,
> while someone else, whose job it was,
> wrote names and dates
> (and what fuel was used to start the job,
> and the final words, if intelligible).
> And if we didn't have the details
> at Hegeman and Sheffield,
> that couldn't be our fault
> that we should have to suffer.

> So *L'Chayim* and again *L'Chayim*.
> The hoax of International Brotherhood. *L'Chayim*.
> The stink in the air shaft. *L'Chayim*.
> The boxcar of broken shoes. *L'Chayim*.
> The traitor baseball team. *L'Chayim*.
> The martyr behind the deli counter. *L'Chayim*.
> The bone in the sea-root's grasp. *L'Chayim*.
> The silent wife at the Sabbath meal. *L'Chayim*.
> The girl in a summer dress
> who passes as you sit in the steamy elevated car
> and makes you remember what you once believed, *L'Chayim*.

And then each man went off to business or breakfast except for
old Mr. Auslander, who stayed to wash the shot glasses and hum

"Bali Hai" at the hallway sink generally reserved for the priests' Holy Day ablutions. While I, damp eyed, happy apprentice to the saints, who had to be in eighth grade and cold sober in an hour, hurried home in the new light among gentile dog walkers, beneath muscled sycamores, in the perfume trail of girls from public high school, home to the dark-eyed mother in a frayed robe, home to the dying sun of butter in the galaxy of the oatmeal bowl.

ROBERT CORDING

Gratitude

from *The Paris Review*

In his prison letters, Bonhoeffer is thankful
for a hairbrush, for a pipe and tobacco,
for cigarettes and Schelling's *Morals* Vol. II.
Thankful for stain remover, laxatives,
collar studs, bottled fruit and cooling salts.
For his Bible and hymns praising what is
fearful, which he sings, pacing in circles
for exercise, to his cell walls where he's hung
a reproduction of Durer's *Apocalypse*.
He's thankful for letters from his parents
and friends that lead him back home,
and for the pain of memory's arrival,
his orderly room of books and prints too far
from the nightly sobs of a prisoner
in the next cell whom Bonhoeffer does not know
how to comfort, though he believes religion
begins with a neighbor who is within reach.
He's thankful for the few hours outside
in the prison yard, and for the half-strangled
laughter between inmates as they sit together
under a chestnut tree. He's thankful even
for a small ant hill, and for the ants that are
all purpose and clear decision. For the two
lime trees that mumble audibly with the workings
of bees in June and especially for the warm

laying on of sun that tells him he's a man
created of earth and not of air and thoughts.
He's thankful for minutes when his reading
and writing fill up the emptiness of time,
and for those moments when he sees himself
as a small figure in a vast, unrolling scroll,
though mostly he looks out over the plains
of ignorance inside himself. And for that,
too, he's thankful: for the self who asks,
Who am I?—the man who steps cheerfully
from this cell and speaks easily to his jailers,
or the man who is restless and trembling
with anger and despair as cities burn and Jews
are herded into railroad cars—can
without an answer, say finally, *I am thine,*
to a God who lives each day,
as Bonhoeffer must, in the knowledge
of what has been done, is still being done,
his gift a refusal to leave his suffering, for which,
even as the rope is placed around his neck
and pulled tight, Bonhoeffer is utterly grateful.

Source

from *The Gettysburg Review*

I'd been traveling all day, driving north
—smaller and smaller roads, clapboard houses
startled awake by the new green around them—

when I saw three horses in a fenced field
by the narrow highway's edge: white horses,

two uniformly snowy, the other speckled
as though he'd been rolling in flakes of rust.
They were of graduated sizes—small, medium,

large—and two stood to watch while the smallest
waded up to his knees in a shallow pond,

tossing his head and taking
—it seemed unmistakable—
delight in the cool water

around his hooves and ankles.
I kept on driving, I went into town

to visit the bookstores and the coffee bar
and looked at the new novels
and the volumes of poetry, but all the time

it was horses I was thinking of,
and when I drove back to find them,

the three companions left off
whatever it was they were playing at
and came nearer the wire fence—

I'd pulled over onto the grassy shoulder
of the highway—to see what I'd brought them.

Experience is an intact fruit,
core and flesh and rind of it; once cut open,
entered, it can't be the same, can it?

Though that is the dream of the poem:
as if we could look out

through that moment's blushed skin.
They wandered toward the fence.
The tallest turned toward me;

I was moved by the verticality of her face,
elongated reach from the tips of her ears

down to white eyelids and lashes,
the pink articulation
of nostrils, wind stirring the strands

of her mane a little to frame the gaze
in which she fixed me. She was the bold one;

the others stood at a slight distance
while she held me in her attention.
Put your tongue to the green-flecked peel

of it, reader, and taste it
from the inside: would you believe me
if I said that beneath them a clear channel

ran from the three horses to the place
they'd come from, the cool womb

of nothing, cave at the heart
of the world, deep and resilient and firmly set
at the core of things? Not emptiness,

not negation, but a generous, cold nothing:
the breathing space out of which new shoots

are propelled to the grazing mouths,
out of which the horses themselves are tendered
into the new light. The poem wants the impossible;

the poem wants a name for the kind nothing
at the core of time, out of which the foals

come tumbling: curled, fetal, dreaming,
and into which the old crumple, fetlock
and skull breaking like waves of foaming milk. . . .

Cold, bracing nothing that mothers forth
mud and mint, hoof and clover, root hair

and horsehair and the accordion bones
of the rust-spotted little one unfolding itself
into the afternoon. You too: you flare

and fall back into the necessary
open space. What could be better than that?

It was the beginning of May,
the black earth nearly steaming,
and a scatter of petals decked the mud

like pearls, everything warm with setting out,
and you could see beneath their hooves
the path they'd traveled up, the horse road

on which they trot into the world, eager for pleasure
and sunlight, and down which they descend,

in good time, into the source of spring.

Grace Notes

from *Notre Dame Magazine*

Is there a richer and stranger idea in the world than grace? Only love, grace's cousin, grace's summer pelt.

Etymology: *grace* is the English translation of the Latin *gratia,* itself a translation of the Greek *charis,* itself a translation of various Hebrew words meaning, collectively, love, compassion, fidelity—all used in context of these gifts being utterly free from God to God's creatures. There are no requisites for grace, no magnets for it, no special prayers to lure it. No guru, no method, no teacher, as the Irish genius Van Morrison sings.

You can be good, bad, or indifferent, and you are equally liable to have grace hit you in the eye. *Non enim gratia Dei erit ullo modo nisi gratuita fuerit omni modo,* "it will not be the grace of God in any way unless it has been gratuitous in every way," says old Augustine, the grace-obsessed bishop of Hippo, Augustine, who considered the whole revolution of his life to be the direct result of a shock of grace. Grace is uncontrollable, arbitrary to our senses, apparently unmerited. It's utterly free, ferociously strong, and about as mysterious a thing as you could imagine.

First rule of grace: grace rules.

Grace lifts, it brings to joy. And what, as we age, do we cherish and savor more than joy? Pleasure, power, fame, lust, money, they eventually lose their fastballs, or should: At our best and wisest we just want joy, and when we are filled with grace we see rich thick joy in the simplest of things. Joy everywhere.

Notice how many saints—whom we assume were and are crammed to the eyeballs with grace—are celebrated for their childlike simplicity, their capacity to sense divine joy in everything: the daily resurrection of light, the dustiest of sparrows.

The undulating grace of horizons and waterlines, of new countries looming up through the mist as the ship nears harbor. The graceful lines of land fleeing in every direction from where you stand in the furrowed field. The smooth sweet swelling grace of a woman with child, the muscular grace of a man's knotted back at work. The cheek of child, the shank of youth, the measured grace of the aged. The thin brave knobbykneed yellow sticks that prop up herons, my wife's elegant neck when she folds back her hair with that unconscious practiced female flip of fingers, the slow pained kneeling of an old woman in chapel. In the lope of an animal loping. In a tree leaping very slowly sunward. In a child's hilarity. In the endurance of sadness. In the shudder of calm after rage.

In the bone of the character of a priest who walks to his breakfast with blood on his shoes, the blood of a student who died in his arms in the night after a drunken wreck, the priest is a wreck himself this bright awful dawn, minutes after he blessed the body, but he puts one foot in front of another and walks into a normal day because he is brave enough to keep living, and wise enough to know he has no choice, and he knows he received grace from the hand of the Lord when he needed it most, first when the boy terrified of dying grabbed him by the collar and begged to be told he would live forever and now, here, in the crack of a morning in a campus parking lot as he hesitates by his car, exhausted, rooted.

But he walks.

God grant me the grace of a normal day, prays my wife.

What would an alphabet of grace include? Acrobatic, blessed, calm, dignified, ecstatic, eternal, epiphanous, flowing, gentle, harmless, inexplicable, joyous, keen, lissome, momentous, near, oblique, opaque, peaceful, quiet, roomy, salvific, tireless, unbelievable, various, xpeditious, yearning, zest.

Grace in the Old Testament is overwhelmingly a visual affair, from its first mention, in Genesis, where Noah finds grace in the eyes of the Lord, to its last, when the Lord remarks to Zechariah that He will pour grace on the House of David, which will then be able to see "Me whom they have pierced"—an evocative foretelling of the Christ. Grace is "found in the eyes of the Lord," "found in thy sight," "found in your eyes," until one sees that the ancient people's sense of grace was favor, and they were constantly checking to see if they were on the good side of the One Who May Not Be Named. A crowd of the most interesting characters in the Old Book asks anxiously after grace: Joseph and Moses, Gideon and the sons of Gad and the sons of Reuben, Ruth and Hannah, David and Joab, Ziba and Ezra.

Only in the psalms and proverbs does grace open up and become something poured into lips and into the body, something to be granted to the lowly: *Though He scoffs at the scoffers / Yet He gives grace to the afflicted. . . .*

In the New Testament the Christ is grace personified—"the grace of God was upon him," according to Luke, and He is "full of grace and truth," says John, who makes a clear distinction between the prophets and the Messiah: "the law was given by Moses, but grace and truth came by Jesus Christ." The apostles in their Acts are infused and suffused (and confused) by grace granted them by God, and they thrash out into the country from Jerusalem teaching and preaching and wrestling awkwardly with their newfound power. Those who were not patient are now patient; those who could not preach now "speak boldly in the Lord, which gave testimony unto the word of His grace"; those who were shy and clumsy are now "granted signs and wonders to be done by their hands."

That most interesting man Paul has the most interesting things to say about grace in the Acts. He wants to "testify the gospel of the grace of God," he says to the Ephesians in his last meeting with them, commending them finally "to God, and to the word of his grace, which is able to build you up, and to give you an inheritance among all them which are sanctified." In one of his densest and most eloquent essays, to the Romans, he notes that faith is the avenue to grace, which saves the soul—"access by faith into grace in hope of the glory of God," as he says. To the Romans he also insists that grace is utterly gratuitous, unearnable: "If by grace, not now by works: otherwise grace is no more grace." He bares all to the Corinthians and tells them that "to keep me from exalting myself, there was given me a thorn in the flesh, a messenger of Satan, to buffet me," and "concerning this I three times entreated the Lord that it might depart from me, and He said unto me, *My grace is sufficient for thee, for My strength is made perfect in weakness.*"

Grace sufficient to the size of your despair, neither more nor less grace than you need!

"Unto every one of us is given grace according to the measure of the gift," says Paul, mysteriously; "He resisteth the proud, and giveth grace to the humble," says Peter, unmysteriously.

The final line of the New Testament speaks of grace, John ending the account of his visions on the island of Patmos with a blessing that has come down familiarly to our time and many times been spoken over the bowed heads of the faithful, in a thousand languages: "The grace of our Lord Jesus Christ be with you all, amen." Thus Scripture ends with grace on its lips.

Can grace be granted all men, all women, all faiths, all nations, whether or no they have the Word of God in their mouths and hearts? O yes O yes, the Church says—interestingly, has always said, no controversies and wrestling matches and murders done over the issue—a miracle. And it has eloquently said it, here and there. Orosius, one of Augustine's many disciples, said that grace was showered upon us all *quotidie per tempora, per dies, per momenta, cunctis et singulis*—daily through the seasons, through the days, through the moments, to all of us, to every one of us.

Each person experiences grace as he or she does human and divine love—which is to say, idiosyncratically, in ways different from all others. So we are all writing essays about grace all the time, in all sorts of languages.

Physical grace: a certain easy carriage, an authority of lightness, a liquid quickness or liability to litheness, a disciplined exuberance of the body, an unselfconscious ease, a comfortable residence in the body and world. All cats and women have it. Nearly all vegetative things. Most children, most animals, most trees. Many men. Generally the larger the entity the less grace; this is why we are agog at grace in the largest athletes and animals; why some people watch professional football; why circuses employ elephants, to wow the populace not with size so much as with unexpected grace in the gargantuan.

I think maybe we are so absorbed and attracted by physical grace because we sense how fleeting it can be, how very many enemies it has.

Graceful creatures: A pine marten racing fast and sure over talus and scree; my wife floating through a road race in a summer by a river; one of my sons, twisting in the air as he falls backward from a porch step, landing on his hands and knees and bouncing up again in a single smooth motion and sailing away at top speed, not a cry, not a scratch, my mouth falling open to see a body so quick to sense and react, so blindingly quick to rearrange itself. A body wholly at home in the ocean of quick.

"I have always been so sure I was right, that I was being led by God," wrote grace-riveted Dorothy Day (whose mother's name was Grace) in her middle years. "I confidently expected Him to show His will by external events. I looked for some big happening, some unmistakable sign. I disregarded all the little signs. I begin now to see them and with such clearness that I have to beg not to be shown too much, for fear I cannot bear it."

One of the few projects she never finished—she was a ferociously energetic woman, flinty, stubborn, not at all sweet, a perhaps-saint made of bone and glower—was a small book to be called *All Is Grace*. "The title really means 'all things work together for good to those who love God,'" she wrote.

Her favorite saint was another flinty woman obsessed by grace, Catherine of Siena, twenty-fourth of twenty-five children, a woman who received the (Dominican) habit at eighteen and then retired to her room for three years, coming out only for Mass. When she *did* emerge finally she was a dynamo, so respected by the Church that cardinals and bishops and priests confessed their sins to her. Catherine had visions during which God spoke to her at great length, and God, it turned out, is as grace obsessed as Catherine and Augustine and Thomas and us: "My mercy is incomparably greater than all the sins anyone could commit," He said to Catherine. "This is that sin which is never forgiven, now or ever: the refusal, the scorning, of my mercy. For this offends me more than all the other sins they have committed. So the despair of Judas displeased me more and was a greater insult to my Son than his betrayal had been. My providence will never fail those who want to receive it."

Grace unfailing, inexhaustible, endless.

Oceans of grace, fountains of grace, rivers of grace. Water is an apt metaphor for grace; it is such a graceful creature itself, sinuous and ungraspable, the first ingredient of life, the substance that composes, cleanses, rejuvenates us, the sea in which we swam before birth.

Karl Rahner's final words on this earth, uttered, it is said, with startling authority and joy from a man minutes from morte: *All is grace!*

Another graceful ending: the great British preacher and writer Monsignor Ronald Knox. Drifting in and out of consciousness, Knox wakes to find a friend by his bedside. The friend asks if Knox would like to have some of the New Testament read to him—an edition that Knox has himself translated from the Greek.

"No," says Knox faintly.

And a few minutes later, even fainter:

"Awfully jolly of you to suggest it, though"—his last words.

God loves some of us violently; perhaps that savage love is a form of grace too. To wrench from you every shred of peace and feed you nothing but struggle sandwiches every day of your life—is that the highest form of Love? If you have the worst life imaginable and struggle ferociously against it, could it be that your fuel to fight is grace? Or that the measure of courage against your lot is the mark of your character?

How else to understand raped children, broken and bloodied and murdered children, children with ancient eyes, children who were never children, children who bear the marks of evil to their graves, children torn by evil as I write, as you read? *How else to understand them?* Tell me why they suffered and died, or suffered and did not die but were haunted and twisted all their lives by evil done upon them. Tell me why there have been so many millions of little broken Christs. Tell me.

And no one will tell me, for no one knows, only the inscrutable Lord, who never shows His hole cards. So I wonder if most grace in the world is spoken for by those who need it most, and those the smallest among us, their pain the greatest sin of our age.

Not-grace: disgrace, graceless. I listen to and read of people telling of the moments when they felt grace arriving and they use words like *calm, serene, harmony, peace, symmetry.* So grace flows, and the lack of grace—not-grace—is a damming of flow, jamming of gears, a stick in the spokes.

The only saint named for grace: Gratia, a fifteenth-century Dalmatian sailor who one day wanders into a Venetian church and is stunned by the sermon (from an Augustinian). Gratia joins the order and is sent to a monastery where he becomes a legendary gardener, and miracles of light and water follow him like puppies until the day he dies.

When have I been filled with grace? One time above all others, when my son was under ether. He was born with a broken heart, an incomplete heart, part of a heart. Not enough to keep him alive. Twice doctors cut him open and cut into his heart. Twice I waited and raged and chewed my fingers until they bled on the floor. Twice I sat in dark rooms with my wife and friends and savagely ate my skin.

The first operation was terrifying, but it happened so fast and was so necessary and was so soon after the day he was born with a twin brother that we all, mother father sister families friends, staggered through the days and nights too tired and frightened to do anything but lurch into the next hour.

But by the second operation my son was nearly two years old, a stubborn funny amiable boy with a crooked gunslinger's grin, and when a doctor carried him down the hall, his moon-boy face grinning at me as it receded toward awful pain and possible death, I went somewhere dark that frightens me still. It was a cold black country that I hope never to see again. Yet out of the dark came my wife's hand like a hawk, and I believe, to this hour, that when she touched me I received pure grace. She woke me, saved me, not for the first time, not for the last.

As I finish writing these lines I look up, and my heart-healed son runs past the window, covered with mud and jelly.

I grow utterly absorbed, as I age, by two things: love, thorough or insufficient, and grace under duress. Only those two. Politics, religion, money, ambition, they fade and are subsumed, consumed, eaten by these two vast and endless subjects: love and grace.

Those are the only things we will take to our graves, the only things that will be on our lips as we die, the only things that will be in our pockets as we walk to the country of the blessed—Tir na nOg it was called by my Irish people before me, the country of the always-young, where death has no dominion.

We love or do not love, we love well or badly, our friendships are a form of love, our enmities a form of not-love, missing love, weak love.

And grace under duress: what else is there?

Age and illness hammer us, tragedy and evil hammer us, greed and cupidity hammer us, we hammer ourselves in guilt and fear. What are we but the stories of how we fought against our troubles? What good do we remember of the dead but their humor, their stories, their courage, their selflessness, their grace?

"One day I am invested mysteriously with my mother's grace," writes Louise Erdrich in *The Blue Jay's Dance,* a gentle and very honest memoir of the first year of her last child. "I am alone with our children. This has been a no-sleep week for each of them. At four in the morning of the fourth night I haven't slept, I sit down, weeping. I fall into a fifteen-minute coma before the next round begins. It happens to be a long crying bout, nothing wrong physically, just growth, maybe teeth. Who knows? Sometimes babies just cry and cry. Morning drags on, our baby continues to cry. Then, in my office, with her in the crib next to the desk, I break through a level of sleep-deprived frustration so intense I think I'll burst, into a dimension of surprising calm. My hands reach down, trembling with anger, reach toward the needy child, but instead of roughly managing her they close gently as a whisper on her body. As though I am physically enlarged, I draw her to me, breathing deeply. The tension drops away. I am invested with my mother's patience. Her hands have poured it into me. The hours she soothed me and my younger brothers and sisters have passed invisibly into me. The gift has lain within me all my life, like a bird in a nest. . . ."

We think of grace arriving like an ambulance, just-in-time delivery, an invisible divine cavalry cresting a hill of troubles, a bolt of jazz from the glittering horn of the Creator, but maybe it lives in us and is activated by illness of the spirit. Maybe we're loaded with grace. Maybe we're stuffed with the stuff. Maybe it's stitched into our DNA, a fifth ingredient in the deoxyribonucleic acidic soup.

Grace at meals, that lovely habit of pausing to thank the Generosity who made the plants and fruits, the beasts of the earth and the birds of the sky and the fish of the sea—"even the *macaroni?*" says my daughter, and I say unto her Yea, even the macaroni, and also the Cheerios and the cheese crackers and the ginger snaps, for these foods have sustained her like no others, not even ye fruits and plants, of which she has cautiously partaken in nibbles that would mortify a mouse.

An ancient urge, the sigh of thanks at the prospect of food, and certainly a habit predating Christianity, but the peoples of the One God gave that whisper of relief and gratitude a graceful name and made it a custom gentle and handsome.

Each home has its own grace or lack thereof, and the litany of formal and informal prayers at table is endless. As a boy I chanted a grace so old in our family that it often suffered hurried hungry editing into one long word—*BlessusOLordandthesethygiftswhichweareabouttoreceivefromthybountythroughChristOurLordAmen*—but as a man graced with small children I ask them to name something for which they are thankful before we further reduce the macaroni population. *For my favorite shirt, for my basketball, for my ballet slippers,* they say grinning, but sometimes they pray *for Mom,* or *for kids who are dead,* and I think not for the first or last time that prayers from the smallest people are heard first.

The greatest of grace-scholars was Thomas Aquinas, a vast man in several senses—he was nicknamed the Dumb Ox as a student for his silence and bulk and apparently was gifted with total recall of everything he had ever read, especially the Scriptures, which he committed to memory while imprisoned for two years. It was Thomas, in his massive *Summa Theologica,* who strove to explicate every intricate layer and corner of grace (*gratia actualis ad actum,* grace granted by God for the performance of salutary acts, disappearing when the act concludes; *gratia gratis datae,* the extraordinary grace granted miracle workers, prophets, speakers in tongues, visionaries, priests, nuns, monks; *gratia illuminationis,* grace of the intellect; *gratia inspirationis,* grace of the will, etc., etc.), and his treatise on the subject remains the primary scholarly tome. Three times in the last years of his life Thomas was miraculously lifted into the air in church, and those present heard a voice from the crucifix say, *Thou hast written well of me, Thomas. . . .*

I ask a group of students from abroad about grace. *Grazia,* says an Italian girl, *nel senso spirituale, nel senso fisico,* the same word carrying the double load it does in English. *Sancteiddrwydd,* says a young Welsh woman, or *truyaredd,* the latter more like mercy; physical grace would be simply *gras.* I tell them the Gaelic word for the name Grace: *Gráinne,* which hails from the oldest spoken Irish and is thought to mean, rivetingly, She Who Strikes Fear.

Grace, says a French boy. *Eun-chong* in Korean, *milost* in Czech, *laun ch* in Chinese, *onchou* in Japanese, *ne'ama elaheiah* in Arabic, my head is spinning happily, the students cheerfully write or draw the word for me and try to explain how the idea feels in their languages, their countries, their hearts

"*Gracia,*" says a sweet shy Spanish girl. "It means the grace that God's catholic has. God has a power to protect and make full happy to people. It's a benediction of God. It's free."

DAVID JAMES DUNCAN

Strategic Withdrawal: A Tool for Restoration

from *Orion*

Any movement inward

—as into a chair by a window the light of which you use only to stare into a cup of tea

—or as into a habit of drinking tea, as opposed to coffee, because the former behaves so much more quietly within the body, so slowly releases its soft opening of eyes and mind

—or as in letting the eyes come to a standstill, in some space on the page of a book you've been reading, in order to stare at nothing or at something inside or at something neither inside nor out—an association-sprung scene, an entire small world, maybe; a place so pungent you leave your body to stand in it for a time

—or as in turning over a handwritten letter, before or after you've read it, to run your hand across the reverse side, blank side, the written words invisible now yet palpable in the impressions the pen left in the paper, the strange backward slant you never think of as being there, the earnest weight of the writer's departed hand still feelable, physical track of her thought still traceable, the fossil record of expended energy, the "handicraft" evident in the paucity of words; the whole page, though we think of paper as smooth, as idiosyncratically and subtly bumpy as the skin of your love's body, in which also dwells a reverse side, unseen side, of breath, blood, unformed thoughts, unthought words, nonverbal language

strategic withdrawal: any movement backward, away from the battle lines of one's incarnation (as in the phrase "spiritual retreat" but without the once-in-a-blue-moon connotations of those two words, because the backward movement needed, the spiritual retreat required, is moment to moment and day to day)

strategic withdrawal: any refusal to man our habitual demographic, political, or psychological trenches and defend our turf, for though the turf is holy, our defenses, when they grow automatonic, are not

any refusal to engage in verbal jousting with that testy or irritating or ideologically loud or theologically bloated person in your life—you know the one: the agitatedly racist or sexist or Selfist or religionist or politically powerful pedant, co-worker, parent, friend, or (God help you) spouse whose opinions are too poorly formed, too loudly held, or just too incessantly divulged to allow you to achieve peace in the presence of so much clanging banging editorializing mental machinery

any retreat (however ignominious it may seem to the will or the mind or the ego), not just from all such exchanges but from the underlying tensions and history that launch the exchanges (*your* side of the tensions and history, anyway: the side you've an inalienable right to retreat from)

any movement away from one's "urgencies," one's "this-is-who-I-am"nesses, one's responsibilities, agitations, racial guilt, sworn causes, shames, strengths, weaknesses, memories, workaday identity, public or secret battlefields

any movement toward formlessness

silence

stillness

emptiness

primordiality

any movement toward a beginning, as in Genesis 1, John 1, Quran Tao Te Ching Diamond Sutra Mahabharata Kalevala Mumonkan Ramayana Torah Gita 1 and toward one's own "in the beginning"

toward one's *origin* (root of *originality*); toward one's ignorance (that underrated state the embracing of which precedes every influx of fresh knowledge); toward one's amorphousness (the state of all clay before the potter conceives a form, wedges the clay, centers it, and begins throwing the bowl, the cup, the urn); toward one's interior blankness (the state of the paper preceding every new image, idea, drawing, sketch, or poem); toward one's wilderness (*wild:* the condition of all worlds, inner and outer, before the creation of the man-made bewilderments from which we are endeavoring to withdraw)

strategic withdrawal:

any attempt to step from a why, however worthy, into whylessness

as in an extemporaneous walk to a destination unknown; a walk during which everything but your movement through God-knows-where becomes the God-knows-what you're doing

or as in going fishing without desire for fish so that desirelessness becomes the prey you're catching

or as in a stroll to a neighborhood café or tavern one or more neighborhoods removed from any in which you're known, which establishment you then enter not to socialize, read the paper, or eat the (probably bad) food, but just to nurse the single slow drink as you soak, without judgment, in the riverine babble of your city and native tongue

strategic withdrawal: any act you can devise, any psycho-spiritual act at all, that embodies a willingness to wait for the world to disclose itself to you rather than to disclose yourself, your altruism, creativity, skills, energy, ideas, and (let's face it) agenda, myopia, delusions, preconceptions, addictions, and inappropriate trajectories to this world

the willingness to drop all trajectories, willingness to boot up with all extensions OFF, willingness *not* to save this world but simply to wait for it to disclose itself to you, whether anything seems, even after long long waiting, to be disclosing itself to you or not

an act of faith, then, really: faith that the world is *always* disclosing itself, faith that lack of disclosure is impossible: faith that what blocks Creation's ceaseless flow of disclosures is, invariably, *our* calluses and callousness, our old injuries and injuriousness, our plans, cross-purposes, neuroses, absurd speed of passage, divided minds, ruling manias, lack of trust, lack of faith—and our overabundance of faith, too, cf. Thomas Merton: "Prayer is possible only when prayer is impossible"

strategic withdrawal: to step back, now and then, from the possible to take rest in the impossible: to stand without trajectory in the godgiven weather till the soul's identity begins to come with the weathering: to get off my own laboriously cleared and maintained trails and back onto the pristine hence unmarked path by moving, any old how, toward interior nakedness; toward silence; toward what Buddhists call "emptiness," Christians "poverty of spirit," Snyder "wild," and Eckhart "desirelessness: the virgin that eternally gives birth to the Son"

strategic withdrawal: this prayer:

When I'm lost, God help me get more lost. Help me lose me so completely that nothing remains but the primordial peace and originality that keep creating and sustaining this blood-, tear-, and love-worthy world that is never lost for an instant save by an insufficiently lost me

"We're all in the gutter," said Oscar Wilde in the throes of such a withdrawal, "but some of us are looking at the stars"
strategic withdrawal:
look at the stars

—Sheperdstown, West Virginia; cross-country
Delta jet; and Lolo, Montana, Summer 1999

JOHN LANDRETTI

Bear Butte Diary

from *Orion*

JULY 6

A wet morning. The clouds scud by, looking dark and broken. They have that startled watchfulness of things flying past. I hunch on the gravel lot, making coffee. Six scoops, and one for the pot. Across the ravine, the yellow grasses of Bear Butte lift into fog: I can see nothing of the high rocks, sacred place of Crazy Horse. On the ceremonial grounds just beyond the ravine are two tents, our little dome, still standing, and one of those large Coleman contraptions that blew down last night and now, deserted, lies drenched across the shapes of coolers and upturned cots.

His time approaching, Jethro submits to a final obligation: he squats at the side-view mirror and begins to snip off his mustache. The last of the whiskers gather on a paper towel that already holds his beard clippings—an impressive collection, enough hair to cover a small animal. When he comes round to the tailgate, he looks like a middle-aged boy, brave and bashful.

"Sure is strange," he says, feeling his face.

I smile at the sight of him and hold out a cup of coffee. He takes it, but his eyes are on the horizon.

"Any time now," he says, again.

We look at the road that is to bring us the Cheyenne holy man called Vernon Bullcoming. The gravel curves up through prairie wildflowers and disappears against the clouds.

The rattletrap Toyota, I notice, is gone. Its owner probably left when the weather turned bad. He was a white man who, like us, had arrived in the heat and stillness of the previous afternoon. Apparently, he'd placed himself on the mountain in order to fast and pray, as the Cheyenne have done since the days before they were called Cheyenne. Or perhaps he had another tradition in mind and had come to seek a vision in the way of the Sioux. Lamenting, they call it. In any case, while helping Jethro collect sage, I'd glimpsed the man through the pines. He lay prone on a blanket: a person waiting for something. At that haunted hour of late day, the entire earth—the golden plains and far Black Hills—seemed itself to be waiting, every needle and seed inclined to contemplation. The air had been full of sun, stunning in its stillness, the sort of afternoon in which the whole world appears finally to have gotten itself to rights. Indeed, anyone would have been hard-pressed to have lain on those slopes and escaped a little circumstantial peace with God.

Many tribes share a spiritual history with this place. The Mandan and Kiowa, the Arikara, and those two old rivals, the Crow and Sioux—all see Bear Butte as a source of divine emanation. But it is the Cheyenne to whom this mountain is most significant; it's their cathedral, built of fire and wind. Their own word for it refers not to a bear (which the mountain is thought to resemble) but to a locus of spiritual instruction—*Nowah'wus*—The Sacred Mountain Where People Are Taught. It's the place, they say, where spirits taught a holy man called Sweet Medicine how to live rightly. They taught him the dance of world renewal, the Sun Dance. They gave him *Maahotse,* the four Sacred Arrows, through which God blazes and gives his strength to the people. I'm told that these arrows are still with the Cheyenne, guarded by a keeper who lives in Oklahoma. During times of renewal ceremonies, the arrows are driven from one sacred place to another. I imagine them—mythic arrows—wrapped carefully and stored in a car trunk, perhaps at rest near something as ordinary as a suit-case or tire jack.

In accord with tradition, a Cheyenne male gets placed on the butte only after having received the instruction of a holy man. It's a time-consuming and expensive tutelage; one has many rituals to complete in preparation for the fast and many giveaways to make in gratitude for the instruction. A man may be inspired to fast for any number of reasons: to pray for the well-being of a loved one, to heal an old sorrow, but always to learn something about what God has in mind for him. (Women, too, fast, and for similar rea-sons, but they do so at the base of the mountain, near the tents.) A man in fasting remains on the slope, exposed to all weather, from sunset the first night until sunrise the fourth morning, and although he may become terrified by what he dreams or sees, he has his religion, his discipline, to guide him through the worst of it. I picture that white man fleeing the storm, his blanket balled up in his arms. What mixture of relief and humiliation had he felt as he drove through the downpour to the highway below?

With the Toyota gone, our truck and a nearby van are the only vehicles left in the lot. There's a coup stick leaning against the van, and a spear decorated with eagle feathers. After a while, the van rocks and a white-haired man emerges. He limps over to us, ad-justing his cap—a cap like those favored by truckers, except that his logo is a dainty peace pipe, complete with minuscule, free-swinging feathers.

"New York," he says, noting our license plate.

"Upstate," I explain. "Four hours from the nearest knish vender."

He takes the mug Jethro offers him, sips appreciatively, then taps out a Marlboro Gold.

"Coffee and cigarettes," he tells us. "It's what keep me going."

Jethro explains that he's here to be placed on the mountain and that I'm the helper. The man introduces himself as Grover Horn Antelope. He tells us that he is Lakota Sioux, that he's here to help those who will come for the July ceremonies. He gazes up past the flattened tent. On higher ground, pines draped with strips of cloth rise toward the rocks. The fog has begun to lift, showing the first glimpses of talus.

"I've been coming here thirty-three years," Grover says. "I placed a lot of people on these slopes. I'm the old man of this mountain." His voice is soft, pleasing to hear. "I don't charge anybody," he tells us. "I never have." This seems to be a point that he needs to establish. He goes on to talk about how Bear Butte is too often abused by charlatans who traffic vision quests to a gullible population of non-Indians.

"We had some protesters here," Grover says. "Activists who came with megaphones. They were angry at the people who had paid some spiritual leaders hundreds of dollars to fast, and they wanted to pull them down from the mountain. Can you imagine that?" Grover shakes his head. "It is a blasphemy," he says.

I am touched by the reach of his assessment, for I take him to mean that he finds the entire situation—the greed of the holy men, the virulence of the activists, the foolishness of the non-Indians—*all* of it an affront to the power that Bear Butte signifies. Grover remains with us awhile, talking about the mountain with a kind of sweet and wistful reverence. At one point he peeks into his mug and confesses that last summer he lost his wife of forty-three years. He thanks us for the coffee then shuffles back to his van.

A vehicle surfaces against the sky, and Jethro rises from the tail-gate. We see that it is not Bullcoming but another Cheyenne elder, a man called Ralph Red Fox. His truck, a beat-up camper, makes its dusty way around the curve and parks next to us. Ralph climbs out, followed by his partner, a woman in blond braids called Dana. They have come to wish Jethro luck, before making their long drive back to Idaho. I show them the coffeepot, and Ralph produces a convenience store mug the size of a Bavarian tankard.

We met them the day before, in front of the visitor's center. When Ralph discovered that Jethro was preparing for a fast, he tarried awhile, talking with us about the power of this mountain. I was struck by the formidability of his presence. In his lined face and mirthful eyes lay a peculiar quality of oldness; it wasn't the venerable quality of human age but rather something much older: the humorous and elemental longevity of hills and sky. He spoke quietly, like Grover, talking about the supernatural in the calm fashion of a man who knows and respects his weather. He told us that he was a shaman, that he had knowledge of an ancient ceremony called the Massaum. He said that each summer he passed a few weeks traveling among the sacred places to talk with anyone who wanted to learn what they meant to the Cheyenne. Like Grover he'd seen his share of sham medicine men.

"So, what do you do when you encounter these people?" I asked.

"I go talk to them," he said.

"And what do they do?"

"They leave."

"They leave?" I said. "Just like that?"

He nodded, then replied in a way that I would have judged fatuous but for the considerable dignity of his bearing. "I speak from the heart," he said. "People know."

As that evening approached—the day still warm and golden—Ralph invited us to join Dana and him for a visit. We finished our supper then drove to their camp at Bear Butte Lake. By then it was nightfall. Lightning blinked along the hills, and the wind plied the stillness, leisurely sweeps of it, fragrant with rain. Dana set out sweet rolls, and the four of us sat at a picnic table where we talked about the day and how good it felt to be at the mountain. When we finished our coffee, Ralph invited us to pray. He produced some sage and began rolling it between his palms. He whispered, speaking in syllables I'd never heard before, a melodic concatenation, one that put me in mind of chipped cliffs against a spatter of clouds. When he finished, he placed the sage in Jethro's palm. He showed him the way to hold it then encouraged him to pray. Jethro was quiet a moment, his lips moving beneath his beard. A moment later, he passed the sage to Dana, who whispered a prayer and then passed the sage to me. It lay in my palm, a slender sphere of crushed leaves that Jethro later told me signified a wolf's tail.

"Just pray?" I asked.

Ralph nodded, so I did, then hoped that what I'd murmured was appropriate. When I finished, Ralph placed the sphere on the table and touched it with his cigarette. As the leaves smoldered, he poked among several sandwich bags in his medicine bundle. "Hmm," he mumbled. "Don't want this . . . better not use that . . . Ah!" He sprinkled what looked like wood shavings over the fragrant smoke. After smudging himself, he motioned for us to do the same, then passed around his medicine bundle so that each of us could cradle it in our arms. When our praying was finished, Ralph lowered his face to the table and blew away the ashes. We were quiet awhile, reflecting on what had transpired. The wind continued to blow—the gusts more powerful than before—filling the cottonwoods with an urgent, lonesome sound. I felt at peace, as I had in childhood, when my family was gathered around the table and outside it was dark and raining.

Ralph lit another cigarette. "I received my bundle in 1937," he said. "That was the last time the Massaum was held."

The Massaum, as he explained it, and as Jethro later recounted from his own reading,[1] was a complex ceremony in which the

---

1 An illuminating book on this subject, to which I owe my synopsis of the Massaum, is Karl Schlesier's comprehensive text, *The Wolves of Heaven* (Norman: University of Oklahoma Press, 1987).

Cheyenne, or the Tsistsistas, reenacted the creation of all things—from the inception of time to the gift of the hunt—and in doing so reaffirmed their covenant with the spirits. Once a year the different bands came together to build a lodge that symbolized Bear Butte. Around this they raised other lodges and tipis, all contained within a circle. Here, for five days, they performed the innumerable rituals required to bring the universe into being. The last day culminated in the Massaum's most effusive ritual: scores of people, all dressed as animals, emerged from tipis and danced in a grand circle, now mimicking wolves, buffalo, magpie, elk, now falling at the hands of contraries—sacred clowns who hunted them with tiny bows and arrows. Beginning with its genesis at Bear Butte, the Massaum took place once each summer for over two thousand years. It is older than the culture of the pipe, even older than the gift of the four Sacred Arrows; in tracing the Massaum to its origins, one traces the forging of a people to its source.

"No one person knew *all* of the Massaum," Ralph said. "It was too big. But for a time there were three of us left who could initiate a ceremony. We each had our part, our power.

"One of us was a shape-changer. You threw a buffalo robe over him and he'd fly off an eagle, then a moment later you'd see him come walking back over the hill."

"You mean you actually saw that happen?" I said.

Ralph nodded. "His power was the eagle. The other's was the wolf. Mine too is the wolf." He smiled at me.

I wasn't sure what to make of this fantastic claim. I was convinced of his sincerity, yet at the same time I doubted that any man could literally, I don't know—puff like vapor? slither like fluid? fold like origami?—*become* a bird. It's a familiar ambiguity, one that I experience whenever credible people tell me about the ghosts they've encountered or about strange and giant lights adrift beneath the stars. At any rate, something within me believes them—the same something that believes Ralph Red Fox—though whether that something has its source in subconscious wisdom or merely credulous desire, I cannot say.

"So," I asked, "where are they now, these two men?"

Ralph waved his hand. "Passed over. A long time ago. What they knew went with them. There was no one to pass their knowledge along to."

He took a puff of his cigarette. I looked at him, more stirred by that bit of news than I had been by the implications of the shape-changer; if what he had said were true, then I was seeing a person who embodied the last living part of a religion that predated Christ. His eyes twinkled, full of humor. "You know," he said, "the days are past when this mountain was for Cheyenne and Sioux only. It's for everybody now."

Later, as Jethro drove us back to our own campsite, I stared out the window at the many different lightnings. In a less peaceful mood, I found myself dwelling not only on the loss of the Massaum but also on the implications of Ralph's pronouncement: The mountain is for everybody now. This sentiment, so childlike, so necessary, nonetheless presents a problem. I see it in the folly of that white man who had fled the storm. Clearly he thought "the mountain is for everybody now." And yet he had not been prepared to face the power to which he was praying. Perhaps Ralph meant that Bear Butte, pursued as a spiritual locus, is for anybody willing to submit to the religious tradition that the mountain informs. In contrast to a literal reading of Ralph's words, this interpretation is more qualified and I'd hazard more accurate. I think it's dangerous to presume that I could walk into any sacred place and under the protectorship of my own goodwill safely engage its deeper mysteries. Sincerity alone is no match for a confrontation with terror. It's not that a person like me, governed largely by humanism, or the Toyota man, governed by who knows what, isn't welcomed to these places, isn't invited into the love they offer—I sense that we are, and abundantly so. But without exercising the appropriate humility we put our lives at risk.

Standing in the lot with his tankard of coffee, Ralph wishes Jethro good fortune; Dana gives him an enviable hug, and then we are watching their old camper trundle up the road, bound for Devil's Tower or some other holy place. The rest of the day we haunt the parking lot, waiting for Bullcoming. The fog burns away, revealing the rocks of the high summit. According to park literature, Bear Butte is a laccolith—the remains of a volcano that never blew. From a distance to the west, this uplift stands like an enormous tipi collared by shelves of upended limestone. As the Cheyenne see it, the summit is so much deep earth—home of spirits—flung high into the sphere of breath: what is hidden elsewhere is revealed here.

In the afternoon I put on more coffee. When it's ready, Grover Horn Antelope limps over, and we three sit on the tailgate, not saying much. Now and then Jethro feels his naked chin. The clouds have slowed. They uncobble and form a haze through which a hawk floats up to a more bracing altitude. It is a lazy time, and I think of that James Wright poem about a wasted life. Grover gives us the scoop on medicine man gossip. Once he caught the famous Fools Crow telling a lie, how he had misled a group into believing that he'd passed corporally through the heart of Bear Butte. Grover gestured angrily, two fingers thrust to one side.

"I have walked through this mountain," Grover announces, gesturing. "But in *spirit.* If I were to do it in person, I'd have to dig with a shovel. My power"—he touches his chest—"is the spotted eagle." He pauses, gazing up at the sky. When the coffee is gone, he returns to his van. Earlier I noticed his medicine bundle—like Ralph's, a beautifully beaded affair—tucked up on the dash amid coffee-stained papers and wads of crumpled cellophane.

At dusk Jethro and I hike from the ceremonial grounds up to the visitor's center. The place is closed; behind us, Bear Butte rises in darkened splendor. There's a trailhead for sightseers. Like the aisles of a temple, the trail is posted with signs that warn tourists away from sacred areas. From our high vantage, the plains open below, the grasses freckled with bison. The haze has passed over, and a star or two shines in a contrite way. As we gaze into the distance, I find that all the worries I cannot will into oblivion now fade without effort. About distances, perhaps Emerson is right: "The health of the eye seems to demand a horizon. We are never tired, so long as we can see far enough." Together, Jethro and I watch the cars as they approach from Sturgis. All day long, people have been arriving for the first of the July ceremonies. Mostly Indians in big Plymouths and low-slung Rivieras. They park their cars and haul gear across the ravine to the ceremonial grounds. A couple of tipis have gone up. On the twilit slope, they glow like lanterns.

We conjecture about Bullcoming's continuing absence. At last report he was in Montana, assisting in a Sun Dance ceremony. Jethro feels the tops of the grass. His expression is composed yet drawn; in a rare moment I witness the strain of the burden that has brought him here. I admire him for the dignity of his restraint, for all that he has not told me. I do not know him well, this colleague. Though we've been acquainted for a number of years, I knew nothing of his spiritual apprenticeship (if that is the word) with the Seneca Indians of western New York. He was, to me, simply a farmer with merry eyes, a librarian with a habit of making kindly asides to bushes and pigeons. Since I agreed to accompany him, he has but once alluded to the brutal violence that his wife had suffered and that has brought him here to fast for their mutual healing.

How Jethro came under the guidance of a Cheyenne holy man occurred in the curious way that a number of coincidences, by force of their collective effect, upgrade to a mystical experience. It begins one spring night with a dream. In it Jethro sees a mountain whose power and beauty remain with him in his waking hours. Weeks later, while reviewing some photographs, he is astonished to discover that this dream mountain is an actual place, Bear Butte. That fall, after a visit to his mother in Oklahoma, he rents a car and begins to drive north. He is bound for no particular place, though there is someone he wishes to find—Roy Bullcoming—a man whose picture he'd encountered while studying a demographic text of the Southern Cheyenne. Like the mountain of his dream, the image of Roy Bullcoming stays with him, though given the number of prints in the text he cannot explain what draws him to the picture of that particular man. Tooling north, he turns to the east or west whenever the urge takes him. At a few crossroads he is unsure about which way to turn, and so he waits until a hawk appears—one always does—and the direction it flies is the direction he goes.

Come late afternoon he arrives in a town called Seiling. Feeling that this is the right place, he knocks at a few doors and does his best to explain himself. A woman tells him that yes, she knew of Roy Bullcoming, that the man died some years ago. But his wife is still alive, she lives just up the road. Jethro walks to the door of Bullcoming's widow. He introduces himself, explains how it is that he has come to Seiling. The woman hears him out, and eventually Jethro ends up in a small room, seated at a table where two other women are at work, beading pipe bags. A television blares in the next room, a western, Jethro notices, complete with whooping Indians. Bullcoming's widow allows that she has a son,

Vernon, to whom her husband passed his medicine, and whom she will tell of Jethro's intentions when he returns home that evening. Jethro thanks her for her time, then takes a room at the local motel. At dusk, Vernon Bullcoming shows up, a big man wearing a ball cap.

"Oh, ho," he says.

They shake hands, then Vernon sits in a chair and listens to what this man from New York has to say. When Jethro finishes his petition, when it is clear that he said all that he intended, Vernon assents: he agrees to place Jethro on the mountain. They arrange to meet the next morning, then shake hands at the doorway.

"I'm grateful for your help," Jethro says.

"I knew you were coming here," Vernon tells him.

Jethro asks how he could have known such a thing.

"I dreamed you," Vernon replies.

Night comes and still Vernon has not arrived. We build a fire. For a while I help Jethro keep vigil. We smoke quietly, waiting for a light to appear in the parking lot. Eventually I grow sleepy and so take a stroll out into the grasses. At the ravine, I gaze upward. Clear again. A sky so starry that it seems as if one night has slightly overlapped another. It is a sky that I have seen in other places: from the Escalante River, the Adirondack Mountains, the red cliffs of Superior's southern shore. If the center is everywhere, as I feel it must be, then what is the point of a place like Bear Butte? Why a Ganges or a Mecca? What vestiges of a bygone spiritual event make any one of these places more divinely central than any other place? Or is sanctification subordinate to the effects of accumulated prayer? I stare into the stars. From their remove, how absurd our geographical distinctions must seem. To think that God, in touching this blue point of light, presses more firmly upon this butte here, that river there. Yet despite my skepticism, I cannot deny the inordinate sense of awe I feel in the company of this butte. Or that I have felt before the windows of Chartres or among the ruins of Incan temples. In all these places, I encountered a powerful and immediate presence, a genius loci, that I must admit does not so apparently grace the common byways, that I cannot explain without producing postulates no more true—and far less interesting—than those plucky nostrums put forth by the old natural philosophers. And so these places exist. And so we covet them. And for that reason soil their names with our inhumanity, as evidenced by Grover's story of the angry protesters and exploited acolytes.

July 7

Dawn. Assuming Bullcoming arrives, Jethro will begin his fast this evening: three nights and two days on a blanket. I turn around and find his sleeping bag empty. Outside, a magpie lifts from the sumac; the valleys look cool and breathed upon. Down at the parking lot I discover him keeping vigil on his tailgate, one leg crossed, the coffee ready. I barely finish my first cup when a sedan surfaces at the ridge. It drifts toward us, slumped to one side, a rack of suitcases twined to the roof.

"It's them!" Jethro says.

The car stops in front of us. A big man steps out and rises slowly to his full height. He greets Jethro, then stretches and looks around. I put him at fifty, a potbellied fellow wearing a short-sleeved dress shirt and reading glasses. Unlike Ralph Red Fox, Vernon does not match my preconception of a Cheyenne holy man; he reminds me, somehow, of an electrician. His car is filled with the Bullcoming family, some sleeping soundly, others newly awake and frowning thoughtfully. Though the sun is just rising, it is clear they've been on the road for hours. While Bullcoming produces a number of folding chairs, I pour coffee for him and his wife, Rhoda. They accept it gratefully. Meanwhile Grover Antelope, coffee-prescient, limps over from his van.

While I cook breakfast, everybody sits in a circle and talks in a pleasant, lazy fashion. We have much to do, and I am anxious to work, but nothing is said about Jethro's fast. Instead, Vernon and Grover exchange stories about hunting mishaps. By degrees, the children empty themselves from the sedan: one after the other, they roll out of the backseat like stowed circus clowns. They are jug-eared and skinny, solemn before this fresh change of events. They go to Rhoda and wait shyly for their oatmeal and fruit.

As the morning grows hot, we go to work hauling gear onto the ceremonial grounds. We establish a fire pit and raise a large tent. Bullcoming fashions an awning, using strips of scrap wood, frayed baling twine, and a ratty tarp. When his work is done, he gives one of the posts an affectionate shake.

"Indian," he says.

We drive to Sturgis for groceries: pounds of meat, sweet rolls, and coffee. Later, while Rhoda cooks, Vernon talks quietly to Jethro. He offers last-minute counsel, his hands drifting in a series of deliberate gestures. An hour before sundown, the ceremony begins. Two other Cheyenne men amble up from another campsite. No introductions are made; they simply join Vernon, Jethro, and me in the tent. We sit in a circle, and Jethro tells the story of his coming to Bear Butte. He talks about the violence visited upon his wife and, so, upon him. While we listen, his voice cracks. We remain silent as he wipes his eyes and continues. He expresses his wish to heal and, in accord with tradition, to pray for the healing of the earth. He ends by thanking us for being with him at this, his first fast. When he has finished, the men grunt affirmingly. Then Bullcoming instructs Jethro to light his pipe—a genuine catlinite pipe that Jethro has spent the year carving. The pipe is passed around the circle. Each man points it in the six directions then puffs with easeful vigor. At last, I get the pipe. I have never held one before. I aim it around at the various directions then take a few tentative puffs. Nobody appears to judge my awkwardness. Bullcoming puts out a bit of food for the spirits, then we feast on grilled chicken and sweet rolls. The meal complete, Jethro takes his last gulp from a plastic bucket containing water from his farm in the Finger Lakes and my old home in the Wisconsin River Valley. He sets it down, gives me a wry grin. He is now a man in fasting.

As the dusk approaches, Bullcoming signals us and a couple of teenagers to his sedan. We drive along a lane to a trailhead hidden by plum trees. Bullcoming removes a buffalo skull from the trunk and starts walking. We follow him up into the grasses: Jethro empty-handed, the teenagers bearing his things, and I at the rear with a flashlight. We walk silently, and I enjoy the comradely pleasure of moving single file through a dusky landscape. The sun, just setting, draws a long shadow from Bear Butte. The shadow is shaped like a tipi. Far below us lies Bear Butte Lake, shaped like an arrowhead. As the land darkens, the tipi disappears, but the lake remains blue and lighted.

Bullcoming seems to use the buffalo skull as a kind of divining rod. When he—or it—finds the right spot, he plants the skull with pronounced finality. As we look on, he kneels and begins plucking away grass. He rubs his thumb into the earth then arranges a bed of sage bundles. At last, he instructs Jethro to remove all but his shorts. While I aim the light, Bullcoming paints Jethro's wrists and ankles. He paints his cheeks blue, his chest red, then ends with a general basting of yellow. We unfurl Jethro's bedroll then tip him, like a pole, backward to the earth. We draw a sheet over his body and, rather tenderly, tuck him in. Near his head, I arrange some matches and his pipe. Then I join the teenagers standing back beside a clump of yucca. They seem detached yet unhurried. When at last Bullcoming finishes the initiation, the four of us walk away as silently as we'd arrived.

To the east a few stars twinkle contentedly. The west glows like lighted blood.

At midnight, I help the Bullcoming family carry gear down to their sedan. They must travel back to Montana to return grandchildren and collect additional cookware. We cross the ravine to the parking lot. On the hill above us, flashlights bob as yet another group makes camp. Rhoda carefully inserts limp children into the backseat. As Bullcoming starts the engine, I step away and peek through the windows. The dash lights, those that work, glow wanly on an array of hands and knees. The back is dark and crowded, the small bodies arranged among thick blankets and pillows. As the sedan begins its backward drift, I glimpse the face of a small child. It peers out blankly at me from deep within its burrow of siblings. What magnificent memories you will have, I think.

JULY 8

After sunrise, I walk up past the plum trees to check on Jethro. I am to do this at dawn and dusk for each day of the fast. I stroll, hands in my pockets, on this fine, chilly morning. Bear Butte Lake sparkles flinty blue, and the giant tipi-shadow of the mountain slants steeply to the west. I find Jethro laid out among the cone flowers.

"How is it?" I say, sitting beside him.

He rubs his face, looks rested and content. "Just fine," he says.

I sit a while longer, and we both look out at the freshly lighted plains. In the far distance, we can see Harney Peak. It was there, in his famous vision, that Black Elk had been shown the hoop of the world: a giant circle of circles containing his people and all the nations of earth. It was a transcendent vision, built upon many images of beauty and vitality—the revolving rows of horses, the flowering trees—but upon destruction and suffering too, for the Grandfathers did not spare Black Elk the heartbreaking sight of his own broken hoop: the dying tree of his people, the spectacle of their bewildered lamentations. I give Jethro's arm a squeeze and start back down the slope.

In camp, I start my chores. There is a pile of scrap lumber in the parking lot, and my task is to carry the boards across the ravine and up the slope to our fire pit. There, I must use my foot to crack the boards into manageable lengths. It is nasty work. I have no gloves, and all the lumber is ungainly and splintered. After stocking our camp, I haul still more lumber to an *inipi,* or sweat-lodge site. I keep at it for quite a while, hauling load after load to the fire pit beside the *inipi* frame. As I work, the two Cheyenne men who attended last evening's ceremonial dinner wander out from their tent. They arrange folding chairs in the shade and for a long time sip coffee and monitor the progress of my labor. Eventually I have accumulated an enormous heap beside the *inipi* frame. I catch my breath then spend time arranging the wood into what looks to me like a neat, spiritual pile. Sweat soaked, I approach the two men to find out precisely how much wood I will need to collect for two sweat-lodge ceremonies. They lean from their chairs, observing my pile. One of them is tall and gray-haired, dressed like a cowboy. The other is a stout, narrow-eyed man with a belly like the Buddha. The gray-haired man says that I'm getting close. I thank him, and he nods agreeably. He then mentions, as an aside, that some other group will simply take all my wood and burn it for their own ceremony. I brush at my arms, imagine tipping him out of his chair. The gray-haired man laughs. His laughter is sharp. He looks to his companion, who smiles sleepily, then back at me: "Your friend is all right?"

"It's getting hot," I say.

The gray-haired man snatches at the air, making a fist. "The sun is watching," he says. "It will try to *beat* him."

He instructs me to sit down—something I do not have to be told twice. The man tells me that he is Gilbert White Dirt, his companion a man called Glen. Gilbert, too, is a Cheyenne holy man. With pride, he gestures at the mountain and lets me know that he has placed many people up there. He touches Glen's arm. "I placed Glen," he says. His companion, who is looking else-where and does not appear to be listening, smiles in agreement. I tell Gilbert that a couple of days ago I didn't know any holy men, and now I know four. I tell him about our evening with Ralph Red Fox, how moving it had been to learn about the Massaum, to sit and pray with him.

Gilbert is unimpressed. He dismisses Ralph with a wave of his hand. Ralph, he tells me, is a fake. Startled by this pronounce-ment, I review my memory of Ralph, and though I sense that Gilbert is both informed and sincere, I cannot abide by his judg-ment. Nonetheless, Gilbert remains adamant, so much so that he finds the subject beneath debate. He will say no more about Ralph but turns with vigor to my questions about worship. Like Ralph, like Bullcoming and old Grover, Gilbert White Dirt appears to relish an occasion for spiritual discourse; indeed, he settles into it as readily as other men settle into talk about sports. He listens to what I offer about my own religious history. I allow that I was raised Catholic but have not practiced that faith in fifteen years. Nonetheless, I have always believed in God and have even re-tained a Christian impression of Him—that is, the impression of an imperious and yet loving presence from whom we have be-come separated and who wishes that we would rejoin Him once again. I do not tell Gilbert how I tend to visualize this presence: as the distortion of a childhood memory, the blue and white swirls of my grandmother's kitchen floor thinned to transparency— God, a kind of etherialized linoleum. It is, I believe, a semblance that can only survive in the head of a person whom hardship has not pressed into forging a more restorative image.

In the end, Gilbert tells me that I must get myself placed on that mountain.

I squint up at the glaring talus.

"You will come back to Bear Butte," he says, pointing at me.

"Well," I say.

He laughs loudly at my equivocation.

I find that I like him, this hard-edged Gilbert White Dirt. The keenness of his conviction makes for a refreshing counterpoint to the soft-spoken natures of the other holy men. More so, the quality of his weathered and aquiline features reminds me of faces that I've seen in my dreams. Like Gilbert's, these faces are always stern and watchful, but, unlike Gilbert, they never tell me anything. Instead, they seem to be waiting for me to act, as if I must rectify a series of temporal deflections that over time have steered me into my current state of spiritual ambivalence.

While the sweat dries on my back, Gilbert tells me about the culture of the Sacred Pipe. He explains its lovely symbolism of red bowl and sumac stem, of breath and smoke. He tells the story of that terrible beauty, the White Calf Woman, who brought the pipe to the Sioux, and thence the Plains Indians. The longer he talks, the more the shadows shrink toward the tree trunks. To escape the glare, I find myself scrunching closer to their chairs. At last, we three are crowded together beneath a tiny cottonwood. Our conversation ends with Gilbert telling a rather lame joke about Indians, hot dogs, and penises.

Although it is lunchtime, the light is so intense that none of us is ready to move. We yield to the silence of the hour, each of us squinting at the peaks. Far away, a raven floats from a twist of juniper. The only sound is that of a few Sioux children crashing about in the ravine—a place surely populated with rattlesnakes and all manner of venomous creatures. Yesterday, Rhoda shook her head at their antics. "Those Sioux," she muttered. "The Cheyenne say they don't watch their kids close enough. They run wild and make the weather change."

At last Gilbert rises. He stretches then tips back his cowboy hat. "Tonight," he says. "You come and pray with us."

In the full heat of afternoon, I stroll up to the visitor's center to view the distant Black Hills. Despite the ferocity of the light, I forego sunglasses. I've noticed that none of the Indians around here wear them. Hat-brimmed or open-faced, all go about their day squinting complacently. It's a signature look, quite distinct from the polarized, mirrory gaze of tourists. I pause to squint at the view, which last night had looked so pleasing. Now, as I peer across that vast cauldron of grasses, I think about Jethro, who surely must be having a time of it.

How peculiar, our use of pain to transcend an early, greater suffering. There are Cheyenne men who have walked in wide circles, dragging behind them a cavalcade of buffalo skulls, each one attached by cord to a slice in his back. What visions of heaven flower from the soil of so great a tribulation? I am always sobered to meet the profoundly religious, those who have voluntarily undergone privation in order to better understand God's will for them. Invariably, these individuals glow with an inner grace not nearly so consistent—or even evident—in the rest of us. *Spiritus lenitatis,* St. Bernard called it. Indeed, the serene clarity and compassion in the eyes of the devout seem testimony to the rightness of their difficult choices.

I glance up at these scorched slopes that have housed so much suffering and transcendence, and I wonder about my own choices: whether it's folly to sidestep religious tradition and instead seek a largely secular path to God by acting on the most magnanimous thoughts of mortals like Emerson or Whitman, by emulating the tradition of all those poets whose passion for life is so mindfully tempered by their address of suffering and death, whose response to the human condition is to live out their days filled with a rollicky mixture of uncertainty, ebullience, compassion, and pride.

In the visitor's center, I drink deep from the icy arc of the water fountain. The interior is dim and cool. There is the usual circumference of glass cases. I regard the stones and dried plants, the assortment of ceremonial garments. There are no tourists around, so Chuck Rambow, the head ranger, spends some time talking with me. He is an affable man. Twenty years on the job, and he still visibly lights up at the prospect of a discussion about the butte. He has about him that air of childlike wonder common among people who have found themselves in a particular landscape. I think of Edward Abbey, bounding up all those slot canyons, or John Muir, striding through the columbine in the Sierras.

While Chuck brews some coffee, I question him about Grover Horn Antelope's dig at Fools Crow, about Gilbert White Dirt's disparagement of Ralph. Chuck smiles, somewhat sadly. Apparently there is a measure of petty rivalry among the various holy men. Some of the more purely traditional sort, like Gilbert, resent the more progressive, politically oriented tactics of an itinerant like Ralph. Others, like Grover and Fools Crow, interpret their religion in ways so distinct from one another that they find themselves at loggerheads.

In any case, Chuck's assessment strikes me as so obvious that I find myself embarrassed for not having figured this out on my own; impressed as I was by the spiritual presence of each, I failed to allow for their humanity and so reduced them to so many religious cartoons. It is that tendency, I imagine, that makes it so easy for spiritual hucksters to swindle a crowd.

At dusk, I hike up the hill to check on Jethro. I find him tucked beneath his sheet. There is no moisture around his lips, just a tacky whiteness. The paints have streaked from his skin, leaving the after-image of a lighter sunburn. I reach over to his pipe bag and set down an extra book of matches.

"How is it?" I ask.

He rises up on one elbow, stares out at the land, blinking. "Awfully warm," he replies. "How about you?"

"Not as bad."

He laughs then lifts his arm, pointing at a place in the sky. "You know that sun? It stayed, right there. In fact, I think at one point it went backward."

We rest awhile, looking out at the prettiness of the valley.

After dark, I light a fire and wait for the Bullcomings to return. I'm just washing my pots when a child runs up to me. He nods to the tent of Gilbert White Dirt then runs away. I follow after him and find Gilbert waiting for me, holding his pipe bag the way a person holds a newborn. Glen is at his side, wrapped in a shawl. We walk past a tent where five Cheyenne women sit under the stars, fasting. We go another twenty paces then sit three abreast in the dry grass. Gilbert faces the sky and begins to sing the Cheyenne "Song of the Buffalo," the sound of it as melodic as the antiphony of any Benedictine monk. Every now and then Glen blows on a whistle made of eagle bone; the device produces a sound so shrill that it must bring even the stars to attention. I am left feeling alert, fully alive.

We each pray aloud in our own turn, I in English, they in Cheyenne. At one point Gilbert's voice cracks, and I realize that he is in tears. He continues his prayers, his voice faltering, hands open to the sky. Then he settles back and we are quiet. The pipe is passed. I puff, feel the joy and peace that I had after rolling the sage with Jethro, Dana, and Ralph Red Fox.

The praying finished, we struggle to our feet. We pause before the tent so that Gilbert can bless the women. While waiting, I stare at the tiny lights shimmering on the plains below and am moved by their beauty and remoteness. Yet unlike the previous evening, I do not experience this spectacle of distance with the tender rejuvenation to which Emerson referred, but rather I am struck by a more troubling acuity as noted by Virginia Woolf, here commenting on the distant twinkling of a beach town: "The lights were rippling and running as if they were drops of silver water held firm in the wind. And all the poverty, all the suffering had turned to that—" How much there is to keep in mind if we are to be true to this world: A swoon inspired by a pretty horizon is never the whole of it but only marks the threshold of a more complicated communion.

As we file back toward the tents, the pale glow of a beacon from Ellsworth Air Force Base sweeps lightly across the back of Glen's old shawl. There is an appeal in the light, something beseeching in its constant return, to which the shawl does not respond. I once lived with a Navajo man who told me one day that I would make a terrible Indian. I laughed, because I saw that he was right, and the observation has had the curious effect of freeing me from ever wanting to become an Indian or of succumbing to the delusion that because a culture appeals to me I could assume the emotional weight of its history, as if all its complexities could be swallowed whole and brought to life inside me. Of course, I may convert to another religion or adopt another culture—but only as an application to the inviolate core of my own heritage. In my case, a heritage that reaches back through centuries of Christian Europe: stones, candles, iron, books.

We emerge from the bushes, walking single file. I gaze up at the butte, am amazed to see an aura sliding like silk along the highest rocks. I tug Glen's shawl and point this out to him.

"It does that," he tells me.

July 9

Dawn. The Bullcomings have returned from Montana, and all are sleeping soundly. Rhoda's pots and pans rest in a ready heap near the fire pit. The air is soft and still. I hear only the delicate questionings of birds and, from somewhere among the tents, a man snoring with astounding resonance. Quietly, I make coffee. I notice that across the ravine, on the slope above the parking lot, yet another camp has established itself. The group—the largest one yet—has arranged a kind of chuck wagon at its center. A small figure stands before it, manipulating different steams and smokes.

Nearer the ravine, the sumac quiver. A row of women emerges. Wrapped in white sheets, they walk single file through the campsite. They move swiftly and without words, the downward tilt of their heads suggesting—from even my vantage—a deep and focused humility. They disappear among some cottonwoods, the sheets twitching at their heels. It is a stirring sight, a human archetype of this hemisphere.

"Boy," Jethro says, when I visit him. "Who was doing all that drumming and singing last night?"

"What drumming and singing?" I say.

He blinks, wipes a crust of skin from his lips. The rocks glow with the first strong blast of sunlight.

I spend the morning running errands for Rhoda. Seated in her chair, she recites a list of goods for the feast that she will prepare to honor Jethro's return. Though it is a long list, there is no hesitancy in her recital.

"You've done this before," I say.

She indulges me with a smile then looks out at the cliffs. I sit with her for a while, and she tells me how she is worried about Jethro. I recall the quiet way she had approved of the ceremonial moccasins that he had spent the year designing and beading. The heat intensifies. It casts a stillness over the entire camp. Even the crickets call it quits. Each of us finds a place under the awning, and I fall into a deep sleep.

When I awake I find that the Bullcomings have left. To town perhaps. There is no movement among the tents. The sun, at least, has slipped to the west. It ignites a ridge of wrinkled limestone. The stone, so deeply creased with shadow, seems alive, composed of faces that shift watchfully. Compared with this subtle and ominous sight, Mount Rushmore seems an even greater travesty than I'd previously judged it. As I gaze across the ravine, I am surprised to see that the new campsite with the chuck wagon is gone. Where once there had been so many tents and people, there now is only a flattened spread of grass, eerily vacant.

Alone before those old watchful rocks, I put on a pot of coffee and find that I am depressed. The shift of mood reminds me of how circumstantial my peace tends to be, how tentative—much like the stillness on our first afternoon at this butte, before the weather turned. Just as the coffee is ready, Grover Horn Antelope appears, strolling through the grass with a walking stick. He joins me under the awning, and I happily hand him a cup. He sips, gazing at the rocks. I absorb what I can of his peacefulness, this old man who lost his wife of forty-three years, who as a Lakota elder has surely seen his share of suffering and injustice.

"Those people across the ravine," I say. "That was quite a spread they had there. What happened to them?"

Grover sets down his cup. He continues to look out at the rocks. "Oh, they had a young girl in their group, and she broke her fast. When that happens, it can bring bad luck for the other people up on the hill. They had to clear out quick." He is quiet a moment, as if to let his account of the mishap come apart in the air and drift away. He lights a cigarette then tells me about the time when he was a boy, how he had lain under the sun for nine days. "It was long," he says, "but I had my vision."

At dusk, when I visit Jethro, he does not lift his head. I worry that he has suffered heatstroke. I squat beside him, watchful. His face is swollen. He opens his eyes and manages a smile.

"The sun," he says. "Stayed right there, all day." He points, as he had yesterday, then lets his arm drop.

"How are you doing otherwise?"

He nods vaguely. "Got some ticks coming around. The same one, I think. Throw him off and an hour later he's back. I took some notes." He gestures at his journal, bookmarked with a pen.

"Tomorrow," I say. "We'll go to town and I'll buy you a milk-shake."

"Now, that's a good idea," he says and closes his eyes.

As the sky reddens, I return to camp just in time for the *inipi* ceremony. Grover Horn Antelope has been asked to conduct it. I join the others, a bunch of loose-gutted men and women standing around in bathing trunks. Grover stands near the fire pit, wrapped in a beach towel advertising Marlboro cigarettes. He holds his pipe aloft, singing loudly to the four directions. We go into the dome, and in the darkness Grover touches sweetgrass to the heated rocks. It gives off a stirring scent, a savor whose mnemonic powers are on par with the pungency of wet juniper or a crush of crisp, brown leaves. We pray and chant. There are four sessions. Each one builds to a kind of spiritual free-for-all; our chanting swirls skyward like flocks of joyful starlings. I think of Ralph Red Fox and imagine the Massaum, all of those whirling animal-people and sacred clowns, all two thousand years of them, rising with our songs and dispersing among the stars. When at last the ceremony ends, I stagger out and see that the day is gone. The sky is cool, and the planets shine, bright and wet. The group picks its way over the stony ground to shake hands with Grover. High above the sweat lodge, a remote sound pierces the air. Looking up, I can just make out the specks of innumerable birds—eagles—source of Grover's power. People point at the sky, agree that it was good ceremony. I make it my wish that what we have done helps Jethro and the others through this final night.

July 10

Two hours until sunrise. The Bullcoming family moves around in the lantern light, preparing the feast. More Bullcoming relatives have arrived late in the night, many young men in cowboy hats. In the cool air these men and I shuffle around in the ravine, yanking deadwood from the tangle of poison ivy.

As the sky lightens, Vernon gathers a number of the men, and we all make the long walk up the hill. Jethro sits up when he sees us coming. We help him to his feet, drape the white sheet from his shoulders. He looks wan and pink but amenable. He gazes out at the landscape whose company he has kept these last sixty hours. The men in the cowboy hats gather up his bedroll, his pipe and tobacco ties. Bullcoming tucks sage into the buffalo skull then hands it to me. With Vernon out front, followed by Jethro and the rest, we file down the hill. Approaching the camp, we are greeted by a row of five Cheyenne men. They are facing the sunrise. They are singing for Jethro, a Cheyenne song of welcome and return: "YOU ARE A MAN NOW!" they sing, "YOU ARE A MAN NOW!"

After the *inipi,* Bullcoming blesses some cloth, which I am asked to tie to a branch of ponderosa pine. And thus Jethro's fast is officially finished. We have our feast, and Jethro hands out his giveaways: handmade shirts and blankets for all those who have helped him. He looks exhausted but serene. Perhaps the long, slow healing for both him and his wife has begun to take hold. Eventually, all of his gift boxes are empty. The children run off to play, while the adults lounge in the shade.

As the afternoon grows hotter, people throughout the camp begin to take leave. We say good-bye to the men in Cheyenne cowboy hats. Gilbert White Dirt strikes his camp and says farewell. In parting, he sets a mirror on a card table, along with a scrap of paper and pencil. He commands me to look into the mirror while drawing a circle. Then Gilbert takes the pencil and does the same. Glen follows him, and then the young boy who had fetched me down for prayers. I look at their results: three perfect hoops next to my crumpled line. Gilbert swats me on the shoulder.

"You'll come back!" he says.

I smile at him, still uncertain but pleased.

By late afternoon, the Bullcomings have left, gone north to another Sun Dance ceremony. All that remains on the campground are a couple of *inipi* frames and a few empty fire pits. While hauling the last of our gear to Jethro's truck, I find Grover Antelope seated in the shade of a cottonwood.

"I'll be here awhile," he says. He gazes out at the fire pits. "It gets kind of lonely when they all go. But I like the quiet." I thank him for his company, give him a fresh pack of Marlboros and a pound of gourmet coffee.

"Come back," he says in his quiet, pleasing way. "I'll drill some more into your head."

In the parking lot, I find Jethro standing by himself, his thumbs in his pockets. We take a last look around before falling into the truck for the long drive home. In the sky, over the ridge of wildflowers, Jethro spots an unusual cloud, brilliantly white. It is shaped like a buffalo in full gallop. The likeness is stunning, requires no effort to conceptualize.

"Jesus," I say. "You want me to get a picture?"

"No, no," Jethro says, "let it be."

And so I do, and we drive up the road, and a moment later the buffalo is only a cloud drifting apart over a hill.

LEAH KONCELIK LEBEC

Stillbirth

from *First Things*

I woke up feeling not too great. The weight of the baby pulled at my back and sides. In the past couple of weeks it had been getting harder to turn over in bed. I wasn't that big yet, but all the weight was so concentrated and unbalanced. I lay there, feeling woozy. What was going on? Aches and pains had settled everywhere during the night. My calves ached, my back ached, my neck ached. My head was heavy.

I got up. The bathroom was warm and steamy, and Alain was shaving. I leaned against the doorjamb. "Don't feel so good," I mumbled.

"What's wrong?"

"I don't know. Maybe I'm coming down with something."

"You'd better take it easy today."

"Yes."

I decided to take a shower anyway. The water streamed over my rounded body. Pregnancy gave me a whole new self: my hair had doubled its volume, my nails grew faster than I could trim them. Everything was pumped up and primed with new life, blossoming. Now, however, the body was heavy, achy, woozy.

I cupped my hands around my smooth, full middle. "What's going on, little one?"

"What did you say?" said Alain, putting away his after-shave lotion in the medicine chest.

"I was talking to the baby. He isn't mov—"

What? What was I saying? Shake off that thought. I patted my hands briskly on top of my tummy. "Come on. Come on. Wake up!" They sleep and they wake, just like we do. They wake when we sleep and jump and stretch and turn. Then they sleep a lot when we move around. He was only sleeping.

I came out of the shower, wrapped myself in a towel. Alain was looking at me, frowning. "Are you all right?"

"I'm sick. I'll go back to bed for a few hours."

"Call me if you need me. And call the doctor."

I lay there, feeling worse as the hours went by. By one o'clock, I realized I had a fever. I took my temperature. A hundred and two degrees. I called the doctor. "Probably just the flu," she said. "There's flu going around. Drink fluids, stay in bed. Take care of yourself." The doctor's name was Shelley. My age, or maybe younger. Very casual, very laid-back. All her patients called her by her first name.

At three o'clock, I started shaking. Chills and fever. Time to call the doctor again. "Shelley's not here. But we paged her at the hospital, and she says to stop by the office. Someone here will check you out." The office was a block away. I put on a dress, sleeveless, flowered. It was August 24, warm and sunny.

A nurse snapped commands at me. "Get on the table. Lie down. You don't have a fever. You're not sick." Was she crazy? Gone were the chummy conversations of the regular staff, of Shelley. Instead we had some female commandant, barking orders and flexing her authority. "The baby's not moving," I blurted out.

"Yes it is," she replied. Who was this woman? Where had they found her? I was passive, conciliatory. "Well, I thought he wasn't moving. And I have had a fever. It comes in waves, then I get chilled."

"The baby's fine. Get up. You can go."

These are the words that would burn in the mind. These are

the seeds of rage. There were to be many more before he died, and was born.

The long afternoon wore on. From the bed, I move to the living room couch. I pull a blanket over me, push it off. Fever mounts, sweat soaks the couch. Every muscle seems to be curling in on itself, contracting around the sickness. The body is fighting hard. The little man inside is fighting even harder, but I don't know that. That ignorance would pound me with grief and guilt, much later. What could anyone have done? Who knows? But the guilt I would later feel had little basis in logic: the heart has its reasons, for guilt as for love as for rage. I kept no loving vigil, I did nothing to stave off death.

Third call to the doctor. "This flu," she says, "everybody has it. Just everybody. Did you take some Tylenol? Remember, Tylenol only, no aspirin." I go back to bed. Now it's seven o'clock. More chills and shaking. I get up to go to the bathroom. I have to hold onto the walls as I move. Suddenly, there is blood.

I stumble out of the bathroom just as Alain is walking in the apartment door.

"I'm bleeding."

He reacts with great urgency, which frightens me even more. When I see Alain's set face and hear his taut voice, I start to panic a little. He calls the doctor, then puts me on the phone with Shelley.

"Well, I think you'd better come down to the hospital. I'll take a look at you. I'm here."

On the elevator up to the maternity floor, I can hardly stand. I lean against the elevator wall and feel the sweat course down my face. It seems that each burning wave of fever leaves me more drained and shaking than the last. I disrobe, put on their little flowered smock with the silly ties in the back, and give them a urine sample in the bathroom next to the treatment room. More blood. "I'm bleeding," I say to the nurse. It seems very important to sound calm and controlled, so I keep my voice steady and informative. There is a tremendous pull to be a good and intelligent patient, and not to give anyone any trouble.

Now contractions are starting. Shelley appears, examines me, and announces that there is significant bleeding from the uterus. The baby's heart is monitored, contractions are monitored, my blood pressure is monitored every fifteen minutes. I am in labor. The baby's heart is beating very fast. I am twenty-eight weeks pregnant, and I am in active labor. No one has the slightest idea what is going on.

Shelley decides to give some medication to stop labor and, finally, an antibiotic. She gives the nurse instructions then leaves for the night. The monitors are removed. Alain offers to stay, but I tell him to go. The night nurse comes to give me a shot. Aftershocks of pain continue to pulse through me. I cry out involuntarily. "I haven't even given you the second one yet," she says, and there is unmistakable fatigue and disdain in her voice.

She leaves. Everything is hurting, everything is dark. Machines are blinking. From another time and space come the faint noises of cars, taxis, buses. People are out there, moving around the city. I am so far from them, from everyone. I don't know what's going on in this room, in my body, and no one else does either. I am afraid. A cry rises up in my throat, something like a sob, but I control it. It seems important to stifle that sob.

And then he died, sometime during the quiet predawn hours. No one wept as he died. No one knew the precise moment when his heart renounced the struggle, and he gave up his spirit.

It is dawn. I lie there, in the little white room with the cabinets and machines, waiting for someone to appear. The weight of the baby is heavy on my back. My hands are held lightly around my womb. I notice that I have no fever. The morning nurse comes in, cheerful and friendly. She picks up the stethoscope and starts to search for the baby's heartbeat. The room is silent.

"Where exactly were they picking up the heartbeat last night?" she asks.

"I don't know. Down on the left side, I think."

"Hmmm . . . just a sec. Shelley's in the hall, I'll be right back."

Shelley and the nurse come in. Shelley is holding the Doppler ultrasound monitor—high-tech stuff that can pick up the heartbeat of an eight-week-old fetus. She moves the monitor over my belly, slowly, methodically. Up, down, across; up, down, across. No one speaks. She repeats the gestures, over and over again. I glance fleetingly at the nurse. Her face is lowered. Her eyes are fixed on the floor.

"Leah . . . these monitors . . . they're very sensitive—extremely sensitive. We don't . . . we're not picking up any heart sounds."

Alain walks into the room. He takes one look. "What is it?"

"The baby's heart has stopped." I say that very calmly, because I am calm. Nothing is real. There was a heartbeat, now there is none. There were some sounds in the universe, but now those sounds are still.

Alain leans over to hold me. The doctor is saying some things—not much more information—evidence of some infection, somewhere—she is sorry—I should go home and await the birth.

There is some kind of play going on, and nobody had given me the lines to learn. I don't know what I am supposed to say or do. I am very removed, and for some reason, I still keep clinging to my insane desire to please everyone, to be polite, good, and co-operative. Okay. Yes. We'll go home and await the birth. I guess I'll call when contractions start again. Is that all right? Is that what I should do? What if they start in the middle of the night? Oh, sorry, silly question, I'll call whenever they start. Yes, definitely, I will finish out these antibiotics: one three times a day for two more days. (Two days? said a doctor later. Two days? Infection strong enough to kill, and you're given antibiotics for two days? And then he stopped talking, abruptly.)

On that first day home, Alain and I move through our life carefully, delicately. We don't know what to do or what to think. We don't even know what to say to people. "The baby died, we're waiting for him to be born"? The belly has become an embarrassment, something shockingly wrong. We don't want people to see us. We go to get the antibiotics, then we go home. I lie on the bed and rest. In the afternoon, I get up and write in my diary, something about how the baby has died, and some sentences of farewell and resignation. They feel completely meaningless. I am not feeling a thing.

It is night. We go to bed. Alain used to kiss the baby goodnight. He used to lean over and lay his head on my middle, his arms cradling me. "Good night, baby," he would say. "Sleep tight. Don't kick your mama too hard tonight"—and then we'd laugh because, sure enough, the baby would start jumping and thrashing around at the sound of his voice.

That first night, we went to bed, and neither one of us knew what to do. There was the lump that used to be "the baby," but it wasn't the baby anymore. We didn't have the words to talk about it. But as I lay back against the pillow, and turned quietly away from him, my heart started beating fast. There was something looming on the edges of my consciousness, but I didn't want it to come any closer.

Suddenly a whisper rose unbidden from my heart: "Good night, baby." I wanted silence. Stonily, I turned to fitful, fearful sleep. But the whisper rose again, even as my mind tried to crush the words: "Good night, little one." And then, with a thrill of fear: "Farewell, beloved."

The next day, we went to a church. We were vaguely wondering what we should do when the baby was born. Should we bury it? Should we baptize it? We talked to a priest. We didn't know him, and he didn't know us. We were not rooted in any religious community then. We stumbled into his church and demanded that he say the right words to us at a time when neither he nor we could know how heavily these decisions would weigh.

"Don't think of it as anything but an operation," he said. "Don't bury it or baptize it. It will only increase the pain." He's right, I thought, even as a more cynical thought nudged its way in: an "operation"? What does this guy know about childbirth? But Alain and I decided to agree with him. We didn't really care one way or another about burial or ritual. The fetus was dead. The sooner its body was taken care of, the better.

Labor started again that evening. All night long, the long birth pangs continued. I thought of nothing but surviving the physical pain. No drugs, no anesthesia, no epidural, no cute breathing exercises—none of us was focusing on this as a "normal" birth. I think we were all concentrating on one thing only: get it over with, get the fetus out of there, and move on.

Finally, he was born. "Push," said Shelley one last time, and he was out. Silence. She cut and clamped the cord. She wrapped him in a towel, wiped the blood off his face, and closed his eyes.

"Do you want to hold him?" she asked.

"Yes," I said. I was exhausted.

She placed him in my arms. Alain stood beside me, next to the narrow bed. I took the baby into the crook of my elbow and felt the weight of his body against me.

I raised one hand and cupped it around his tiny head. There was a kind of downy hair on his head. I touched the swirling soft pattern with the tips of my fingers. I caressed his head, then his cheek. I stared into a perfect face.

His eyes were closed. I touched the lids, then bent to kiss them: first one, then the other. He looked asleep. There was a dimple in his chin; the little mouth was shaped like his father's. A rosebud mouth, so still and quiet.

No cry, no sound, my son?

I ran my hand down from his shoulder to his hand. I picked up that hand and stared at the fingers. They were feather-light. Each had a tiny, pink, translucent nail. The little hand curled softly around my finger. I had never known such vulnerability, such fragility. I am holding your hand, little one. You are so small, and I am here. I am your mother. I am a mother. To you. You are my son.

I cradled his head closer, closer. My hand cupped his face. He was silent, still. His weight was in my arms. The weight of his body, his face, his hand, his fingers—these stay with me, forever.

I looked up. Alain looked stricken. "I can't hold him," I said, flatly. I meant: I will not hold him in this life. He is gone from me. I will not be able to hold my baby.

Shelley thought I meant "I can't bear to hold him" and immediately came over and took him out of my arms. She wrapped the towel around him more firmly. She wrapped it all the way around him and covered his face. She laid him on top of a cart, covered with shiny instruments. She turned to the nurse.

"Take this to Pathology. Tell them to send me a report."

The nurse complied. She wheeled the cart out of the room. And that was our farewell.

The day wore on. My heart went into a fluttering arrhythmia, clocked at two hundred beats a minute. Monitors, machines, cardiologists, ceaseless activity, everyone bent now on finding out "what was going on."

Nothing was going on. I had a minor heart condition, which chose that moment to show up and deflect attention over to my heart, instead of to what had just happened to "the fetus." Nevertheless, Shelley and all the hospital personnel treated the tachycardia as though it were a full-fledged coronary, and we went through the rest of the day never once mentioning the stillbirth.

Finally, it is night. My heart has calmed down. I have been placed in a room on another floor, someone having kindly understood that the maternity wing was probably inappropriate at this time. Alain, exhausted, has gone home again, to an empty apartment and his own thoughts. My mother, on vacation in Vermont, has finally gotten through to me. She is crying. I say some things to comfort her, then hang up, turn out the light, and turn to sleep.

It is dark. There are no machines, no doctors, no nurses, no one to be polite to, no heart problem to talk about and explain, no husband to hover worriedly over my bed, no tests, no monitors.

There is no baby.

There, in the dark, it hits me. The grief is a physical thing. It comes in waves—wave after wave, shocking my spirit, shattering my heart. I curl my body around its emptiness. Its center is gone. Its womb is empty. My arms are empty.

But you were here! I held you! Where have you gone, beloved? Where are you, my little son?

There is no one in the room with me, but even so, I try to muffle the wrenching sobs. His vulnerability, his fragility, his weight are more than I can bear. I feel him in my arms, but he is not here. My son. I am a mother, but my child is gone. Where are you? He is not here, but I cannot let him go. Who is holding that hand? On what breast are you cradled tonight? Are you afraid, wherever you are? Are you crying? Is someone there to hold you? Please, God, hold him, rock him, cradle him, soothe him, whisper to him, caress him. Love him for me, please God.

The storm passes, but I am changed forever. It sufficed to hold him, to look into his face, and he entered my heart forever. I am a mother, and my son has died. Where there was no knowledge of him before, now there is a river, coursing through my mind and heart, bearing the memory and the loss of him forever.

For the first few months, the river is a torrent, crashing through my life, shattering friendships, straining family ties, reconfiguring my marriage, leaving devastation everywhere. People say the most painful things, and I have no words to make them understand. "You'll have another." "It was probably for the best." All these statements seem to spring from a similar source: the speaker's desire to minimize the trauma—for me, he thinks, not understanding that he is also minimizing it for himself. He cannot see what there is to grieve about. He cannot imagine "the baby," and therefore there is nothing to mourn. What's more, he finds reasons why the stillbirth was a "good thing."

This is not malevolent behavior. People genuinely think they are helping when they tell me that "You'll have plenty more." But the words wound, and they are relentless. "All better now?" chirps a friend ten days after the birth. "How's your thesis progressing?" asks another, avoiding the subject altogether.

But if friends and casual acquaintances seem to lack understanding, the presumptions of the wider culture batter the heart of any woman who has ever mourned a preterm child. A mother who mourns a pregnancy loss learns to carry her grief silently, as if ashamed of her sorrow. Who cares if a child dies before it is born? Aren't there too many children in the world already? And who says she lost a real baby anyway? In reading through some insurance papers after the birth of our son, I stopped at one sentence, a description of how the pregnancy had ended. *Fetal Wastage* was the term.

We named our son Damien. We understood, too late, how healing and important are the rituals of death. We tried to find his body, to have him baptized and buried, but, true to the monumental mishandling they had displayed from the beginning, Shelley and the hospital staff had lost the baby's body and had no records of where he had been taken. "Where are you?" became both a literal and figurative cry. My dreams were dominated for months by desperate searches, through darkness, through strange lands, with empty arms stretched out in front of stumbling feet.

Of course time heals, and grief gives way to peace. Slowly, I allowed myself to let him go, as I drew comfort and strength from art and song and prayer, those tentative human recreations of the sacred. I had a tape of the soprano Janet Baker. Her voice wove a gentle web of love around my child—the tremulous, reverent "Ave Maria" allowed another mother's arms to take him up and hold him; the lullaby cadence of "Close Thine Eyes" permitted both censored grief and thwarted love to simply be, unhindered and unjudged:

Close thine eyes
And sleep secure
Thy soul is safe
Thy body's sure
He that guards thee
He that keeps
Never slumbers, never sleeps
Then close thine eyes
And sleep secure.

Only through such rites and symbols could I begin to give him over into the arms of his Maker. Slowly, I allowed myself to turn back to this life, this time, this valley.

The river is calm now, its torrents still and peaceful. There are seeds to sow, harvests to reap, and work to do before our own nightfall. Gabriel, Christina, and Xavier have come to bless us. Their upturned faces and sweet eyes ground us, center us, and fill us with purpose. But Damien changed the landscape of my hopes and my dreams and my thoughts. My children speak of him naturally and happily, without the embarrassment or fear that so many adults feel in hearing his name. They expect to see him one day, "on that mountain," where every tear is washed away. He is not here, yet he is with us. I bear him forever, my firstborn son, and my children speak his name.

Stillbirth. There is such paradox in the word, such death. The first syllable cancels out the second. All that newness, that unfurling life, is canceled out already, from the beginning. All that sweet force, gathering, gathering, month after month, now silent, still.

And yet, triumphing over that tragic paradox, I have found an astonishing, infinitely more paradoxical joy, embedded even in that memory of my first child, unmoving in my arms.

What possible joy? The realization, for me, of how strongly God loves us. Yes, loves us, all six billion—whatever—of us, teeming over the earth. I have come to understand the love for Damien that pierced my heart as a dim reflection of God's love for us. Such love is instantaneous, it is absolute, it has no care for how many of us there are or what we have accomplished. It has no care for how long we have been alive. Young or old, sick or well, we are lovely in His sight, worthy to His heart. The love that overwhelmed me, even for a seven-month-old stillborn baby, also deepened my understanding, comforted me, and, in the end, held up for me a mirror of the divine. Our capacity to grasp the humanity, the luminous beauty, of every child who comes into being is our capacity to love as God loves—with a strength that is primal, unreasonable, and unshakable.

God loves us as a mother loves her child—because we are there, because we are His, because we are ourselves: irreplaceable, forever unique, never, ever to be forgotten. "The Lord called me from the womb, from the body of my mother he named my name" (Isaiah 49:1).

Toward Humility

from *Fourth Genre*

5

Once it's over, you write it all down in second person, so that it doesn't sound like you who's complaining. So it doesn't sound like a complaint.

Because you have been blessed.

You have been blessed.

You have been blessed.

And still you know nothing, and still it all sounds like a complaint.

4

You are on a Lear jet.

It's very nice: plush leather seats for which leg room isn't even an issue, the jet seating only six; burled wood cabinets holding beer and sodas; burled wood drawers hiding bags of chips, boxes of cookies, cans of nuts; copies of three of today's newspapers; a stereo system loaded with CDs.

Your younger son, age thirteen, is with you, invited along with the rest of your family by the publicist for the bookstore chain whose jet this is. When you and your wife and two sons pulled up to the private end of the airport in the town where you live, there on the tarmac sat a Lear jet, out of which came first the publicist, a young and pretty woman in a beige business suit, followed by the pilots, who introduced themselves with just their first names—Hal and John—and shook hands with each member of your family.

"You're all welcome to come along," the publicist had said, and you'd seen she meant it. But it was an invitation made on the spot, nothing you had planned for. And since your older son, fifteen, has a basketball tournament, and your wife has to drive, it is left to your younger son to come along.

Your younger son, the one who has set his heart and mind and soul upon being a pilot. The one whose room is plastered with posters of jets. The one who has memorized his copy of *Jane's Military Aircraft*.

"I guess we can get you a toothbrush," you'd said to him, and here had come a smile you knew was the real thing, his eyebrows up, mouth open, deep breaths in and out, in his eyes a joyful disbelief at this good fortune. All in a smile.

Now here you are, above clouds. In a Lear jet, your son in the jumpseat—leather, too—behind the cockpit, talking to Hal and John, handing them cans of Diet Coke, the publicist talking to you about who else has ridden in the corporate jet. Tom Wolfe, she tells you. Patricia Cornwell. Jimmy Carter. And a writer who was so arrogant she won't tell you his name.

This is nowhere you'd ever thought you might be. Sure, you may have hoped a book you wrote might someday become a bestseller, but it wasn't a serious hope. More like hoping to win the lottery. A pretty thought, but not a whole lot you could do about it other than write the best you knew how.

But getting on a list wasn't why you wrote, and here, at 37,000 feet and doing 627 miles an hour over a landscape so far below you see, really, nothing, there is in you a kind of guilt, a sense somehow you are doing something you shouldn't be doing.

Riding in a Lear jet to go to a bookstore—four of them in two days—to sign copies of your book.

Your book: published eight years before, out of print for the last two. A book four books ago, one you'd thought dead and gone, the few copies left from the one and only hardcover print run available in remainder bins at book warehouses here and there around the country.

A book about your family, based on the life of your grandmother, who raised six children, all of whom were born in a log cabin your grandfather built, the last of those six a Down syndrome baby, a daughter born in 1943 and for whom little hope of living was held out by the doctors of the time. It is about your grandmother, and the love she has for that baby, her desire to see her live and her own desire to fix things for her daughter as best she can, if even at the cost of her other children and, perhaps, her husband.

A book recently anointed by a celebrity talk show host. Not a celebrity but an icon. Not an icon but a Force. A person so powerful and influential that simply by announcing the name of your book a month ago, your book has been born again.

Bigger than you had ever imagined it might become. Bigger than you had ever allowed yourself even to dream. Even bigger than that. And bigger.

Guilt, because it seems you're some kind of impostor. Even though it is based on your family, you had to reread the novel for the first time since you last went through it, maybe nine years ago, when it was in galleys, you sick of it by that time to the point where, like all the other books you have published—there are eight in all—you don't read them again. But this one you had to reread so that you could know who these characters were, know the intricate details of their lives so that if someone on the television show were to have asked you a question of an obscure moment in the whole of it all, you would have seemed to them and to the nation—Who would be watching? How many people? As many as have bought the book? And more, of course—to be on close terms with the book, with its people, its social context and historical and spiritual significance.

You wrote it ten years ago.

And yesterday you were on this talk show host's program.

Tom Wolfe, you think. Jimmy Carter, and you realize you are dressed entirely wrong, in your dull green sweater and khaki pants, old leather shoes. Maybe you should have worn a sport coat. Maybe a tie. Definitely better shoes.

You can see the soles of your son's skateboard shoes, worn nearly through at the balls of his feet, him on his knees and as far into the cockpit as he can get. He's got on a pair of cargo shorts, the right rear pocket torn, and a green T-shirt. He'd been lucky enough to wear a polar fleece jacket to the airport this February morning in the sunny South.

This is all wrong.

The publicist continues on about who has ridden in the corporate jet, and you nod, wondering, How did I get here?

All you know is that you wrote this book and received a phone call the first week in January, a call that came on a very bad day for you, a call that found you out a thousand miles from your home, where you were teaching others how they might learn to write. A job in addition to the daily teaching job you have so that you might make ends meet, and so that your wife wouldn't have to work as many hours as she has in the past.

The Force found you there, on a very bad day, and gave you unbelievable news. And now your book is on the lists.

You think about that day. About how very bad it was, how empty, and hollow, and how even the news that was the biggest news of your life was made small by what happened.

And now the plane begins its initial descent into the metropolis, and your son returns to the seat beside you, still with that incredulous smile, though you have been airborne nearly an hour. Hal and John happily announce you'll be landing in moments, the landscape below hurrying into view—trees, highways, cars, homes. Nothing different from the view out any airplane window you have looked before, but different all the way around.

Everything is different.

The jet settles effortlessly to the ground, taxies to the private end of an airport you've flown into before, the public terminal out your window but far, far away, and you see, there on the tarmac as the jet eases to a stop, a Mercedes limousine.

Yep. A Mercedes.

You look at your shoes, and at your son's. His cargo shorts. This sweater you have on.

"When we were here with Jimmy Carter, the lines were all the way out the store and halfway around the building," the publicist says. "This is going to be fun," she says, and smiles, stands, heads out the door past smiling, nodding Hal and John.

Then John asks, "What would you guys like for dinner?"

You and your son look at each other—he's still smiling, still smiling—and then you look to John, shrug, smile. "Subs?" you say, as if the request might be too much to manage.

"No problem," John says, and both he and Hal nod again.

Here is the store: brick, tall, a presence. A single store in a huge bookstore chain, every store complete with a coffee bar and bakery, a gift shop with coffee mugs and T-shirts and calendars.

And books.

You climb out the limousine before the chauffeur can get around to open your door, because you don't want to make him feel like you're the kind of person who will wait for a door to be opened. Then you and your son, the publicist in the lead, make your way for the front doors.

Inside is a huge poster in a stand, the poster two feet by four feet, advertising your being at this store for a signing. In the center of the poster is your picture, formidable and serious, it seems to you. Too serious. This isn't you, you think. That person staring pensively off the photographer's left shoulder is somebody posing as an author, you think.

There are a few people in the store, and you wonder if the line will form a little later on, once the signing gets under way, and you are ushered by a smiling store manager in a red apron to the signing area.

It's in the middle of the store. There is a table stacked with copies of the anointed book, and with reprints of the earlier three books, and of the four that have come out since the anointed one first appeared all those years ago. Your books, you see, are piled everywhere. Books, and books.

"Look at this!" the manager exclaims, and points like a game show hostess to a rack of paperback books beside you, the bestseller rack. "You're the number one book," the manager says, and you see the rows of your book, beneath them a placard with #1 printed on it.

You look at your son to see if he's as impressed as you are beginning to be.

He smiles at you, nods at the books, his eyebrows up.

He's impressed.

You take your seat behind the table laden with your books and see between the stacks that there is a kind of runway that extends out from the front of your table to the other end of the store, a long and empty runway paved with gray-blue carpet. Big, and wide, and empty.

"We'll get you some coffee and cookies, if that's all right," the publicist says to you, then, to your son, "Hot chocolate sound good?" and your son says, "Yes ma'am," and, "Thank you."

You are here. The signing has begun.

But there are no customers.

You wait, while the manager announces over the in-store speakers your presence, fresh from yesterday's appearance on national TV. This drives a couple of people to the runway, and they walk down the long corridor of gray-blue carpet toward you. It seems it takes a long time for them to make it to you, longer even than the flight up here from your hometown, and you smile at these people coming at you: a young man, tall and lanky; a woman your age with glasses and short brown hair.

They are smiling at you.

You know them. Students of yours from the program where you teach a thousand miles from home. They are students of yours, friends, writers. Both of them.

You stand, hug them both, introduce them to your son, to the manager back from the announcement, and to the publicist returning now with that coffee and hot chocolate, those cookies. Then the three of you remark upon the circumstance of your meeting here: they live in the same city and have been waiting for your appearance at the store; how wonderful and strange that your book has been picked, what a blessing!; when Jimmy Carter came here, the line was out the door and halfway around the building.

You talk, sip at the coffee, don't touch the cookie. There are no other customers, and the manager promises they will come, they will come. He's had phone calls all day asking when you will get here, and if the lines will be too long to wait through.

You talk more, and more. Talk that dwindles to nothing but what is *not* being said: where are the customers?

Now, finally, fifteen minutes into a two-hour signing, you see an older woman rounding the end of the runway. She has bright

orange hair piled high and wears a tailored blue suit. She's pushing a stroller, and you imagine she is a grandmother out with her
grandchild, the child's mother perhaps somewhere in the store
right now, searching out children's books while Grandma takes
care of the baby.

It's an expensive suit, you can tell as she moves closer, maybe
thirty feet away now, and you see too the expensive leather bag
she carries with her. The baby is still hidden under blankets, and
you smile at the woman as she moves closer, closer, a customer
heralding perhaps more customers, maybe even a line out the
store and halfway around the building by the time this is all over.

Maybe.

Then here is the woman arriving at the other side of the table,
and you see between the stacks she is even older than you believed. Heavy pancake makeup serves in a way that actually makes
her wrinkles bigger, thicker; watery eyes are almost lost in heavy
blue eye shadow; penciled-in eyebrows arch high on her forehead.

And you are smiling at this person, this customer, as she slowly
bends to the stroller and says in the same moment, "Here's the famous writer, Sophie, the famous writer Mommy wants you to
meet," and she lifts from inside the blankets, the woman cooing
all the while and making kissing sounds now, a dog.

A rat dog, a pink bow in the thin brown fur between its pointy
ears.

"Sophie," the woman says to the dog, "would you mind if
Mommy lets the famous writer hold you?" and her arms stretch
toward you between the stacks of your books, in her hands this
dog with a pink ribbon, and without thinking you reach toward
her, and now you are holding Sophie.

The dog whimpers, shivers, licks its lips too quickly, tiny eyes
darting again and again away from you to Mommy.

You don't know what to say, only smile, nod, and let your own eyes dart to your students, these friends, who stand with their own smiles, eyes open perhaps a little too wide, and then you glance behind you to the publicist, whose chin is a little too high and whose mouth is open, and to the manager, who stands with her arms crossed against her red apron. She's looking at the gray-blue carpet.

And here is your son. He's standing at the end of this line of people, hands behind his back, watching. He's not smiling, his mouth a straight line, and your eyes meet a moment.

He's watching.

"Sophie would love it," the woman begins, and you turn to her. She's plucked a copy of the anointed book from one of the piles, has opened it to the title page. Those watery eyes are nearly lost in the wrinkles gathering for the force of her smile. "I know Sophie would absolutely love it," she continues, "if you were to sign this copy to her."

You swallow, still smiling. "For Sophie?" you say.

The woman nods, reaches toward you for the dog, and you hand it out to her while she says, "She'll love it. She'd be so very proud."

Here is your book, open and ready to be signed.

You look at your students. Their faces are no different, still smiling. They are looking at you.

You look at the publicist, and the manager. They are both looking at you, too.

And you look to your son. He has his hands at his sides now, his mouth still that thin, straight line. But his eyes have narrowed, looking at you, scrutinizing you in a way that speaks so that only you can hear, *This is what happens when you're famous?*

These are the exact words you hear from his eyes, narrowed, scrutinizing.

"She would be so very proud," the woman says, and you look to her again, Sophie up to her face now, and licking her cheek, that pancake makeup.

You pull from your shirt pocket your pen.

3

Everyone is here, your living room choked with friends, maybe fifty people in all, all there to watch the show. You and your wife have laid out platters of buffalo wings, fresh vegetables, jalapeño poppers, various cheeses and crackers and dip; there are bowls of chips, a vast array of soft drinks. Cups have been filled with store-bought ice, paper plates and napkins and utensils all spread out.

They are here for the celebration. You, on the Force's talk show, your book the feature.

Kids swirl around the house and out in the yard, their parents laughing and eating and asking what it was like to meet her, to be with her, to talk with her. Some of them tell you, too, that they have finally read your book, and tell you how wonderful your book was.

You've known most of these people for years, and there are moments that come to you while these friends tell you how wonderful your book was when you want to ask them, Why didn't you read it when it came out eight years ago? But you only smile, tell them all the same thing: thank you, thank you, thank you.

You tell them, too, that the Force was incredibly intelligent, disarming, genuine, better read than you yourself are. A genuine, genuine person.

This was what she was like when you met her, when you taped the show for three hours two weeks ago, you and her book club guests—four women, each of whom wrote a letter about the effect of your book on their lives that was convincing enough to get the producers of the show to fly them in, be these book club guests—and there were moments during that whole afternoon when, seated next to her and listening to one or another of the guests, you stole a look at her and told yourself, *That's her. That's her. I'm sitting next to her.* Moments that startled you with the reality of this all, moments that in the next moment you had to shut down for fear that thinking this way would render you wordless, strike you dumb with celebrity were the conversation to turn abruptly to you.

Then the show begins. Kids still swirl, and your wife has to pull two preschoolers from the computer in the sunroom off the living room, where they are banging two-fisted each on the keyboard, no one other than you and your wife seeming to notice this, everyone watching the television. There are no empty chairs left, no space on the sofa, the carpet in front of the TV spread with people sitting, paper plates in hand heaped with buffalo wings and jalapeño poppers and veggie sticks, and you have no choice but to stand in the back of the room, watching.

Here is what you were warned of: this episode of the book club show—your episode—happens to fall during sweeps month, when ratings are measured so as to figure how much to charge for advertising time, and since the viewership for the monthly show featuring the book and the author always plummets, the producers have decided to spend the first half of the hour with bloopers from past shows. "Forgettable moments," these fragments have been called by the promotional ads leading up to the air date.

This was what you were warned of, two weeks ago when you were through with the taping. Officials from the show told you all this, and you'd nodded, smiling, understanding. What else was there for you to do? Demand equal time with everyone else?

No. You'd nodded, smiled, understood.

Now the Force introduces video clip after video clip of, truly, forgettable moments from past episodes: two people argue over whether the toilet paper is more efficiently utilized if rolled over the top or out from beneath; a woman tells a Viagra joke; the Force marches down the street outside her studio in protest of uncomfortable panty hose.

Your guests look at you.

"I had nothing to do with this," you say, too loud. "It'll be on the last half of the show," you say, too loud again.

They are quiet for a while, then return to ladling dip onto plates, loading up wings and poppers, pouring soda, until, finally, you are introduced, and the book, and there you are for two minutes talking about your grandmother, and your aunt with Down syndrome, your voice clear and calm, and you are amazed at how clear and calm you are there on the television, when you had wanted nothing more than to jump from the sofa you were seated on in the studio and do jumping jacks to work off the fear and trembling inside you. Now comes a series of family photos, a montage of images with your voice over it all, calm and smooth, the images on the screen pictures your family has had for years.

Pictures of your grandmother, and of your aunt.

The people you wrote about, whose lives are now here for the world to see, and you realize in this moment that you had nothing to do with this. That these photos—of your grandmother, your aunt, and your grandfather and aunts and uncles and your father, too, all these family photos that have existed for years— simply bear testament to the fact they were lives lived out of your hands, and all you had to do was to write them down, getting credit for all those lives led.

You think about that bad day in January. About how this all began, and how all this credit has come to you.

Yet you are still a little steamed about losing the first half of the show, when every other author you've seen featured on the show has gotten most of the program. You are a little steamed, too, about not having some place to sit here in your living room, and about those kids banging on the keyboard. You are a little steamed.

Then the discussion with you and the four women and the Force begins, and you see, along with everyone in your house, and everyone in the country, the world, a discussion that had lasted three hours squelched down to eight minutes, and six or so of those given to a woman who gave up her Down syndrome child at birth because of the "life sentence" she saw being handed her. You see in your living room choked with your friends this woman crying over her life, her decision, and see her somehow thank you for your book and the meaning it has given her life.

You knew this would be what was included on the air. You'd known it the moment her voice wavered and cracked that afternoon two weeks ago, there in the studio. You knew it then, and now here it is: this woman, crying over giving up her baby, and thanking you for it.

And you see yourself nod on the air, looking thoughtful.

She makes great TV, you think. This woman who missed the point of your book entirely.

2

You are answering the phones for a while, because of the terrible thing that has happened this bright, cold January day.

"We'll send you a brochure," you say to someone on the other end of the line, no one you know, and as she tells you her address you do not write it down, only sit with your back to the desk, looking out the window onto the late afternoon world outside: snow, sky.

A little after lunch, this day turned very bad, a turn that has led to you here, in the office of the program in which you teach a thousand miles from home, to answer the phone for the administrative director.

She is in the other room, too much in shards to answer the phone, to field the bonehead questions that still come to a program such as this one no matter what bad things happen and when. People still call to ask about the program, about costs and applications, about credits and teachers. About all things.

Earlier today, before you began answering the phone, before lunch, your agent called here, where you are teaching others to write because it seems you know something about writing, to tell you the novel you have just finished writing is awful.

You are here for two weeks, in workshops and seminars, lectures and readings, the students adults who know what is at stake. Though they have lives away from here, just as you have your own, you and they converge on this New England campus from all over the country, the world, twice a year to study the word and all it can mean. They come here to study writing, because they want to write, and some of them become friends to you and to the other writers teaching here, because it is this love of the word that unites you all.

Some of them become your friends.

Your agent said to you this morning, "What happened to this?" She said, "Where was your heart?"

Her call, you'd recognized with her words and tone, had not surprised you. You knew it was coming. You knew the book was dead and gone to hell in a handbasket, had known it for the last month as you'd tried to get to the end of the thing. You knew it had gone to hell in a handbasket even before you missed the deadline last week.

You knew.

The novel: a sequel to the last one you published, early last year. That one had done well, better than any of the others you've published this far. A novel you'd had a tough time trying to get published, seeing as how your books have never done that well. You're a literary author, and publishers know that means you don't sell many books. You're not a best-seller, they know. You write well enough, but you're just not a best-seller, a fact you reconciled yourself to many years ago.

But the first hardcover run of this latest book—a run in the low five figures—sold out in a few months, the publisher electing not to reprint. They'd sold as many as they'd believed they could sell, had also sold it to paperback with another publisher.

Everything was great, with selling out the print run. So great they asked ten months ago if you would write a sequel to it, and you agreed, though it wasn't anything you'd thought much about. Not until you saw how well the book was selling.

Now, here you were, ten months later, teaching people to write on a day cursed with the sad and empty curse of a startlingly blue winter sky. A day in which you have been informed of what you have known all along: this one didn't work.

You know nothing about writing.

But this is not the bad thing. It had seemed bad enough to you, walking across campus to lunch after the phone call, three hours long, from your agent, a phone call in which you both reconnoitered the train wreck before you, pieced out what was salvageable, shrugged over what was lost.

The day seemed bad enough then.

And then.

Then, after lunch, one of the students was found in his room, dead. Not one of the students, but one of *your* students.

Not one of your students, but a friend.

Some of them become your friends.

You were to have had dinner in town with him tonight, to talk about the novel he is writing, the novel you had been working on with him all last semester, when he was a student of yours and during which time he became a friend. A big, ambitious, strange, and haunting novel.

A novel that will go unfinished now.

He was found in his dorm room, sitting at his desk, having gone to his room the night before, students have said, complaining of a headache.

He was found sitting at his desk, reading a copy of one of your books. A novel. A lesser-known one, one it seemed no one really cared for.

Your friend was reading it.

He was found at one-thirty on this blue and cursed January afternoon. Now it is four o'clock, between that time and this a somber and hushed chaos breaking out all over campus. Everyone here knows everyone here. No one has ever died here before. He was too young. He was your friend.

And now you are answering phones for the administrative director who is in the other room. You told her you wanted to answer the phone to give her time away from the bonehead questions, but you know you offered as a means to keep yourself from falling into shards of your own. You offered so that you would have something to do, and not have to think of this very bad day, when the loss of your own book, you see, means nothing. A book means nothing.

You have lost a friend. A friend who is here, a thousand miles from home, too. A friend not much older than you, his death a complete and utter surprise. He lives with his mother, you know, where he takes care of her, an invalid, and where he is writing a big, ambitious, strange, and haunting novel.

The phone rings. You are looking out the window at the afternoon sky growing dark, the blue gone to an ashen violet, and you turn to the phone, watch it a moment as though its ringing might change how it appears, like in cartoons when the phone jumps from its place and shivers.

It rings, and nothing happens, rings again, and you pick up the receiver, hold it to your ear knowing another bonehead question is on its way.

"May I speak to ____ ____?" a man says, all business, a solid voice that carries authority with it, and you think perhaps this is an official from the college, calling on business. Not a bonehead.

"Hold on," you say, and place the phone down, go to the room next door, where she is sitting, gathering herself.

"Can you take a call?" you ask, and try to smile. "It's for you," you say, and she nods, sniffs, tries at a smile herself. She stands, and you follow her back into her office, her domain, you only a brief tenant this afternoon of a very bad day.

She picks up the phone, says "Hello?" and her eyes go immediately to you. "You were just talking to him," she says, and hands you the phone, trying to smile.

You take the receiver, bring it to your ear, say, "Yes?"

"I'm calling from Chicago," the businessman's voice says to you, "and my boss is working on a project she needs to talk to you about. I need to break her from a meeting. Can you hold?"

A meeting, you think. My boss. What is this about?

You say, "Sure," and now music comes on the line, and you glance up at the director, who is looking at you, wondering, too, you can see, what this might be about. You don't live here. You're a thousand miles from home. Who knows you are here, and why?

You shrug at her in answer to her eyes, and then the music stops with a phone connection click, and a voice you think you may recognize says your name, then her own, then shouts, "We're going to have so much fun!"

Who is this? Is this who you think it is? Is this who she says she is?

Is this *her?*

"Is this a joke?" you shout. "Is this for real?" and your eyes quick jump to the director, who sits in a chair across from you, watching you in wonder.

This makes the woman calling—*her*—laugh, and she assures you this is no joke, this is for real, and that she has chosen a book you have written as her book of the month next month.

It's a book four books ago, a book out of print. A book about your grandmother, her Down syndrome daughter, your family.

This isn't happening. It hasn't happened. It will not happen.

But it has happened: you have been chosen. Your book has been anointed.

"This is secret," she says. "You can't tell anyone. We'll announce it in twelve days. But you can't tell anyone."

"Can I tell my wife?" you manage to get out, and she laughs, says you can, but that's all, and she talks a little more, and you talk, and you cannot believe that you are talking to her, you here a thousand miles from home and with a secret larger than any you have ever had lain upon you. Even bigger.

Yet all you can think to say to her is, *A friend of mine died today. A friend of mine died. Can I tell you a friend of mine died?*

But you do not say it. You merely talk with her, *her,* about things you won't be able to recall five minutes from now.

And then the phone call is over, and you hang up, look at the administrative director.

She knows who it was, you can tell. She knows, but asks, "Was it *her?*"

"It's a secret," you say, your words hushed for fear someone else in the office might hear. "You can't tell anyone," you say, and you are standing, and you hug her because she is the closest person to you and you have this secret inside you, and because she is the only other person on the planet to know.

You will call your wife next. You will call her and tell her of this moment, of this delivery. Of this news beyond any news you have ever gotten.

You let go the director, and see she is crying, and you are crying now, too. You are crying, and you are smiling, and you look back to the window, see the ashen violet gone to a purple so deep and so true that you know none of this is happening, none of it. This is what you finally understand is *surreal*, a word you have heard and used a thousand times. But now it has meaning.

A friend has died. The Force has called. The sky has gone from a cold and indifferent blue to this regal purple. A secret has been bestowed. A novel has been lost. Another gone unfinished.

This is *surreal*.

You go to the window, lean against the frame, your face close enough to the glass to make out the intricate filaments of ice crystals there.

You want to feel the cold on your cheek, want evidence this is real, all of this day is real. You want evidence.

You listen again to her voice on the phone, the words exchanged. You feel this cold.

A friend has died, and you did not record his passing with the Force.

And now you cry openly, watching the sky out there in its regal color, regal not for anything you have done. Only assigned that value by your eyes on this particular January day. That color has nothing to do with you, exists as it does as a kind of gift whether you are here to see it or not.

What does a book matter?

Still you cry, and do not know if it is out of sorrow or joy, and decide in the next moment it is out of both.

I

Your newest book is pretty much going to hell. In a hand-basket.

Late afternoon, December, and you and your wife are in lawn chairs at the soccer field, watching your younger son play in one of the last games before Christmas.

Christmas. Your deadline for the next novel. The advance you were given, a sum the same as you were paid for your last book, even though it sold out its print run and sold to paperback as well, was spent months ago. Ancient history. Now here's Christmas coming hard at you, the novel going to hell.

Your son, a wing, is out on the field, your wife sitting beside you on your left, your older son a few feet farther to your left and in a lawn chair, too, and talking to a schoolmate sitting on the grass beside him. Long shadows fall from across the field toward you, cast by the forest there. Other parents, schoolmates, brothers, and sisters are spread across your side of the field, those shadows approaching you all. Maybe thirty or forty people altogether. It's a small school, new and with no field on campus, this one a municipal field at a city park. Lawn chairs is the best anyone can do.

And of course here with you, too, is your book pretty much going to hell, and this fact, its lack of momentum in your head and heart coupled with that looming deadline, might as well be a dead body propped in yet another lawn chair sitting next to you for all its palpable presence in your life. The world knows, it seems to you, that you are flailing.

You are cranky. That's what you would like to think it is. But it is more than that, and you know it, and your wife knows it, and your children do, too. You are angry, resentful. You are in the last fifty pages, but the book is leaving you, not like sand through your fingers, but like ground glass swallowed down.

You believed you had something, going in to the writing of it nine months ago. You believed you were headed somewhere.

You thought you knew something: that you could write this book.

So, when you see your son lag behind on a run downfield, you yell at him, "Get on the ball! Get in the game!"

It's too loud, you know, with the first word out of your mouth, and you turn to your wife, say, "Why doesn't he get into the game?" as though to lend your outburst credence. As though to find in her some kind of agreement that it's your son slacking off, when you know too well it's about a book you are writing going down like ground glass.

She looks at you out the corner of her eye, says nothing.

Your older son gets up from his lawn chair and moves even farther away with his friend, and you look at him, too. He's got on sunglasses, a ball cap on backward. He's embarrassed by you, you know.

You would have been, too, were you him.

But the book is dying. It is dying.

You yell, even louder, "Let's GO! Get in the GAME!" and feel your hands in fists on the arms of the lawn chair.

This time your younger son looks over his shoulder, though far downfield, and his eyes meet yours. Then, quickly, they dart away, to others on the sidelines, then to the ground, his back fully to you now, him running and running.

"He's always just hanging back like that," you say to your wife, quieter but, you only now realize, with your teeth clenched. "It's like he's always just watching what's going on." You know your words as you speak them are one more attempt to give your anger, your resentment a clear conscience: you're yelling because of your kid. Not because of you.

And now your wife stands, picks up her lawn chair, moves away, settles her chair a good fifty feet from you.

This is no signal to you of the embarrassment you are. It is nothing cryptic you are meant to decipher. It is her truth and yours both, big and dumb: you are a fool.

And it is because of a book. A stupid book. There are more important things, she is shouting to you in settling her lawn chair that far from you. There are more important things than a book.

You are here in your chair, alone with yourself. And the corpse of your book propped beside you.

You look off to the right, for no good reason but that it's away from those you have embarrassed, and those who know you for the fool you are.

And see there near the sideline, almost to the corner of the field, a blond kid, down on one knee on the sideline, his back to you. He's maybe ten yards away, the sun falling across the field to give his blond hair an extra shimmer to it, turning it almost white.

He's talking to himself, you hear, his voice quiet but there, just there. He's got on a black T-shirt, cargo shorts, skateboard shoes, and though his back is to you, you can see he has in one hand a plastic yellow baseball bat, in the other a plastic Day-Glo orange squirt gun.

He's holding them oddly, you can see, the bat by the thick end, where the ball makes contact, the handle up and perpendicular to the ground, like a flagstaff with no flag; the squirt gun he holds delicately, thumb and first finger at the bottom of the grip, as though it might be too hot.

He's still talking, and you can see the gun and bat moving a little, first the gun, his hand shaking it in sync, you hear, with his words, then the bat, the movement small, like the sound of his voice coming to you across the grass, and over the shouts of players at the far end of the field. Then the gun shakes again, and you see, too, by the movement of his head that he looks at the gun when he moves it and talks, and looks as well at the bat when he moves it and talks.

What is he doing?

Then he turns, rolls toward you from the knee he is on to sitting flat on the ground. He's facing you now, still holding the bat and gun in this odd way, and you see, now, now, he is a Down syndrome boy: almond eyes, thick neck, his mouth open.

He speaks again, looks at the bat, moving it with his words, and you only now realize he is speaking for the bat, that the bat itself is talking, this boy supplying the words, and then the gun answers the bat.

They are talking one to the other: a yellow bat, a Day-Glo squirt gun.

The boy is about your younger son's age, you see, and see, too, the shimmer of late afternoon sunlight in his hair the same as a few moments before, when his back was to you, and you hadn't known. You hadn't known.

You look at him. Still they talk one to the other, the words nothing you can make out, but there is something beautiful and profound in what you see. Something right and simple and true, and just past your understanding.

It's a kind of peace you see, and can't understand, this moment.

I wrote a book about that, you think. I wrote a book about a Down syndrome person, my aunt, and her mother. My grandmother, you think.

That was a good book, you think. That one was a gift, given to you without your even asking.

A gift, you think, and you wonder who this boy is with, who his own family is, who he is a gift to, and just as you wonder this you hear a rise in the crowd.

Parents and children in lawn chairs are growing louder now, clapping, hollering, though nothing as bombastic as what you knew you let out a few minutes before, and you turn to the sound, see your son's team moving and moving before the goal down there, the ball popped to the left and then right, and now you hear from the boy the word, "Go," then louder, "Go! GO!" and you look at him, see him turned to that end of the field now, too, see the bat and gun held still, this boy back up on one knee and in profile to you. "GO JOHNNY!" he yells, and you know he has a brother out there.

The gun and bat talk to each other again, while the shadows from the far side of the field grow closer to you all, to everyone, and now you know you knew nothing in writing that book. It was a gift, this story of a mother and daughter, but has it made you a better father to your son? Has it made you a better husband to your wife?

The answer, of course, is no, because here you are, chewing out the world around you because a book is going down like ground glass swallowed.

This is when the boy happens to glance up from the dialogue he creates and lives at once, to see you looking at him. Your eyes meet a moment, the talking toys now still, and you say, "Hi." You say it just to be nice to him. You say it because your eyes have met, and he has seen you watching him.

But you say it to try and save yourself.

He looks at you, looks at you, and even before he goes back to the dialogue at hand, his friends these toys, you know he won't say a thing.

You are a stranger.

You look beside you. There is no corpse of a book here, not anywhere around. Your wife is gone, too, her to your left and away from you, your older son even farther away. And there is your younger son, out on the field and running away from you as best he can. Your son, a teammate to this boy's brother.

There is, you know, only you here with you, and though you wish it were possible, pray it might be possible, there is no way for you to stand and lift your lawn chair and walk fifty feet away from you.

Which is what you want to do. To be away from you, here.

Because you have been blessed.

You have been blessed.

You have been blessed.

o

You have everything to learn.

This will be what keeps you. What points you toward humility: knowing how very little you know, how very far you have to go. As far now, in the second person and once it's all over, as on an afternoon soccer field, shadows growing long.

I know nothing. I know I know nothing.

I have been blessed.

for Jim Ferry

VALERIE MARTIN

Being Saint Francis

from *The Atlantic Monthly*

> *A genuine first-hand religious experience . . . is bound to
> be a heterodoxy to its witnesses, the prophet appearing as
> a mere lonely madman. If his doctrine prove contagious
> enough to spread to any others, it becomes a definite and
> labeled heresy. But if it then still prove contagious enough
> to triumph over persecution, it becomes itself an ortho-
> doxy; and when a religion has become an orthodoxy, its
> day of inwardness is over: the spring is dry; the faithful
> live at second hand exclusively and stone the prophets in
> their turn.*
>
> —William James,
> The Varieties of Religious Experience

INTRODUCTION

When Saint Francis—San Francesco—lay dying, he asked to
be moved from the bishop's residence in Assisi to the chapel at the
Portiuncula, a distance of about two miles outside the city walls.
As they passed the city gates, he bid the friars carrying him to set
him down on the road so that he might say a final farewell to the
place of his birth. "This town," he began, "has the worst reputation in the whole region as the home of every kind of rogue and
scoundrel." Then he begged God to bless the place and to make it
the home of all who sincerely honored his name.

According to a contemporary brochure put out by the commune's busy tourist agency, Assisi is a city that cannot just be "seen"; it must be "experienced" as a place, perhaps *the* place, where "the spirit of St. Francis pervades all." Every year hundreds of thousands of visitors, art lovers, tourists, and pilgrims from all over the world flock to see the famous basilica where the saint is buried. The narrow streets in which Francesco begged for bread are lined with hundreds of shops selling all manner of atrocious trinkets and some of the worst food to be found in Italy, at prices as breathtaking as the view from the Rocca Maggiore, the late-medieval fortress that glowers over the prosperous, crowded town. The spirit that pervades these streets is the same one that whistled down the stone staircases and across the Piazza del Commune in Francesco's lifetime, the same spirit that drove him straight into the outspread arms of Jesus Christ: the cold, relentless, insatiable, furious spirit of commerce.

Francesco di Pietro Bernardone was born in Assisi, toward the end of 1181, to a wealthy cloth merchant, Pietro Bernardone, and his wife, Pica, who may or may not have been French. He had an ordinary childhood, helping his father at his business and attending the church school near his house, where he was an unremarkable student. He grew to be a lively young man, fond of music and parties, given to romantic tales, dreams of knighthood, fantastical treasure quests, but also to prayer in solitary chapels. During one such occasion, at the dilapidated Church of San Damiano, God spoke to him from a crucifix, bidding him to repair the church. Francesco took some bolts of cloth from his father's warehouse, sold them, and delivered the money to the priest who lived there to pay for the repair of the chapel. Pietro, enraged by his son's extravagance, brought a complaint against him, which was resolved in the public square of Assisi. When the bishop gave Francesco the money and advised him to return to his father what was his, Francesco declared, "My Lord Bishop, not only will I gladly give back the money which is my father's, but also my clothes." He stripped off his clothes, placed the money on them, and standing naked before the bishop, his father, and all present, announced, "Listen, all of you, and mark my words. Hitherto I have called Pietro Bernardone my father; but because I am resolved to serve God, I return to him the money on account of which he was so perturbed, and also the clothes I wore which are his; and from now on I will say, 'Our Father who art in heaven,' and not 'Father Pietro Bernardone.'" The crowd wept in sympathy, and the bishop covered the naked and rebellious youth with his own cloak.

Francesco then took refuge in the poor church, where he devoted himself to making repairs; he begged for food and oil on the streets of Assisi. His former neighbors mocked him and drove him away, but one rich young man, Bernardo of Quintavalle, impressed by Francesco's sincerity and evident contentment in his new life, decided to join him. Together the two men gave away all of Bernardo's money and possessions to the poor.

More followers joined them. When they numbered twelve, the group walked to Rome to ask the Pope to approve a rule by which they might live as liegemen of the Church. After a dream in which he saw the Lateran Basilica collapsing and Francesco holding it up, the Pope, Innocent III, gave them an oral and very conditional approval.

Francesco's brotherhood, the Fratres Minores, grew rapidly. Within a few years the original twelve had grown to 5,000 (in comparison, the Dominican order, the Friars Preachers, as they were known, founded at roughly the same time, had fewer than fifty friars by 1220). They met each year during the feast of Pentecost for chapter meetings at the Portiuncula, a wooded area owned by local Benedictine monks and leased to the friars for one basket of fish a year. At these meetings Francesco delivered various admonitions; the friars were assigned to different regions; the *custos,* or caretakers, and ministers were appointed; and problems of administration were addressed. Between meetings the mission of the *fratres* was to wander homeless over the world, preaching repentance, begging for their food, offering themselves as servants to all. This, they believed, was the way the early apostles had lived, the way Jesus had adjured all his followers to live—giving the world an example of virtue, loving poverty, making no preparations for the next meal or the next bed, but leaving everything to God.

A Rich Young Man on the Road

In the morning, when he leaves Foligno, on the last leg of his journey from Rome to Assisi, Francesco's horse plods along at a steady pace, requiring neither guidance nor urging. Francesco is in no hurry, for his home has none of the charms of the adventure he brings to a close with his return. Everyone will want to hear about what he has seen; even his father will listen to his descriptions of Rome, the city of wonders, of the towers and bridges, the palace of the Laterano, and all the shrines and sacred relics he visited. But he will not mention the event that most fired his imagination, because anyone who hears of it will say it was a shameful, foolish exploit, the folly of a wealthy and useless young man who hasn't the sense to appreciate his position. Suppose, his father would exclaim, just suppose some neighbor from Assisi had recognized him. How could he hold his head up in the town?

Something has been coming to him now for some time. He cannot be sure what it is or when it began, but he can feel it moving toward him, gathering momentum. His dreams are full of triumph; voices speak to him and counsel him, showing him scenes of great glory and making a promise: All this will be yours. But when he is awake, there are no triumphs, though he is free to indulge himself in whatever pursuits and amusements his father's money can buy. Nothing obstructs him; no one contradicts him. When he made up his mind to visit the holy places in Rome, he met with no objections. His mother provided him with a pouch full of bread and sweets, and his father encouraged him to take the better of their horses; both parents were anxious that his clothes be the finest and that he carry enough silver to make proper offerings at the shrines.

His horse shakes his head, as if to remind Francesco that he has at least some small obligations as a rider, and he comes to himself with a start. It is a spring day of stunning perfection; the air is cool and fresh, the sky overhead as blue as the mantle of the Holy Virgin, and on either side of the road the fields stretch away pleasantly, olive trees on one side, grain on the other, bordered by ranks of cypress and pine. There are contingents of chaffinches chirping in the dusty leaves of the olive trees, and swallows whirling overhead in undulating formations, like fallen leaves twisting and turning in a stream. He passes two peasants digging mud by the side of the road and another leading a reluctant goat by a bit of dirty rope. They glance at him as he goes by, a rich young man, carefree, and they give terse responses to his friendly salutations. The goat gives a strangled cry, struggling at the end of his rope while his owner curses and threatens him. Francesco looks away, wounded, as he always is by displays of pointless ferocity. He has seen too many the past few days in Rome, where men and beasts are crowded together and tempers flare at the most innocent remark. At the Basilica of San Pietro he saw two men fighting on the very steps, and later, when he came out, there was such a quantity of blood, though no sign of the combatants, that he thought one had surely killed the other. And it was there, as he stood looking around nervously, that a voice called out to him from the shadows of the vestibule, and the peculiar and wonderful adventure began.

"Have you given it all to the thieving priests?" the voice inquired. "Or is there a coin to spare for those that may truly have need of it?"

Francesco stepped away from the blood soaking into the paving stones and approached the man—if he was a man, for all he could see of him was one bare foot, so swollen and bruised that it looked more like a rotten vegetable than human flesh. "I have not given it all," he said, stepping in under the arch. He could see nothing, for the bright daylight had dazzled his eyes and now the shadows confounded them, but he heard the harsh laughter of several men. One of them said, "Here is the last honest man in the world," and another responded, "It proves what I have been telling you, that the Judgment Day is near, for here is the new Christ among us to prove it."

"And the Pope is the Antichrist," the first speaker declared. Francesco gazed down at them as his eyes became accustomed to the dark. There were three of them; two were old fellows, or so they appeared. The third, the one who had announced the imminence of the Judgment Day, was a youth of perhaps Francesco's age with thick blond hair, scarcely any beard, and an open, ingenuous expression. He looked Francesco up and down with a bold, rapacious eye. "Now, that's a fine cloak such as only a nobleman could afford," he observed.

"I am not a nobleman," Francesco replied. "But my father is a cloth merchant."

The young man got to his feet awkwardly, pressing his hands against the wall behind him. When he was halfway up, he hopped forward onto his one good leg. The other was stunted and shriveled. He could put his weight on this leg long enough to make a quick step; he crossed the space with a rolling, out-of-kilter gait, and then propped himself against the wall. "Wouldn't I look a prince in such a cloak as that?" he said, smiling up into Francesco's face. His lower right teeth were missing, and when he smiled, his lower lip fell in over the gap.

"For the love of God," one of the old men said, "give us a coin if you won't give us the cloak."

Francesco turned to look at the speaker, narrowing his eyes to make him out in the shadows, crouched beside his friend, who rubbed his face with his palms and echoed, "Yes, give us a coin, for the love of God."

"For the love of God," Francesco said.

He looked into the eyes of the ragged young man who imagined no greater glory than to have such a cloak as his. "Will you trade your clothes for mine?" he said. In reply the youth gave a hoot of delight. The old men cackled together; here was an odd business. "Will you let me sit here with you?" Francesco continued, as he pulled off his cloak, his doublet, his leather girdle. The young man began stripping off his rags, which took no time at all, because he wore only a short sackcloth tunic and a pair of filthy breeches embroidered with holes. "I will have to take my other clothes back when I go," Francesco explained, examining the contents of his purse, "but I will leave you my cloak and all but two of these coins; I will need that much for my journey home."

"Giuseppe is right," one of the old men remarked. "This proves that God's judgment is nigh on this world."

Francesco laughed. Half-naked, he bent over to pull off his leggings. Giuseppe had already donned his shirt. "And will you share your food with me?" Francesco asked. This sent them all into a riot of laughter. "Oh, yes," they agreed. Giuseppe slid down the wall to the stones, clutching his new cloak, which he had bundled in his arms like a baby. "You are welcome to everything we have," he announced, with the casual grace and courtesy of a lord offering hospitality to some bedraggled traveler.

Francesco stayed with them all day, and the people who saw him took him for one of the beggars. What was this sensation, so delicious and unexpected, when a passing lady paused to look down at him with a haughty yet pitying eye? As he stretched out his hand to her, she turned away, drawing her heavy skirt in close, lest he should touch it. Did she thank heaven that no son of hers would ever be found in such disgraceful circumstances? And what would she say if she knew that this importuning beggar was a sham, deserving neither charity nor pity, for he had a horse, a purse, and fine clothes, and would return in a day or two to his father's comfortable house, where a servant would greet him at the door?

When evening came, two more men joined the group, and they all sat down in the street to share the food they had begged. It was poor stuff, black bread and a little grain, which they made into a porridge, for one of them owned an iron pot, and another had begged some sticks of firewood. Francesco listened to their lively conversation, full of profanity and derision for the vanity of the world. Though he was wealthy, they included him, as if he, too, did not know when he would find a meal again. After they had eaten, he changed back into his own clothes and laughed with them over the miracle of his transformation. Yet he felt an aching, premonitory sadness as the crisp linen settled across his shoulders; it was as though he were putting on a costume that would deceive only a fool, for a wise man would see at once that it did not suit him, that it must belong to some other man, an elegant, stylish young man, and that Francesco was an impostor in his own clothes. He folded his cloak and laid it in Giuseppe's lap, accepting his enthusiastic blessing and the boisterous farewells of the others, who promised him their hospitality whenever he should return. Then, bowing and waving as they repeatedly called his name, he wandered out into the dark streets alone.

Now he is himself again, but not himself; something has changed, and the world looks different because of it. He has acquired, among other novelties, a memory he will not share. His horse carries him back over the same road he traveled before. His senses are open; he is prey to sudden and conflicting emotions. He sees himself from the outside, and he is not entirely gratified by what he sees.

THE LEPER

His back is stiff and sore from days of riding and from the long rounds of the shrines. He shrugs his shoulders, attempting to shake out the soreness, and rolls his head in a slow circle, easing the knotted muscles in his neck. As he does this, his horse starts, making a panicked sidestep that nearly unseats him. He catches up the reins as he lifts himself out of the saddle and then, when he drops back into his seat, he loosens his knees, gripping the horse's flanks with his calves. He knows as he goes through these automatic calming responses that there is something in the road just ahead, something that was not there a moment ago. The horse comes to a standstill in a cloud of dust that rises to his knees, and he stands working his head back and forth against the bit. Francesco rests a hand on his mane and says his name softly, reassuringly, as he looks down past the foaming lips to see what has so terrified this normally sedate and reliable creature.

The leper stands in the middle of the road, perfectly still. One hand rests on the bell cord around his neck, the other hangs limply at his side. He is dressed in a filthy garment, patched together from bits of sacking and undyed wool, which hangs loosely on his emaciated body. He regards Francesco and his horse steadily, his head slightly turned and his chin lifted, the better to see them, for his disease has eaten away half his face and he has only one eye.

Francesco does not speak. He cannot move. They face each other on the road, and the bright sun pours down great quantities of light over them, so there are no shadows anywhere, nothing to soften or dim the harsh reality of this encounter, and nowhere to hide from the necessity of playing it out. The leper's eye drills into Francesco. From childhood he has had a horror of lepers, and he has always avoided the *lazaretto* at the foot of Mount Subasio, where they sometimes congregate in the road, rattling their wooden bells and calling out for alms. He dreams of the foul stench rising from their rotting flesh, their grotesque faces, their phlegmy, guttural voices. He wakes sweating and shouting for help.

He glances back down the road and into the neat ranks of the olive trees. All is uncommonly empty and still. Even the birds, twittering only a moment ago, have been silenced.

He could ride on. There is no reason to stop. He could throw down his last coin to the leper as he passes. His horse lifts one hoof and paws the hard dirt. It is time to go on, to go home. As Francesco drops his hand to the reins, his eyes fall on his own well-fitting glove, and it dawns on him that this leper is not wearing gloves, which is odd, because he and his kind are required always to wear them when they leave their hospitals, just as they are required always to wear and ring their bells to warn unwary travelers of their approach.

Again Francesco looks down on the solitary figure of the leper, who has not moved. His hand is wrapped around the cord, his head arrested at an angle. He is like a statue, lifeless and weatherbeaten, and Francesco has the sudden sense that he has been standing there, in his path, forever.

Something has been coming toward him, or he has been coming to something; he has known this for some time, and he has bent his energy in the direction of finding out what it might be. This was the reason for his pilgrimage to Rome. At the shrines he had recited the requisite prayers; gazed upon the relics, the bones, the bits of hair and cloth, the vials of blood and tears; and proffered the proper offerings. But he had not felt the burden of his sins lifted, and this spiritual restlessness drove him on. Only when he was with the beggars in the vestibule of the basilica had he felt some respite from this condition of tense and urgent expectancy.

He is in the grip of it again as he swings one leg over the saddle and drops to the ground beside his horse. The stillness of the world makes every sound acute—the clinking of the bridle chain as he leads the animal to a green patch nearby, the sound of grass tearing, and then the big jaws grinding. Francesco runs his hands through his hair, bats the dust from the front of his surcoat, and turns to face the man, who is there waiting for him.

The leper watches him with interest. His blasted face is bathed in sunlight: the black hole that was his eye has a steely sheen, and a few moist drops on his scab-encrusted lips glitter like precious stones. He moves at last, releasing his cord and extending his hand slowly, palm up, before him.

This supplicating gesture releases Francesco, for it dictates the countergesture, which he realizes he longs to make. Without hesitation he strides across the distance separating him from his obligation, smiling all the while as if stepping out to greet an old and dear friend. He opens his purse, extracts the thin piece of silver inside it, and closes it up again. He is closer now than he has ever before been to one of these unfortunate beings, and the familiar reaction of disgust and nausea rises up, nearly choking him, but he battles it down. He can hear the rasp of the leper's breath, rattling and wet. The battle between Francesco's will and his innate reluctance overmasters him: he misses a step, recovers, and then drops to one knee before the outstretched hand, which is hardly recognizable as a hand but is, rather, a lumpish, misshapen thing, the fingers so swollen and calloused that they are hardly differentiated, the flesh as black and hard as an animal's rough paw.

Carefully Francesco places his coin in the open palm, where it glitters, hot and white. For a moment he tries to form some simple speech, some pleasantry that will restore him to the ordinary world, but even as he struggles, he understands that this world is gone from him now, that there is no turning back. It was only so much smoke, blinding and confusing him, but he has come through it somehow; he has found the source of it, and now, at last, he is standing in the fire. Tenderly he takes the leper's hand, tenderly he brings it to his lips. At once his mouth is flooded with an unearthly sweetness that pours over his tongue, burning his throat and bringing sudden tears to his eyes. These tears moisten the corrupted hand he presses to his mouth. His ears are filled with the sound of wind, and he can feel the wind chilling his face, a cold, harsh wind blowing toward him from the future, blowing away everything that has come before this moment—this moment he has longed for and dreaded, as if he thought he might not live through it.

He reaches up, clinging to the leper's tunic, for the wind is so strong and cold that he fears he cannot stand against it. Behind him the horse lifts its head from grazing and lets out a long, impatient whinny, but Francesco does not hear it. He is there in the road, rising to his feet, and the leper assists him, holding him by the shoulders. Then the two men clutch each other, their faces pressed close together, their arms entwined. The sun beats down and the air is hot and still, yet they appear to be caught in a whirlwind. Their clothes whip about; their hair stands on end; they hold on to each other for dear life.

In Hiding

We can hear their voices, angry and exultant, over the terrified cries of their prisoners, like the shouts of butchers one to another when they are herding squealing, struggling pigs into the slaughtering pen. These captors are neither men nor beasts; in spite of their hairy backs, black horns, brutish snouts, and birds' feet, they stand upright and brandish in their large human hands the tools of their trade: lashes; slashing hooks; glowing, red-hot irons. One digs his talons into the neck of a naked man who writhes beneath him, his face swollen and blue, his body drawn up in an impossible arc. The man's mouth is opened wide in a howl, for his captor has forced a thick rod between his buttocks and is bearing down hard upon it. Behind these two a woman has fallen to her knees as she struggles to release her shoulder from the jaws of another demon. The creature's thick reptilian tail is wrapped around her torso, holding her fast against his thighs. He mocks her suffering, pointing out her destination: a black tube with teeth, like the mouth of an enormous serpent, down which two of his fellows have thrown another victim—whether male or female is uncertain, because only the legs and feet are visible. The feet are curiously flexed. All but two of the prisoners are naked: a man in rich garb, carrying a sack across his shoulders and entering the awful scene through a flaming gate at one side, and another man crawling on the ground near the serpent's mouth, naked but for the bishop's miter still firmly in place on his head, his torso wrapped tightly in the coiled tail of another demon. The bishop is gazing at another man, who has a demon crouched on his stomach. The creature is positioned so that his buttocks are poised just over his victim's face; his sharp talons are sunk in the man's genitals. The sufferer's mouth is held open by an iron device, and his eyes are rolled back in agony and horror. From the demon's anus flows a stream of gold coins, filling the open mouth, choking the man with gold.

Francesco lets out a soft huff of amusement as he examines this last image. He looks up from the dark and lurid sufferings of the damned to the bright sunlit window next to him, but he does not notice the limpidity of the light that illuminates the book and the table he is bending over, because he hears the sound of footsteps on the gravel outside. Hurriedly he crosses the room and drops down into an open recess in the floor, a space so narrow and shallow that he has to curl himself in a ball to fit into it. He reaches up to slide the flat stone that serves as a lid for this, his own personal hell, into place, closing his eyes tight against the dirt that always showers down when the stone's edge lodges in the earth.

The door has opened, the intruder has paused, and then the footsteps come purposefully to the hiding place. Two sharp raps bring down a fresh shower of dirt. Francesco pushes against the stone, lifting it, while his friend grabs the edge and pulls it back across the floor. Francesco sits up in his hole and rubs the dirt from his eyes.

"Your father has not relented," the old priest says. "He knows you are in hiding hereabouts, and he has sworn to find you if he has to pay the entire guard."

"He won't have to pay anyone," Francesco says flatly.

The priest throws up his hands. "What will you do?"

"I'm going to Assisi," Francesco says. "He will find me in the street easily enough."

Ingrate, Thief, Scoundrel

Inside the gates of Assisi two boys, returning from the forest, each burdened by a large dead hare, push past Francesco, and he is so weak that he staggers into the wall. Their heads come up like those of young wolves alerted by the misstep of a sheep, their eyes fix coldly upon him, and their nostrils quiver, testing the air, deciphering the scent of vulnerability and fear. "Idiot," one observes to the other. Francesco rights himself and continues up the street, holding the skirt of his tunic so that he will not trip on it. The boys fall into step behind him. Each is half his size but has twice his strength. "You know who this is," one says to the other. "This is the son of Pietro Bernardone, the one who has robbed his father and disgraced his name." Francesco plods on, his eyes on the paving stones rising ahead of him.

"Why have you come back, madman?" one of the boys taunts him. "Do you think your father will welcome you?" The other steps up quickly, overtaking Francesco and dancing out ahead of him, brandishing his hare. He squeezes his nose with his free hand and whines, "God, how he stinks."

"He stinks of his friends at the *lazaretto*," his companion offers. "He is searching for his new love among the lepers." At this Francesco looks briefly over his shoulder, his expression a mixture of exhaustion, fever, and irony. The boy feels the hot black arrow of this regard as a momentary hesitation, instantly banished by the arrival of a boisterous trio clattering down the steps from San Giorgio. They are just released from school and wild from a morning of Latin declensions, intent now on merriment or mischief, whichever comes easier. At once they spy Francesco and his persecutors and rush forward to join in the game, shouting imprecations—"Idiot," "Swine," "Thief," "Madman." Circling Francesco, they pluck at his sleeves, bump him hard with their hips and elbows, mock his efforts to keep his footing and to continue on his way. His resistance is feeble and he does not protest, which excites their contempt. They speak for him, grinning and winking at one another, "Oh, do not push me so, my dear Giorgio." "Matteo, why are you so rough with me?" The racket brings women to the upper windows along the street. "It is Pietro Bernardone's son," one observes to another. Like a feather riding on the air, this phrase is borne away along the streets, fluttering across the piazza at San Giorgio, sucked into the narrow passageway and puffed out across the marketplace, where the stalls are closing for the day. Old women, trudging homeward with their baskets half empty—summer is over, and already there is little to buy but turnips, apples, and quinces—lift their sharp faces to hear the news: "Pietro's son, Francesco, has come back."

As Francesco makes his way through the town, the mocking entourage thickens around him, and he can scarcely see what is ahead. The children pick up stones and clods of dirt, which they pitch at him, shouting with delight when they hit their mark. He plods on, indifferent to all provocation; but when they pass the ancient columns of Minerva's temple, the press in front of him suddenly parts, and he is faced with a sight that weakens his knees, though not his resolve. His father rushes toward him, bellowing, cursing, calling on God and on all his neighbors to witness his disgrace and his fury. His face is bright red, his eyes bulge in their sockets, his lips are pulled back over his teeth like an enraged dog's. Francesco stands his ground, but at the last, as his father charges down on him, he throws up his hands to protect his face.

"Ingrate!" Pietro shouts, grabbing his son by the hair. "Thief! Scoundrel!" He knocks Francesco to his knees with a backhanded blow and then jerks him up and slaps him across the ear. Francesco does not struggle or cry out. He has been living in a hole for a month, refining his courage for this confrontation, and though the father has superior strength, the son's will has been formed as igneous rock is formed, under pressure, and it is unyielding.

The crowd now takes the side of youth against age and chides Pietro for his anger. This criticism stings him, and he protests vociferously. How could they know what he has been through day after day, with this good-for-nothing boy who claims he has God's blessing to steal from his own father? He grips Francesco by the elbow and pulls him forward so roughly that he feels the sinew pop at Francesco's shoulder, but he will not be stopped now. If his son resists, he will take his arm right out of the socket. Francesco reels, his eyes roll back in his head, and he stumbles forward, endeavoring to keep up. Pietro rains down curses on his son, on his neighbors, on his town, on the world, on God himself, who has cursed him with the infamy of an ungrateful son.

THE FRIAR AND THE POPE

They have arrived at the Lateran palace, a city within the city, and have made their way through the outer courts and inner vestibules to the great hall where the Lord Pope receives the never-ending tributes and entreaties of the horde that constitutes Jesus Christ's Church on earth. Clerics and prelates, secretaries and legates, lords and guildsmen, each in the costume suitable to his condition and rank, occupy themselves with the ceremonies required to command for even one moment the sublime attention of His Holiness. Bishop Guido guides Francesco and his brothers through the crowd, exchanging a word with a guard here and a secretary there, until they stand before a pair of doors as tall as trees, which open before them ponderously and with an impressive creaking of hinges, like the long-unopened gates of Paradise. They are herded inside by the bishop and passed along by a series of papal functionaries. The Lord Pope, seated at the far end of the great room on his high throne, leans forward to watch their approach. The babble of conversation does not entirely cease, but the volume drops appreciably as all eyes are gradually drawn to this ragged, uncouth, unwashed collection of bumpkins, whose bare feet slap the polished marble floors. Their small, dark, bright-eyed leader steps out ahead of them, his eagerness so barely contained that he seems to execute a bizarre new dance step as he charges forward. The Pope sends Cardinal Giovanni, who stands at his side, an incredulous and skeptical look: This is his discovery? This shabby, inelegant creature fresh from the sty? This is his idea of what the Church will require if it is to stem the flood of heresy and dissension that is washing down from the north? Truly, God's wonders have not ceased.

When Francesco reaches the foot of the steps leading to the Pope's throne, his progress is checked by a terse command from a guard. He looks up to Cardinal Giovanni, who nods at him distantly. He sweeps back the skirt of his patched and unsightly tunic as if it were the robe of an emperor and inclines his head and shoulders in a lordly bow. He can hear the cardinal's introduction: "Here is our Brother Francesco di Pietro Bernardone of Assisi, whom I have examined, and who begs the ear of Your Holiness." Francesco keeps his head down but raises his eyes and looks directly into the Lord Pope's opaque and chilly scrutiny. The Pope's golden corona is studded with jewels, and it rises like the dome of a gleaming beehive high above his head. The rigid collar of his cope is so high that it obscures the lower part of his face, so he appears to be a small mound of gold, brocade, and jewels from which peer steadily two heavy-lidded, skeptical eyes above a long aquiline nose. As Francesco stares, uncertain whether to speak, genuflect, or back cautiously away, the folds of the cope rustle, and a small, pale hand appears, the index finger extended, pointing at him. Then the finger crooks once in a summoning gesture. He casts an anxious look at the cardinal, who lifts his chin, reinforcing the Pope's command. Eagerly Francesco climbs the wide steps to the foot of the papal throne.

Francesco stands before the Lord Pope, nodding his head at something the cardinal is saying. Pope Innocent listens, his neck bent forward beneath the weight of his corona, his shoulders drooping beneath the weight of his robes. His gaze wanders from the cardinal to Francesco and then out to the brothers, huddled together nervously like dull sheep liable to panic and run off a cliff if their shepherd isn't quick about his business. He looks back at the shepherd in question, a dreamy fellow at best, full of enthusiasm, lacking judgment, doubtless barely literate, though Bishop Guido and Cardinal Giovanni have assured His Holiness that these penitents do much good in their district, nursing the poor and even the lepers, repairing churches, preaching repentance and, more important, respect for the Holy See. How much harm could they do if sanctioned, and how much more if refused? He presses his eyelids with his fingertips, listening to the cardinal, who seems determined to keep his protégé from speaking for himself.

The brothers have begun to feel more at ease and to look around curiously. Brother Egidio, gazing up into the gloom, makes a discovery, which he brings to the attention of Brother Angelo. Up there, on the capital of that column, can he see it? Angelo cranes his neck; he doesn't see anything. Then, as Egidio raises his arm to point, Angelo does see it. But what is it? Is it a sparrow or a wren? The bird hops from one marble leaf to another and then takes off in the direction of the doors. It is a sparrow. They follow its dizzy flight as it sails through the cloudy upper atmosphere of the room.

"It seems to me that your way of life is too hard," the Pope comments at last, addressing himself pointedly to Francesco, who smiles as if he expected just this objection, though he says not a word to refute it. Straightway the cardinal offers his unsolicited opinion, which is that it might cause painful and unnecessary misunderstandings among the laity if the Holy Father should decree that the way of life recommended in the Gospels is too difficult for a Christian to undertake. This is not, the Pope concedes, an insignificant point. And as he considers it, his gaze wanders again to the brothers huddled out there in the aisle—surely an unpromising lot. One of them is rubbing his eyes with two fists, like a sleepy child, and two others stand apart, gazing up at the ceiling with their mouths ajar, like simpletons in a field making fantastic pictures out of the clouds.

Stigmata

The shadows have lengthened, and the night birds have begun their plaintive chorus. Brother Leone lights the lamp, adjusts the flame, and returns to his occupation, cutting long strips from a square of white wool. Francesco sits next to him on a stone, his hands resting palms up in his lap. Leone's method is to cut the edge and then rip the strips away. The repeated complaint of the tearing cloth is the only sound in the dim cell. Francesco dabs at his eye with the sleeve of his robe.

It is always worst on Saturday, because Francesco refuses to have his bandages changed on Friday, the day when the Lord Christ suffered on the cross. Leone has removed the cloths from his hands and feet without much difficulty, but they both know that the wound in his side is the most painful to clean, because it bleeds more copiously than the others. So they leave it for last. Leone lays out his strips, takes one up, and kneels at Francesco's feet. Because the nailhead protrudes from the flesh, he lays the strip beneath the iron, passing the cloth around the foot until it is level with the hard black disk. He does this carefully, gently. Moving the nail is excruciating to Francesco, though he never complains, only draws his breath in sharply.

When he has finished with Francesco's feet and hands, Leone helps him pull his tunic over his head, so that he can change the wide bandage that wraps his torso. Francesco groans as he lifts his arms, and Leone winces, apologizing for the pain. Francesco's fingers flutter around the waist of his breeches, touching the edge of the bandage. Leone bends over to inspect it. The blood has soaked through and dried.

Leone has confessed to Brother Rufino the anxiety in his heart when he thinks of his own sinful nature and how unworthy he is to serve so holy a man, yet he is convinced that only through the grace of Father Francesco has his poor soul any hope of salvation. God has chosen Francesco as his instrument to save many souls that would otherwise be damned, and Leone's most fervent prayer is that through no merit of his own but through his devotion to Francesco he will be one of that select company of the redeemed. Yet even as he nourishes that hope, he knows that he has no right to it, because he is so sinful and plagued by temptations.

Now, as he studies the bloodstained bandage, he feels a welling up of emotions: fear, pity, devotion, heart-smiting love. For a moment he does not move, and Francesco asks, "What is it, brother lamb of Christ?"

Leone shivers, drawing away. "It's dry," he says. "But when I unwrap it, it will open again."

Francesco straightens his spine and opens his arms out from his sides as if he were praying, and perhaps he is. Leone unfastens the end of the bandage and slowly pulls away the outer layer. It comes loose easily, but with the next layer he feels a slight resistance, and Francesco's knitted brow tells him what he already knows. "Forgive me, Father," Leone says, pulling the cloth free with a quick jerk. Francesco bites his lower lip without speaking. There is one layer to go, and it will be the most painful. Leone brings the loose part of the bandage just to the edge of the wound, and then pulls it lightly to find the deepest part. Francesco's face has gone white, but he does not flinch. Instead he raises one hand and lays it on Leone's chest, just over his heart. "My dear son," he says softly.

Leone looks down at the bandaged hand pressing gently against his chest. The wonder of the moment overcomes him. Francesco's hand is like a burning sword plunged into his heart, inflaming him with such passionate devotion that his vision blurs and he gasps for air. How is it possible that he is here, tending the miraculous wounds of this new Christ, who is also his dearest friend and companion, his brother, father, and mother, who in- spired him, when they were both young and in love with Lady Poverty, to follow him on a great adventure of the soul? They have walked a thousand miles in this quest, only to come to this cell, where Francesco touches Leone's heart with the hand that bears the proof that he is the most dearly loved of all those who serve the Lord Christ, because of all the saints only he has been chosen to share in Jesus Christ's own suffering.

"Francesco," Leone says, leaning into the hand that presses, that holds, his heart, and meeting his beloved's eyes, which, though they can scarcely see him, still pour forgiveness, love, and perfect understanding over him like warm rain. Brother Leone is swooning. He fears he will be destroyed by the power of this love. Yet his hands are still engaged in their task. With a cry of terror commingled with joy, he pulls sharply at the cloth, freeing it from the wounded flesh. As he loses consciousness, he sees the blood gushing forth, and it seems to him that his whole body and his soul are bathed and refreshed in this blood, which is shed for him, and which he cannot deserve.

Epilogue

Some see the stigmata as the crowning achievement of Francesco's life, signaling his complete identification, and hence union, with his beloved Jesus Christ. Others suggest that there was an element of despair in the miracle—that Francesco saw himself as crucified by the unrest and infighting in the great movement he had founded. His contemporaries, though they had never heard of such a thing before, seem to have accepted it as well within the realm of possibility, and even in keeping with what they understood to be the nature of God's continual interference in the world of men. Francesco had, in their view, been singled out and marked by Jesus as his own. It proved what everyone already suspected—that he was a living saint. Two years later, in October of 1226, Francesco died peacefully at Assisi, revered by all, his devoted friars gathered around him. He was forty-five years old.

ALANE SALIERNO MASON

The Exegesis of Eating

*And thou shalt treat the food that touchest thy lips with
reverence, in recognition of the labors and traditions of
thine ancestors, and in communion and fellowship with
those to whom thou art tied with ties of blood and love.
Thou shalt not neglect to share the fruits of the earth with
thy neighbor. Thou shalt not neglect to feed the old and
the sick. Thou shalt serve first the pasta, then the meat,
fish, or fowl, then the salad, and thou shalt sprinkle no
grated cheese on the fish. Thou shalt give thanks before the
meal and kiss the hand that feeds thee. Except in condition of necessity, thou shalt not eat in haste, in distraction,
or alone.*

These are some of the commandments I took in at my grandparents' table, along with string bean salad, chicken cutlets, potatoes and eggs, stuffed and roasted mushrooms, thinly sliced beef
rolled and tied with string. But in my adult life, I've broken them
all, except for the commandment not to use the grated cheese on
linguini with clam sauce, which I've kept faithfully. In the kitchen
(where so many Italian-American women once ladled out the
years in one meal after another) I spend only a little time at the
beginning and the end of the day, eating while reading the mail,
paying my bills, and listening to radio news. It takes me longer to
do the dishes than to cook, which is not saying much; and what I
cook, I eat alone, heedlessly. I don't bemoan my freedom from the
ancestral bond to the pot waiting to boil, and yet . . . And yet, in
my gut, semolina nourished from infancy, I know there's some-

thing wrong with the way we eat now, the way I feed myself and so rarely feed others.

I spent much of my childhood in my grandmother's kitchen. That was where I returned from school to announce, to her distress, the human beings were descended from the apes. That was where we pulled up chairs to watch through the oven window as her cookies baked. Even her sewing machine and the typewriter on which she made out checks were in the kitchen. Outside the kitchen door, my dog waited with ears pricked for my grandmother to spoil him with treats, as she sometimes spoiled me. She was blamed for making me fat as a child, though I think it was not her fault. Even if she had a taste for sweets, our diet was not especially indulgent. As I watched her cook, she would give me something from her preparations to assuage my hunger—a carrot, a piece of celery.

At lunch, she'd want to know what we wanted to eat for dinner. Most of the foods she prepared took time. They needed first to be "cleaned," trimmed of fat or organs or bones in the case of chicken or meat or fish, or of stems and seeds in the case of vegetables. Then basted in egg and bread crumbs, for cutlets or zucchini flowers, or stuffed, for mushrooms. Then cooked, then dressed, in the case of pasta or salad. For escarole pie, first she cooked the escarole then made the pie crust then layered the vegetable with garlic and anchovies and capers. It all took time. String beans had to be snapped at both ends, and after they were cooked, each one had to be carefully sliced along its length; for artichokes, every leaf had to be trimmed then stuffed with chopped garlic and bread crumbs. Even the homely potatoes with eggs required first cutting the potatoes into small cubes then frying them with oil then draining them on a paper towel before scrambling them with the eggs. (I always take the shortcut: I use less oil and add the eggs directly so it all sticks to the bottom of the pan.)

The foods all became associated with the time it took to prepare them. "Such a big bag of string beans your grandfather brought me, it's a lot of work to clean so many, he doesn't know the time it takes, a whole hour it took me!" Or "He brought home calamar', still with all the bone in, it took me all morning just to clean them and cut them up, doesn't he know you can ask the fish market to do it for you?" She often cleaned the foods under running water, and her hands were rough. Once I tried to squeeze the peeled tomatoes through a strainer the way she did when making sauce; I couldn't do it, it made my knuckles raw.

She never loved to cook in the way she loved to sew. With sewing, the work, the time, didn't disappear when it was done but was laid out in satisfying rows.

"All the time it took to make it, and we ate it in no time!" she'd exclaim as soon as our plates were empty. These were often the first words to break the silence my grandparents preferred while eating. When I chattered, merrily rushing through my food to get my words out faster, they'd both chasten me: "Eat slow, you can talk after. It's no good to eat fast."

My grandmother was always rotund; she took pleasure from eating if not from cooking. Her flowing bosom made for an especially comforting embrace. She snacked through the day, from nervousness, perhaps, but when her depression—what she called her "nervous tension"—became overwhelming, that was when she lost her appetite for sweets as well as for life and when she went on strike from the kitchen. The depression then could feed on itself, as she punished herself with the idea that by not cooking, she was a terrible disappointment to us all.

The thought of preparing the Christmas Eve meal always undid her, disabling her with "nervous tension," as she called it, a blend of fatigue, anxiety, and tears. At ninety-one, as pain in her feet and legs made it increasingly difficult for her to stand long enough to cook, her depression returned with a vengeance, more difficult than ever to treat. That year she was hospitalized twice for trying to die. Left alone for several weeks each time, my grandfather (younger than she but only by a month) struggled to learn to cook.

My grandmother was born in New York of Italian parents; my grandfather was born in Naples, where his mother and father had a little restaurant, a trattoria. There they served pasta marinara, veal scaloppine, chicken cacciatore, zuppa di pesce . . . "everything," my grandfather says. His father's family was in the wine export business and his mother's in the grocery business. The maternal family nickname was "Cocchiamichele," which probably meant that once upon a time, someone in the family named Michele made "cocchia," round loaves of bread with a split across the top.

His father and mother fought over the trattoria. Gennaro thought he should greet the customers out front, a public relations job, while Giuseppina stayed back in the kitchen, doing all the work. She didn't agree.

So Gennaro left for America, and my grandfather's mother took the children back to her hometown, where she ran a tiny grocery from the corner of her house and sold bread, which she baked in a large wood-fired oven across the street. During the First World War, she sold the bread to soldiers. The children fired the oven, and they baked both white bread and scagnozzi, a corn-bread. "The soldiers didn't like it, but we liked it better than white bread," my grandfather remembers. Almost all of his stories of Italy have to do with the preparation of food—the few cents a day he made picking grapes, and how they made wine by crushing the grapes with their feet; how his mother would wring the neck of a chicken, and how she would slit the throat of a pig while he stood with a bowl to catch the blood she would use to make blood pudding, sanguinaccio.

It was his mother's relatives, who had set up a grocery in Brooklyn, who made it possible for him to come to America. Later their grocery business became a chain of supermarkets. My grandfather, who had gone into contracting, built the first of the Danza supermarkets on Avenue X in Brooklyn at the end of World War II. At the groundbreaking, he said to his cousin Albert, "Compare, what are you going to do with this big store?"

"Compare, la gente . . . " Albert said and made a gesture toward his mouth with the bunched fingers of one hand—a gesture to say, "People always need to eat."

My grandfather always hated the idea that Americans think of pizza as Italian food, even though his birthplace is famous for it. He always claimed it wasn't Italian, wasn't real food. "I never heard of pizza before I came to this country. Pizza, pizza, that's junk. Why do you go out for that kind of junk when you can come over here and have a good dinner with us?" he'd say. Pizza is everything he doesn't like about America: quick, sloppy, cheap, eaten on the run, away from home. (He makes a gesture like a turkey gobbling to show what people do when they eat on the run.) "Eat and run, eat and run, that's what they do in this country," he says.

Real food takes time, preparation, care, he might say. A good Italian restaurant can be trusted to provide it, especially when you've gotten to know the owner—when he comes out front to chat with the customers. But best of all is when it is made at home, for the family. His cousins in Naples say coffee from "il bar," the café, will rot your gut, but coffee made at home is good for the stomach. Wine, no matter how acidic, is ottimo if home-made from pure grapes; if you buy that expensive stuff in the bottle, you don't have any idea what the vintner might have put in it.

Home preparation is what makes it good, what slakes hunger and thirst.

While my grandmother was in the hospital the second time, I went over to visit my grandfather, bringing a box of linguini and a jar of marinara sauce. My mother, from her own sickbed, made sure I also brought a baked chicken. "Bring whatever we have," she said.

My grandfather was trying to cook. He had some tomato sauce on the stove, and he had out some other jars and packages of alfredo sauce and bags of egg noodles; I think he was going to mix it all together, whatever was in the cupboard. He likes to do that, mix everything together. For my grandfather to cook is like a second crossing to the New World, bringing his life experience with him: his idea of cooking is mixing, the way he used to mix plaster or cement.

A home care assistant might come a few days a week after my grandmother was released from the hospital, my grandfather told me. "But do they cook?" he asked rhetorically. "Those people, they know nothing about cooking. At most, they open the can of soup at most. Do they know how to prepare the spaghetti marinara, the veal scaloppine?" He laughed.

We had some linguini in the tomato sauce, and we had some of the chicken. But his stomach was bothering him; nothing seemed to sit well. "I have to push it down with a shovel, with a stick," he says, making a gesture like pushing a balled-up rag through a length of pipe. "Not to enjoy it, just to live, just to stay living." He'd lost his appetite for eating since my grandmother had lost hers for life.

After our lunch, he took an ice cream roll out of the freezer. "I have some Friendly ice cream for you to take home to your mommy and dad." This was part of the meal, too—the necessity of sharing it with those who are absent.

"Oh, that's all right, Grandpa, they don't need it, really," I started to say, but he was taking a baked hen out of the freezer too. "Take this home to your mommy, also," he said.

"Grandpa, she just gave you a chicken, and now you want me to bring one back home to her? You keep it, you'll need it."

"Why not? Here, take whatever you want, I have so much stuff here," he said, gesturing to refrigerator shelves that were almost empty.

"Like father, like daughter," I tried to tease him. "If you and my mother had your way, I'd spend all my time carrying food back and forth from one house to the other."

But I did as I was told and took the ice cream and the frozen hen back to my mother. Who am I to argue with the currency of their concern for each other?

A few months before, my grandmother had been feeling so well, she made vanilla cookies to bring to some people they knew. She put them on a paper plate covered with tinfoil, which she carried on the tray in front of her four-wheeled walker.

"I want to show you something you never saw before, something special," my grandfather said. "I want you to meet some wonderful people, some friends of mine, you won't believe what they do. They do things the old-fashioned way, the real, old-fashioned way," he continued, as he drove slowly in his brown Cadillac with SALIERNO on the license plate. "They even have chickens. And you want to see how many peaches he had from his peach tree, my god, how many peaches! Three hundred peaches he had on one tree, you want to see how many he gave Grandma and me the last time, and eggs from his chickens, tomatoes from the garden—what a big garden! So much stuff he gave us, that's why Grandma baked him the cookies. But I don't want to tell you, I want to surprise you."

We crossed over the railroad tracks into the East Village, an Italian and Slav hamlet of neat one-family houses built close together, with tiny gardens sprinkled with lawn ornaments and whirligigs, and stopped in front of a white cottage with a clothesline along the side. A trim middle-aged man in slacks and T-shirt came out to greet us.

They greeted each other with buongiornos and handshakes that went halfway up the arm, and my grandfather said we weren't stopping, we didn't want to interrupt them, we were just dropping off something Grandma made to thank them for everything they did, and so on, and naturally the man insisted that we get out of the car just for a minute, and my grandfather said he told me all about the peaches and the man took us to see his garden.

The garden was perfectly enclosed in a chain-link fence to keep out the deer, and though it must have already been September the tomato plants still had that sweet-bitter smell as strong as pine. His basil plants were small bushes, and he still had some zucchini, overgrown now, very fat and yellow on the underside—maybe he was keeping them for seeds for next year.

Before we left, the man insisted my grandfather take a dozen fresh eggs, and he leaned into the car to give my grandmother two jars of homemade marinara sauce (one with eggplant) and a jar of preserved peaches.

"You see?" my grandfather said as we drove away. "What did I tell you, dear? You don't find people like that anymore these days. They do things the old-fashioned way, like I remember, the real Italian way."

My grandmother was in the hospital for a long month. After those weeks gone by without good food cooked at home, without balanced meals—a month of food as if it were pizza, eaten just to survive, not to savor or celebrate, of food eaten alone—something went out of my grandfather. He started to feel confused, off balance; he no longer felt like driving or grocery shopping or planting his garden, all things he had loved to do. Even with my grandmother home again, he was not the same. I called before going over to visit to see what I could get from the store, but "no, we don't need anything, we have everything here, don't worry about us, you just come over and have a nice lunch with us," my grandmother insisted. But there wasn't, for lunch, the usual bounty of fresh things to eat. For lack of other ingredients, my grandmother had made a soup from pastina and egg. In the toaster oven, she was reheating a half piece of leftover chicken parmigiana one of my uncles had brought from a deli.

"All he wants is soup," my grandmother declared. "He says he's not hungry for anything else. He just wants soup, soup."

"Nothing," my grandfather said. "I have no appetite whatsoever, I have to force myself to eat to live."

I scanned the scanty items on refrigerator shelves—no fruit, no vegetables, no cold cuts—and later in the afternoon claimed to have to go out on a nameless personal errand.

In the supermarket, I found the sliced Italian bread from Arthur Avenue, the ground turkey with which my grandmother likes to make low-fat meatballs, the cold cuts and lettuce and tomatoes, the grapes and pears, the waffles they like for breakfast, the bananas easy for my grandfather to digest, the zucchini easy for my grandmother to prepare, the beets they mentioned that they like—not the artichokes, since the moment she looked at them she would see "a lot of work" to trim and stuff them, a burden and a reproof. Some fresh corn on the cob, some frozen peas, some thinly sliced beef, some Progresso soups, some extra olive oil, and chicken, carrots, celery, spinach—the fixings for a homemade chicken soup.

I was raised in my grandmother's kitchen, and I am the only daughter of her only daughter. My mother's own illness now keeps her from fulfilling her traditional role, and I often think I should be living with them, shopping and cooking for my grandparents and my mother, too. That's how things went in the old country, and who's to say there isn't a poetry and justice in it? To prepare, for one's elders, the kind of food they prepared for you in the way they taught you to prepare it is something that goes beyond food for survival. It can't be replicated by meals on wheels (which doesn't go to their neighborhood anyway) or home-care nurses or store-bought preparations ready to heat. It is the richer nourishment of memory, love, and gratitude.

So I think, but I live over an hour away, working in one of those jobs that devours time and is never satisfied. A professional job, a privilege. And yet a dozen times a week I eat alone, in a way that is against my cultural religion. Should I tell the priest, next time I go to confession, the number of times I took my food in vain? I make quick 'n' easy versions of Italian comfort food— frozen tortellini or gnocchi, boiled then sautéed in the same pan with some garlic and oil and frozen peas. The results are unlike anything I knew in childhood, and each time I cook, I make enough for three. The leftovers harden in the fridge.

My friends remind me that the needs of my family, too, could devour me, that I'll never be there enough to take care of them, not without more self-sacrifice than I am prepared for, more than my grandparents declare themselves willing to accept. But my friends don't say this about my job, which is just as consuming. They are New Yorkers; they assume the job is identical with the self—the independent self that women have struggled so hard to earn.

As I drove to the supermarket to do my grandparents' grocery shopping that day, a strange, potent fear washed over me—fear of having a car accident, of never returning with the groceries that might sustain my grandparents until I saw them again. I'm not usually afraid of driving. Was it a fear of losing myself in their love and need—the fear that if I set off down that road of caretaking, I might never come back? Or was it the fear that no matter what, despite my best efforts and intentions, I would end up failing them—the knowledge that I wouldn't be there each time they needed me?

I wasn't quick enough in getting back to make them dinner. Since my grandfather began feeling unwell, he'd become ever more insistent on eating at particular hours: noon and 5:00 P.M. At 5:30, he was already eating some glutinous egg and pastina soup leftover from lunch. Still I made a salad with some ricotta salata sprinkled on top, and the beets and corn on the cob, and the salad seemed to go into him like water into the leaves of a drooping plant. He perked up.

"A balanced meal is very important," he declared. "I think that's part of why I got so weak. You can just eat pasta and pasta and pasta. You need to have a balanced meal."

"I'm sorry I wasn't around more these last few weeks," I said, feeling the unimportance of the travels and obligations that had occupied me while he had gone into his decline. "I'm sorry I wasn't around to cook something once in a while."

"Oh, no, my dear," my grandfather said. "When opportunity knocks, you have to take it. That's the way it goes. One leads to another. You have opportunities, you take them."

I took most of the skin off the chicken and baked it first so the soup wouldn't be oily, as my grandmother taught me, and I got the garlic, onions, celery and carrots simmering. Then I added the cooked chicken and the spinach, and boiled it awhile. The broth turned a rich, auburn, olive color: it smelled delicious.

"So much cooking you did," my grandfather said to me, "now you can stay away for a month! Don't come back!" Then to my grandmother, "She fooled you, dear. She said she was going shopping for herself, but she was going shopping for us. She pulled a fast one on you." Then to me: "Take some home to your mother. All these things you bought, take some home." Before I could stop him, he had begun packing up a bag for me to bring back to my mother: several packages of frozen waffles, half the fruit, half the package of cookies.

"You pulled a fast one on us," he said again as he walked me to the door.

"I do as I was taught by my elders," I said. "If you taught me the wrong way, you're just going to have to live with it."

"Oh, no, sweet-aht," he replied (he never pronounces an English *h*), "you learned the right way."

Whenever we hear of a friend concerned with family illness or need, we Americans have learned to say, "Don't forget to take care of yourself, make sure you take care of yourself"—but it rings to me a little unconvincing, a little hollow. It's a calorie-counted no-fat meal that doesn't completely satisfy. Is others' need really such a threat to the self, to our idea of what the self is? The American self is the doing, achieving, self-realizing, independent self. A self rattling freely in the large jar of the world. Zooming along in a car, stopping off to refuel with gas and pizza before getting on the road again, the forever youthful, autonomous American self, needing for true nourishment only the air of liberty. A self I can never really believe is something other than a well-intentioned lie, a deceptive seduction.

The ideal farm, for Jefferson, was one that produced everything it needed, not one that gave and took from others. America was meant to be a nation of such self-sufficient farmers. Yet the world is continually telling us that its truth is one of universal need, of mutual dependency.

What if the self does not stop at the borders of the body but is a small constellation of elements including those who need us? Then in taking care of others, we'd be taking care of ourselves, too. Such care is rewarding, we know; it nourishes us also, we know this for a fact. Women have always known it, have always attended to the larger self, doing whatever is required, and yet we also know that, too often, they've lost themselves completely, burying their own talents and desires; they've become nothing other than a means to satisfy their families' needs, and then when they're no longer needed, what are they? Frustrated, angry, depressed—I sometimes think there is an unspoken epidemic of depression among older Italian American women, those who've ladled the pot of nourishment dry. A lifetime spent feeding their families, and somehow they're left without sustenance, feeding on old losses.

When my grandfather started to feel better again, my grandmother's sister died, and my grandmother slowly took a turn again for the worse. Eventually it became an effort to get her out of bed to eat, though my grandfather tried his best to nurse her. Sometimes he ordered pizza or Chinese food or heated restaurant leftovers or trays of lasagna or manicotti that his sons brought by. Just to have to think about it was beginning to wear on him. "Cooking is a problem," he admitted. "Three times a day, someone has to cook!" he said in amazement. Even accounting for illnesses and occasional meals out, my grandmother had prepared almost seventy thousand meals during nearly seventy years of marriage. No wonder she had gotten tired.

But with practice my grandfather was getting better at it, coming up with his own recipes. On Sundays, he didn't give me a chance to cook but already had pots bubbling on the stove when I arrived. He put a bag of store-bought baked chicken in a pot of marinara sauce from the jar and added a lot of a lemon-pepper-garlic spice. It was surprisingly good. He said he was going to open a trattoria like his parents had in Naples. As my grandmother, on new medication, began to feel better again, she criticized his cooking without mercy. "He can't cook, he doesn't know the first thing about cooking," she began to repeat. He prepared meatballs shaped like squat sausages, which I left too long in the oven. "He can't cook at all, those meatballs were terrible," my grandmother said. That she took enough interest to complain was the first good sign.

"I just don't feel like cooking," she lamented the following week. "But he can't cook. He's a man, what does he know about cooking?" We told her men cook, too, even became famous chefs, but she wasn't convinced. Anyway, she didn't want to be convinced, she wanted to be needed; she was on the mend.

I, too, want to be needed, of course, but not too much. When my grandfather tells me women in the workplace have put an end to family love, the family meal around the table, I ask him if he thinks it would be a good thing for me to spend my life in the kitchen. He doesn't have an answer. Nor do I have one for him, for his sense of a world wobbling free of its axis of the family dinner table, a world starved of women's self-sacrifice. I only try to convince myself that it is necessary, also, for me to do the other things that I do, to share some of what I find foraging outside the kitchen and the store. If they are a larger part of me, it must also follow that I am a larger part of them—the part of them writing this essay; the part of them out in the world, with opportunities still before me. Words, I am sure, can be another currency of love. And yet not words alone, for all the worlds and opportunities they bear. For what are words, without flesh?

To feed each other as we have been fed, to eat and be eaten, a good priest says, is an embodiment of our greatest commandment.

In his words nourishment is spiritual, metaphorical, yet palpable and real. Still the literal hungers of those near to us seem infinite, recurring daily. The vat of soup is soon empty again, and washed. Love refills it. How many times? Seven times seventy times, or a thousand times seventy?

Eat slow, my grandmother would say, and tell me afterwards.

DAPHNE MERKIN

Trouble in the Tribe

from *The New Yorker*

I've been trying to lose my religion for years now, but it refuses to go away. Just when I think I've shaken it—put it firmly behind me, a piece of my obscurantist past no longer suited to the faithless life I now lead—it turns up again, dogging me. You'd think it would be easy, particularly in a city like New York, where no one cares whether or not you believe in God; even my friends who do would be hard put to explain why, other than by alluding knowingly to Pascal's wager, in which the odds favor the believer. But as the world becomes a more bewildering place almost by the week, I find myself longing for what I thought I'd never long for again: a sense of community in the midst of the impersonal vastness, a tribe to call my own.

To add to my confusion, Joseph Isadore Lieberman, the first Jewish vice-presidential candidate of a major party, and Abraham Foxman, the national director of the Anti-Defamation League, are noisily airing questions that I've been debating internally for decades: How Jewish is too Jewish? Does a public declaration of religious allegiance always come across as self-serving—a sales technique custom-made for the age of identity politics? Whether Lieberman calls himself a Jewish American or an American Jew is a matter of hairsplitting, a preoccupation of the leery. (Will he look out for the country's welfare or only for the interests of his own kind?) What *is* of significance—to Jews and Gentiles alike— is the fact that Lieberman is observant, a man of religious conviction: he keeps kosher, doesn't turn on lights or travel in a car on

Shabbos, and regularly attends synagogue services. In doing so, he has given the beleaguered Modern Orthodox Jewish establishment something to be truly proud about, a reason to kvell. At the Nashville announcement rally, the Connecticut senator exuberantly (or presumptuously, depending on your tolerance for direct appeals to the divine) invoked God, "maker of all miracles," and praised Gore's "chutzpah" in naming him. Suddenly, the press was brimming with folksy Yiddishisms worthy of Leo Rosten, references to abstruse Jewish concepts, and discussions about whether Lieberman would be able to attend his inauguration, which falls on a Saturday.

As if I didn't have enough conflicts already about having strayed from my Modern Orthodox upbringing, there now looms the temptation to reclaim it and avail myself of ready-made cultural cachet. I can already picture those "revolving-door" Jews, staunch secularists who disdain visible signs of affiliation, suddenly lining up to take a closer look at the quaint religious customs long ago left in the care of tottering relatives in Miami Beach. A few days after Gore announced his choice of a running mate, for instance, I was meeting my mother for dinner at nine. She hadn't eaten for the past twenty-four hours, in observance of the Jewish fast day known as Tishah B'Av. (All Jewish holidays begin and end after sundown.) While she was waiting on Park Avenue for me to pick her up in a cab, a well-coiffed neighbor—whose ethnic origins had been obscured by years of Upper East Side polish—asked her why she was going out to eat so late. My mother explained that she had just finished fasting in commemoration of the destruction of the first and second temple, thousands of years ago. The woman looked startled and then commented, with no small degree of chagrin, "I guess we'll all have to learn about these things now, won't we?"

It's difficult to imagine a sustained resurgence of serious interest in either the sober letter or the confining spirit of the law, but for the moment things are looking up for the "frummies"—which is one of the terms that Modern Orthodox Jews use for their less modern compatriots. (Other shorthand designations include "yeshiva-ish," "*charedi*," and "black hats.") The minute gradations between one subset of observant Judaism and another are suddenly the object of intense national scrutiny, even if they are frequently misunderstood. More irritating to me are the know-it-all remarks of my sedulously lapsed acquaintances to the effect that Lieberman doesn't wear a yarmulke in the workplace and that his wife doesn't cover her hair, as though these practices would in any way disqualify him from being a member in good standing of his synagogue.

In the earliest days of Modern—or, as it is sometimes called, centrist—Orthodox Judaism, the public and private demonstrations of one's religious beliefs were kept separate, like the dishes for meat and dairy food. As it happens, the Modern Orthodox movement was founded, in the 1850s in Frankfurt, Germany, by my great-great-grandfather Rabbi Samson Raphael Hirsch, as a response to the increasingly dominant Reform movement. (The fact that I am a direct descendant of Hirsch gives me sterling *yichus*—the Jewish version of lineage, like having a blood relation on the Mayflower.) Hirsch, an influential theologian and community leader who admired Schiller almost as much as he did Maimonides, cautiously embraced modernity while insisting on the obligation to observe Jewish law. His credo, *Torah im Derech Eretz*—Torah Judaism in harmony with secular culture—was a bow in the direction of both God and Germany. Hirsch founded the first modern Jewish day school, which was based on an innovative curriculum of secular and sacred studies. My mother, who attended the school in the thirties, remembers that the boys took off their yarmulkes for secular classes. Although such a radical distinction between church and state is no longer made, Hirsch's educational model remains the inspiration for Jewish day schools in cities across America.

By the midfifties, when I was born, Modern Orthodoxy was booming. My five siblings and I went to Ramaz, a Jewish day school on the Upper East Side, where we learned to read and write Hebrew. We were also trained in the advanced decoding skills—a pointillist method of inquiry—that were needed to comprehend the voluminous interpretative texts that had swelled, century by century, around the Old Testament: expansive commentaries, colorful Talmudic parables, and competing Midrashic riffs. Why, for instance, when the Torah ascribes righteousness to Noah, does the narrative qualify the description by specifying that he was a righteous man *for his generation?* Everything, it appeared, had a meaning if one only understood how to tease it out.

At home, we recited the Sh'ma before going to sleep and said the blessings over everything from breakfast cereal to our evening snack of Educator's Smokey Bear cookies (the kosher version of Oreos). But although my brothers wore the ritual fringes known as *tzitzis* beneath their shirts seven days a week and went to synagogue on Friday night as well as on Saturday, homogeneity and camouflage were the prevailing themes of the Zeitgeist. Ethnic pride, coming in on the wave of the late sixties, had not yet asserted itself. (The manifestations of specifically Jewish pride— like the wearing of *kippot s'rugot,* crocheted yarmulkes—followed the euphoric Israeli victory in the Six-Day War.) My brothers wouldn't have been caught dead wearing a yarmulke on the crosstown bus or to a Mets game at Shea Stadium. Even so, my family's uneasy concessions to the wider American world led to inevitable tensions. After my older brother graduated from high school, he was deemed insufficiently pious—mostly on the basis of my mother's claim that she had overheard him listening to the radio in his room late one Friday night—and was shipped off to Israel for a corrective program of yeshiva study.

A great deal of the complicated story of modern American Jewry, wherein the lure of assimilation vies with an ingrained tradition of separatism, is recounted by Samuel Freedman in his ambitious new book, *Jew vs. Jew: The Struggle for the Soul of American Jewry* (blurbed, serendipitously, by Senator Lieberman). Freedman, a professor of journalism at Columbia, appears undaunted by the welter of irreconcilable impulses and conflicting reports that awaits anyone who hopes to clarify the recent history of this disputatious bunch. In the author's view, the "ancient bond" that united Jews of every stripe through six thousand years of precarious existence in a hostile world has ceased to do so in a more tolerant one; as the American Jewish community has become increasingly affluent, educated, and successful, its internal divisions have become increasingly rancorous. (Indeed, just contemplating the number of people Freedman must have interviewed—one voluble and tendentious Jew after another, arguing the world—is enough to make a sympathetic reader shudder.)

Freedman has organized his book into six thematically linked sections, centered on specific Jewish neighborhoods across the United States where the "crisis of legitimacy" has been escalating over the past four decades. He touches down first in the Catskills of the postwar era, where he evokes the last gasp of a Jewish identity forged in purely ethnic terms: the working-class Farband movement. He captures the essence of the movement's kibbutznik style, with its twin allegiances to Palestine and to socialism, in a quickly sketched portrait of the Labor Zionist summer camp Kinderwelt. The camp, founded in 1925, flourished for almost half a century, on a combination of Yiddishist sentiment and Israeli folk dancing (with a few classic Americanisms such as Color Wars and panty raids thrown into the mix), before it was razed to make way for a housing development. But, when a small group of Kinderwelt loyalists get together for a reunion in a Manhattan apartment in 1998, Freedman finds that, with one exception (a woman whose son became Orthodox and moved to a settlement on the West Bank), they have only the vaguest notion of Jewishness, and it is predicated mainly on trips to Israel and a lingering collective spirit.

With these scenes, Freedman establishes a context for the often repeated thesis of his book. Ethnic Judaism ("*Seinfeld* and a schmear") has decisively failed, as evidenced by the whopping statistics on intermarriage; at the same time, the Orthodox experience—dismissed in 1955 by one eminent sociologist as "a case study of institutional decay"—is enjoying a wholly unanticipated revival. This shift toward the fundamentalist, God-fearing sort of Judaism is reflected both in the actual demographics (the high birth rate among the Orthodox and ultra-Orthodox, especially compared with the stagnant rate among nonobservant Jews) and in the reconfiguration of American Jewish identity.

Freedman's milling throng of interviewees includes doom-pronouncing traditionalists; entrenched assimilationists; Conservative and progressive Orthodox leaders committed to the notion of a Jewish life "with wiggle room"; an impassioned wacko or two; and a feminist activist who scandalized her ostensibly enlightened Conservative congregation by including the neglected biblical matriarchs—Sarah, Rebecca, Rachel, and Leah—in her invocation of Jewish ancestors. All these disparate figures have felt the effects of the Jewish drift to the right.

Perhaps the most admirably principled—and, for me, guilt-inducing—character in Freedman's book is Daniel Greer, an Ivy League–educated white-shoe lawyer turned religious-school

dean. Greer's trajectory is an example of an intracommunity phenomenon known as "flipping"—converting from a more liberal
form of Orthodoxy to a more stringent one. Reared in a typical
Modern Orthodox Upper West Side home in the forties and
fifties, Greer was the first graduate of the Manhattan Talmudic
Academy to enter Princeton. He went on to Yale Law School
(where he bunked with Jerry Brown), held several high-ranking
positions under Mayor Lindsay, ran for local Democratic office,
and campaigned for McGovern—all the while wearing a hat
rather than a yarmulke in public. But although his career might
appear to be a shining testament to the modern Orthodox ideal of
synthesis, Greer became increasingly uncomfortable with the
compromises it required. He stopped practicing law, grew his
beard, began wearing *tzitzis* outside his clothing, and devoted
himself full-time to religious leadership and community service.
"So many American Jews were first-generation and so concerned
with fitting in," Greer says. "We want to restore a more demon-
strative, open, all-encompassing experience." In 1997, one of his
daughters became a litigant in the controversial Yale Five case, in
which a small group of Orthodox students brought a lawsuit
against the university on the ground of religious discrimination.

At the other end of the spectrum is Harry Shapiro, one of the
lost souls who latch on to the ultra-Orthodox movement because
they have little else to anchor them. The son of a supermarket-
chain executive, Shapiro was a gifted mechanic but an academic
failure. While still in his teens, he bought a one-way ticket to Israel,
but, even after two attempts, he couldn't carve out a tenable existence there. Back in New York, he enrolled in a remedial program
at Yeshiva University, only to flunk out; he opened a butcher shop
in Florida called Kosher Kuts, but the business went under in less
than two years. The only bright spot in Harry's life was his commitment to a fanatically hawkish brand of Zionism, which

culminated in a radical but ineffectual gesture of protest. In 1997, he was arrested for placing a homemade bomb in the Jacksonville Jewish Center, on the eve of an appearance by the former Israeli prime minister and renowned peacemaker Shimon Peres. Shapiro's bizarre religious journey landed him in federal prison with a ten-year sentence.

Jew vs. Jew is an assiduously researched, up-to-the-minute report, and if it finally fails to cohere in the reader's mind that may be because it is too faithful a reflection of the dilemma it describes. The author is so intent on gluing together the splintered pieces of a once-intact community, so determined to transcribe its babble of voices and views, that his book is at times overrun by its own informational anxiety. After I finished it, I felt relieved to be back on my familiar lonely turf—spiritually bereft, perhaps, but safely beyond the din of battle.

Is it ever too late to reclaim your roots? It seems that everyone with even a smidgen of Jewishness in his or her background is doing just that these days, writing a memoir of salvaged ancestral kinship, with the word *Exile* or *Chosen* or *Journey* somewhere in the title. Among such bittersweet reckonings are Mary Gordon's *The Shadow Man,* in which the writer learns that her beloved father was a virulently anti-Semitic Jew; Stephen Dubner's *Turbulent Souls,* wherein the author, having been reared as one of a large Catholic brood by parents who left the synagogue for the Church, reinvents himself as a committed Jew; and Susan Jacoby's *Half-Jew,* in which a secret family history of religious denial is gradually uncovered.

I have been more moved, however, by memoirs that explore a different transformation, in which the narrator questions the presumptions underlying the enterprise of Jewish assimilation. These include Joshua Hammer's *Chosen by God* and David Klinghoffer's

The Lord Will Gather Me In. Both books offer fascinating glimpses into the growing *ba'al tshuva* movement, in which young men and women from devoutly secularist backgrounds decide to become practicing Jews. In *Chosen by God,* which is narrated with bewildered and occasionally self-incriminating candor, Hammer attempts to come to terms with this phenomenon as it is exemplified by his younger brother, Tony. The siblings grew up in a cosmopolitan, nonreligious Manhattan household, but Tony eventually rejected their background and was reborn as Tuvia, an ultra-Orthodox Jew. Hammer, a *Newsweek* correspondent, is scrupulously fair, conveying both his initial sense of horror at his brother's religious makeover—in which Tony, "the most resolute atheist I had known," comes to resemble "a Hasidic Willy Loman"—and his qualified, begrudging comprehension of his brother's motives in seeking out an insulated life of study and prayer.

Klinghoffer's memoir, on the other hand, charts his growing disenchantment with the flabby values and ostentatious lifestyle of the southern California–style Reform Judaism in which he was reared by his adoptive parents. Klinghoffer was five years old when he was told that neither of his birth parents was Jewish; while still in high school, he decided—in an act worthy of inclusion in *Ripley's Believe It or Not*—to perform a ritual conversion on himself. He soaped up a razor blade and gingerly cut at his penis until "a very small bead of red" convinced him that his circumcision was a success and then immersed himself in a bathtub, allowing the water to cover his face. (He later underwent a real circumcision at the hands of a *mohel.*) The author is a junior-division neoconservative (he is a contributing editor at *National Review*), and his book is marked by a trenchant wit and an astringent refusal to buy into the liberal nostrums on which he was brought up. Although he announces that he is "the only person I know of who came to Orthodox Judaism via Friedrich Nietzsche," his argument is essentially a fideist one—that the apprehension of a divine presence at work in the world can be explained only on the basis of faith.

I do think that Klinghoffer's newfound zeal leads him to romanticize certain aspects of his chosen creed; for example, he holds up Orthodox bar mitzvah celebrations as exemplary occasions of piety and modesty. His own Jewish coming of age, by contrast, is derided as part of an emotionally bankrupt "circuit" involving a "mass expenditure of cash and credit"; a hammy and insipid speech (often written by the bar mitzvah boy's mother or father); and a knock-'em-dead theme party, pandering to the pop cultural obsession of the moment. Having attended mostly Orthodox bar mitzvahs growing up, I can attest that I never had the good fortune to witness the sort he describes, where, after a solemn ceremony, the celebrants "adjourn to the synagogue social hall for pickled herring and shots of whiskey." This astonishingly humble repast sounds to me like a story out of I. L. Peretz or Sholom Aleichem, but then isn't it the disillusioned who are most in need of someone or something to idealize?

While reading Hammer and Klinghoffer's memoirs, I tried to envision myself as a kind of double-jointed female returnee, a *ba'alat tshuva* whose odyssey is a curvy variation on the usual linear pattern—a journey from A to B and then back again to A. It's precisely the doubling back on myself that I have trouble with, however, the undoing of accommodations that, for better or worse, I have made. I try to imagine myself bidding good-bye to worldly friends and wanton pleasures, voluntarily tethering myself to outmoded rituals and circumscribed possibilities. But it feels, even at this hypothetical distance, too much like playacting, as though I were an understudy in *Fiddler on the Roof,* tying a kerchief under my chin and taking care of the younger children while waiting for the matchmaker to make me the perfect match.

I suppose some part of me has always thought of my twenty-odd years of religious uncertainty as a passing phase, something I had to wade through in order to get to the other side—which would prove to be, like the most elegant of Zen constructs, my beginning in another guise. But how long can a phase last before it calcifies into a permanent condition?

I've been at play in the fields of heresy ever since the end of my third year in high school, when I walked into Zum Zum, part of a German chain famous for its nitrate-heavy delicacies. It was a fine June day, shortly before I was to go off to work as a junior counselor at Morasha, a strictly Orthodox summer camp, where the boys and girls weren't permitted to swim together. I had always liked everything about Zum Zum, from its faux-pewter plates to its hearty Heidi-influenced aesthetic, complete with waitresses dressed in dirndl skirts and aprons. Now I sat down at the counter with its little clay pots of mustard, "Das Hot" and "Das Sweet," and ordered myself a hot dog—an unkosher hot dog—on a caraway seed bun, accompanied by nicely seasoned potato salad, pepper-flecked sauerkraut, and a tart pickle. It was a revolutionary moment, and by rights I should have been jumping out of my skin. But I wasn't; my hands were steady and my heart was beating at its usual pace. I took my time, savoring every bite.

After this momentous transgression, I quickly reverted to a Morasha girl-camper persona. We *davened* the *shachris* service first thing every morning, clumped together on hard benches in the camp's makeshift shul, having been yanked awake by the Hebrew imprecation to *"Kumu, kumu"* (arise, arise) coming over the loudspeaker, followed by blaring Israeli dance music. Given that we were all normal sex-driven teen-agers, as well as good Jews in the making, the hot topic of *negiyah*—the prohibition on physical contact between unmarried men and women—dominated the late-night conversations. That summer, I myself indulged in my first, highly publicized French kiss, which led to a private talk with my agitated counselor about the ethics of desire.

I felt least ambivalent about my religion when I listened to the merry band of counselors turned musicians who regaled us daily and who were, indeed, one of the camp's main attractions. The band, made up of Yeshiva University college students with names like Label, Eli, and Yitzi, performed what I thought of as inspired music, consisting of melancholy but punchy tunes based on a few minor chords and lyrics from the Hebrew liturgy. To the extent that I believed in something called a soul—I waffled on this, just as I waffled on the idea of God—I felt my soul being wrenched as I listened. I floated upward—away from my resistance to a system that seemed more concerned with tiresome strictures and sexist rabbinical rulings than with virtues like kindness and empathy—and found myself on a cloud of benign camaraderie. This, then, was the real thing, the gratification that awaited you if you bought into the whole kit and caboodle, from keeping kosher to sitting shivah. These were my people, after all, and for a brief while I wanted to be one of them.

Such havens in the wilderness of my disaffection became increasingly rare, as I veered between an escalating strategy of religious defiance and passing myself off as an uncorrupted product of an Orthodox upbringing. My real break came while I was at Barnard; since it was my parents' conviction that an out-of-town college would end their control over my religious life, I effected my rebellion while remaining close to home, practically under their very noses. I moved on from Zum Zum hot dogs to Szechuan dumplings and Indian curries, swooning over the sheer abandon of being able to order anything on a menu that caught my fancy. In the middle of all this, I opted to live in one of Barnard's kosher suites, with four other girls. My suitemates hailed from Queens or Brooklyn, homey boroughs that I chauvinistically supposed to present less of a temptation to stray than Manhattan. Instead of taking part in the bacchanalias of sex and drugs that the rest of the campus was presumably enjoying, they made Friday night dinners to which they invited Orthodox Columbia boys. If I didn't go home for Shabbos, I joined them.

I felt like an impostor, but I would have felt like an impostor among the non-Orthodox. My frame of reference, beginning with something as basic as the calendar, was marked not by Thanksgiving turkeys or Christmas trees but by the mostly solemn round of Jewish holidays, characterized by endless services, heavy meals, and long quiescent afternoons. Rosh Hashanah was followed by Yom Kippur, which was followed by Succos, Chanukah, and then by Purim, Pesach, and Shavuos (which no one had heard of outside the tight circle of the initiated). Truth be told, the flight into freedom seemed as threatening as it was alluring. I feared being overcome by vertigo—falling off the end of the earth, with no one to catch me. What if it turned out that my early training had left me fundamentally unequipped for a world of wide open spaces? What if I was so imprinted by dogma that I needed the very narrowness against which I strained?

It went on like this for years, daring violation followed by guilty compliance. In retrospect, I wonder that my flimsy on-again, off-again self didn't simply rip in two, like a piece of paper. It wasn't that I believed in an angry God, looking down at me with a face like Abraham Lincoln's and plotting his revenge. It wasn't that I feared parental rejection, either, although I'm not sure my father ever knew the extent of my sacrilege. (He surely didn't know that I had begun to make it a habit to eat on Yom Kippur and once, in an especially angry period, felt an urgent need for a manicure.) What haunted me was an insistent and morbid sense that I was an outcast—albeit by choice, which only made it worse. I had willed myself into a cold and dark hallway, inches away from a closed door. I could see the light spilling out from underneath it, and if I could just bring myself to open the door and step inside I would come upon some semblance of earthly grace, an imposed order that would feel natural if only I surrendered myself to it.

I've been nonpracticing for more years than I've been Ortho-dox, but, come Friday evening, wherever I am and whatever I'm doing, I'm always aware that Shabbos is starting. This awareness goes beyond simple nostalgia, yet I have been unable to find an adult definition of Jewishness that I can reconcile with the rigor-ous standards of my childhood. I have gone once or twice to ser-vices at a Reform temple that is affiliated with my daughter's school, and I can't get used to any of it: the mixed seating, the music, the recitation of prayers in English, even the word *temple* instead of *shul*.

Recently, I have begun thinking about making the kitchen in my next apartment kosher. My daughter, who is ten, has wanted us to become more religious for a while now; this summer, she asked me to arrange extra Hebrew lessons for her. I'm sure that some of her interest has been spurred by her desire to *daven* and *bench* along with her first cousins (all nineteen of them), who are being brought up in observant households. But I also think some of it has to do with her own proclivities, just as my discomfort with Orthodoxy had to do with mine. Although part of me balks at the idea of having a child who hankers after a tradition I have spent half a lifetime throwing away, another part feels something resembling pride. When I mentioned these developments to an older friend of mine, an avowedly atheistic Jew from a Camp Kinderwelt sort of background, she reacted with undisguised hor-ror, as though I had declared my intention to join a deranged militant sect in Nebraska. "You're not serious," she said. I shrugged the subject off, slightly embarrassed.

I still have time to scrap my plan to keep kosher—to review the situation in all its unappealing aspects—but I'm not waiting for one of those transcendent, "Aha!" moments to strike, bringing with it a vision of the eternal. I'm not that kind of person, nor is my religion that kind of religion. Judaism is nothing if not down-to-earth in its approach and sets more store by behavior than by belief. It's either a weakness in me or a strength—I haven't decided—that I still haven't figured out where I stand on so consequential a matter as the quality of my Jewish life. But if I should happen to die before I've made up my mind, I'm counting on my family to give me an Orthodox burial.

Neither Here nor There

from *Parabola*

There are places in this world that are neither here nor there, neither up nor down, neither real nor imaginary. These are the in-between places, difficult to find and even more challenging to sustain. Yet they are the most fruitful places of all. For in these liminal narrows a kind of life takes place that is out of the ordinary, creative, and once in a while genuinely magical. We tend to divide life between mind and matter and to assume that we must be in one or the other or both. But religion and folklore tell of another place that is often found by accident, where strange events take place, and where we learn things that can't be discovered in any other way.

Sometimes the transitional places are physical and fairly obvious. An elevator, for instance, is a peculiar place where speech can be difficult and social posture odd. An escalator offers several moments of interstitial existence, when you can see everything but can do nothing. As a writer, I search for the liminal places where ideas, words, and images are stored and ready for use. For many, the shower seems to be such a place, but it doesn't work for me. There I am all sensation and no reverie. Playing the piano places me on a threshold where thoughts multiply and come to life. But a dull lecture is best of all, even one that I am giving.

Emotion is a good vehicle to the places in between. People tell stories of discovering unknown strength when they are trying to save a child. I have stepped beyond the ordinary in times of depression, when I was so withdrawn that an unfamiliar sense of self suddenly arose as from the shadows. Christmas and Halloween, when they really work, can cast a spell that makes ordinary awareness recede into the background on behalf of momentary magic. I believe that the fantasy exuberance in these two festivals, apart from their religious meanings, keeps our overly rational society sane.

A mode of entrance is crucial. A door. A window. We need a chink in the otherwise unbroken surface of what we consider real and proper. Recently a woman wrote to tell me her dream. She was in a garden, holding a child's hand and moving toward a break in a hedge, when a butterfly landed on her nose and covered over her face. There is step one: we need something serendipitous to veil our usual identity. The Greeks thought that the soul was a butterfly—a perfect covering.

The break in the hedge opened to a central area where the sun shone brilliantly. The gap need not be physical, but it is required. In the dark wood at the beginning of his comic journey, Dante says, "I don't know how to describe my entering there, I was so sleepy at that point that I lost track of the actual path." Before I go to sleep, ideas come out, and I wonder sometimes if the drug problems in our society are nothing more than a quest for Dante's somnambulance.

Religion is in the business of finding and constructing methods of getting sleepy, feeling lost, arriving and departing: pilgrimage, procession, fasting, incense, chanting, illuminated books. Psychoanalysis similarly makes use of transference, which means "to carry across," a word easily linked to a bridge, which Sandor Ferenczi interpreted as the movement from what is to what will be. In ordinary life we need methods tailored to our temperaments that effectively take us off the treadmill and the beaten path.

On the same day I got the hedge dream letter, I heard from a man who was deciding whether to quit his law practice and become an art historian. He was on an elevator of sorts and didn't feel comfortable being between places. But there lies yet another aspect of thresholds—insecurity seems to be the emotion proper to the place. I wrote back saying that I felt both envy and relief not to be in his place.

I think that the curse of liminality asks for treatment in kind. We need to enter more fully and more willingly into that realm under the rocks and behind the mirror. We are too sincere, too productive, and too realistic. In his aptly named little book *A Celtic Twilight*, W. B. Yeats tells many disorienting stories about figures who are neither faeries nor human, or who are both, and who would make good role models for us all:

> By the Hospital Lane goes the "Faeries" Path. Every evening they travel from the hill to the sea, from the sea to the hill. At the sea end of their path stands a cottage. One night Mrs. Arbunathy, who lived there, left her door open, as she was expecting her son. Her husband was asleep by the fire; a tall man came in and sat beside him. After he had been sitting there for a while, the woman said, "In the name of God, who are you?" He got up and went out, saying, "Never leave the door open at this hour, or evil may come to you." She woke her husband and told him. "One of the Good People has been with us," said he.

During hours of psychotherapy, I have heard several dreams of doors left ajar and windows cracked open. The dreamer was deathly afraid of who or what might come in because of this negligence, and of course as therapist I suspected that whoever it was, it was probably someone useful and necessary. Often we attain thresholds best through inadvertence. If we want their benefits, we might not always aim for consciousness and awareness but rather a gap in our attention. In my view, the emphasis in some spiritual communities on continuing consciousness defeats the purpose.

I have a fascination for doors, doorways, and vestibules. In another life I'd like to be a maker of extraordinary doors. They are actual thresholds and at the same time images for the deep transitional passages. Standing in a doorway, you are forced into the imagination, wondering what you will find on the other side. It is a place full of expectant fantasy. Gaston Bachelard said, "If one were to give an account of all the doors one has closed and opened, of all the doors one would like to reopen, one would have to tell the story of one's entire life." William Blake made an etching of death's door, showing an old man about to walk under the lintel, with the subscript: "The Door of Death is made of Gold, that Immortal eyes cannot behold."

The foyer of a building is another place of special liminal appeal and magic. It brings you in from the heat or cold and prepares you for a human climate and interaction. In a theater it is also a place of conviviality during the intermission—liminal itself—of a play or performance of music, where you can once again talk and eat and move your body around. It is delicious, restorative time-out.

Some reckless etymologizing discovers that *foyer* is the same word as *focus,* which means hearth or fireplace and is closely connected to the goddess Hestia, who is emotional warmth deified. Interestingly, Kepler used the word *focus* for the center spot of a magnifying glass, probably because it is the place where you can burn a leaf or a bug, as I confess I used to do when I was a boy. The foyer is therefore the hot spot, the alchemical athanor where things happen, the oven or grill of transformation.

This is the key point about thresholds: they are not the place of life and not the place of death. In their narrow confines you may find fantasy, memory, dream, anxiety, miracle, intuition, and magic. These are the means by which the deep soul prospers— neither in life nor entirely out of life. This is a good place from which to make a decision and get a hunch. It is the true home of creativity. It is also the claustrophobic place of greatest fear. Anything of moment takes place in these interstices—in the tunnels and passages and waiting periods. They are indispensable and yet must be kept tangential.

It takes considerable courage to stay as long as needed in a place between, and it requires a degree of holy foolishness to seek one out. We may need a threshold experience just to find the needed threshold. My personal favorites are a piano, a Gothic cathedral, a megalith, dessert, a forest path, an Irish pub, a dark bedroom, Guillaume Dufay, a candlelit bathtub, Lord Peter Wimsey, aftershave, the moors, and honeysuckle. Each of these stands to the side of life's central concerns, and yet each makes life worth living.

HOWARD MUMMA

Conversations with Camus

from *Christian Century*

During several summers in the 1950s, Howard Mumma, a Methodist pastor, served as guest minister at the American Church in Paris. After Sunday service one day, he noticed a man in a dark suit surrounded by admirers. Albert Camus had been coming to church, first to hear Marcel Dupré playing the organ, and later to hear Mumma's sermons.

Mumma became friends with the existentialist Camus, who by then was famous for his novels The Plague *and* The Stranger *and for essays such as* The Myth of Sisyphus. *The two men met to discuss questions of religious belief that Camus raised. Mumma, now ninety-two, kept the conversations confidential for over forty years before deciding to share them.*

Soon after the following conversation on baptism, Mumma returned to the U.S. In 1960 Camus was killed in a car accident.

One day toward the end of my summer in Paris, the concierge's wife prepared supper for Camus and me. We had planned to take a ride that afternoon, but after we finished our meal, we could not bring ourselves to leave. We chose instead to sit and enjoy the view of the river. We were both relaxed and enjoying the weather when Camus broke the silence: "Howard, do you perform baptisms?"

For a moment I thought I was going to fall off my chair. "Yes, Albert, I do," I answered with some tension and surprise.

"What is the significance of this rite?"

I had become accustomed to his questions, and by now we had developed a kind of routine. Still, there was something different about this question. He seemed more than merely curious, rather contemplative, as if this question was more personal to him.

"Baptism is not necessarily a supernatural experience," I began. "The important thing is not the heavens opening up or the dove or the voice. Those are the externals, oriental imagery. Baptism is a symbolic commitment to God, and there is a long-standing tradition and history involved."

"Yes, I remember some of it from my readings."

"First of all, let me say a word about why the average adult seeks baptism. I think, Albert, that you are a good example. You have said to me again and again that you are dissatisfied with the whole philosophy of existentialism and that you are privately seeking something that you do not have."

"Yes, you are exactly right, Howard. The reason I have been coming to church is because I am seeking. I'm almost on a pilgrimage—seeking something to fill the void that I am experiencing—and no one else knows. Certainly the public and the readers of my novels, while they see that void, are not finding the answers in what they are reading. But deep down you are right—I am searching for something that the world is not giving me."

"Albert, I congratulate you for this. I encourage you to keep searching for a meaning and something that will fill the void and transform your life. Then you will arrive in living waters where you will find meaning and purpose."

"Well, Howard, you have to agree that in a sense we are all products of a mundane world, a world without spirit. The world in which we live and the lives which we live are decidedly empty."

"It does often seem that way," I conceded.

"Since I have been coming to church, I have been thinking a great deal about the idea of a transcendent, something that is other than this world. It is something that you do not hear much about today, but I am finding it. I am hearing about it here, in Paris, within the walls of the American Church.

"After all, one of the basic teachings that I learned from Sartre is that man is alone. We are solitary centers of the universe. Perhaps we ourselves are the only ones who have ever asked the great questions of life. Perhaps, since Nazism, we are also the ones who have loved and lost and who are, therefore, fearful of life. That is what led us to sense that there is something—I don't know if it is personal or if it is a great idea or powerful influence—but there is something that can bring meaning to my life. I certainly don't have it, but it is there. On Sunday mornings, I hear that the answer is God.

"You have made it very clear to me, Howard, that we are not the only ones in this world. There is something that is invisible. We may not hear the voice, but there is some way in which we can become aware that we are not the only ones in the world and that there is help for all of us."

Camus leaned forward until his elbows rested on his knees and said, "In the Bible, I have read about people who were not at all self-confident. Men who did not feel as if they had the world by its tail or that they had all the answers. Fact is, one of the things that I have noted in the Bible is that many of its chief characters were confused—just like the rest of us. We are on a pilgrimage. We are all seeking something, whether it is confidence or knowledge or something else entirely. I've read the Old Testament at least three times and I have made many notes on it. In its pages I have found some people who were absolutely confused about life and what they should do and what God wanted them to do.

"There is Jonah, a guy who stood up and refused God. He didn't want to go to Ninevah! He didn't understand what it was all about. He felt that there was no chance for the Ninevites to be redeemed and that God was mistaken. Then there was Moses. God wanted him to go to Egypt to free his people but Moses complained that he stuttered. He couldn't speak well and therefore no one would believe him. And then there was Isaiah. I have read Isaiah a number of times. When God wanted him—in the sixth chapter, I think—to go and work for him, Isaiah said, 'You have the wrong man! I am not worthy, I'm a man of unclean lips!' So even these great men were confused."

Then Camus said, "And I don't understand it to this day—this man Nicodemus!" I was very pleased when he brought up Nicodemus. I got out the Bible and turned to the third chapter of the Gospel of John and we reread it. We discussed it. He said to me, "Now here is a wise man of Israel! He is seeking something that he does not have. I feel right at home with Nicodemus, because I too am uncertain about this whole matter of Christianity. I don't understand what Jesus said to Nicodemus, 'You must be born again.'"

I said, "Albert, let's think about this expression 'to be born again,' because we are moving back to the significance of baptism. What was Jesus' reply?"

Immediately Camus said, "Well, you know what it was! He simply said that you must be born again! I know the exact words: 'Except a man be born of water and of the Spirit, he cannot enter the Kingdom of God,' whatever that is. And he said, 'That which is born of the flesh is flesh and that which is born of the Spirit is spirit.' I simply marvel at it—that you must be born again."

"To me," I said, "to be born again is to enter anew or afresh into the process of spiritual growth. It is to wipe the slate clean. It is to receive forgiveness. It is to receive forgiveness because you have asked God to forgive you of all past sins, so that the guilt, the concerns, the worries, and the mistakes that we have made in the past are forgiven and the slate is truly wiped clean.

"I don't know what the French term would be for a bond or an encumbrance, but the person who accepts forgiveness now believes that there is no mortgage, no encumbrance on him. The slate is clear, your conscience is clear. You are ready to move ahead and commit yourself to a new life, a new spiritual pilgrimage. You are seeking the presence of God himself." I was nervous and intense.

Albert looked me with tears in his eyes and said, "Howard, I am ready. I want this. This is what I want to commit my life to."

Of course, I rejoiced and thanked God privately that he had come to this. I had a difficult time maintaining my composure. The man had been questioning me now for several years about Christianity and had attended services. He had heard my sermons on many occasions and had studied the Bible. Perhaps I should not have been shocked, but it did give me a sense of wonder and amazement that he would be considering taking this kind of step toward Christianity. Yet for some reason, I was unable to commit myself fully to the idea. "But Albert," I said, "haven't you already been baptized?"

"Yes," said Camus, "when I was a child but it meant nothing to me. It was something done to me, no more meaningful than a handshake."

"Well, the baptism of a child is not performed because the child has faith in God or in Christ, which a baby clearly does not have. It is given because God loves the child and welcomes him into the family of God. The baptism begins a process in which you begin to grow, even as an infant, into a new life, the gift which has been given to you."

"But it seems right that I should be baptized now that I have spent these months reading and discussing the Bible with you—"

I had to interrupt, though I could not express my full thoughts. Christian doctrine holds that one baptism suffices; there is no reason for rebaptism. Only if there is some doubt that person has been given a valid baptism do we rebaptize, and we call it a "conditional baptism." So on one hand, I wanted to deny his request for baptism on the grounds that it wasn't necessary. On the other hand, I sensed that Albert needed the experience. My compromise was to bring up the matter of joining a church and experiencing the rule of confirmation. That proved to be a mistake.

Right away, he jumped on me and said, "Howard, I am not ready to be a member of a church! I have difficulty in attending church! I have to fight people all the time after a service, even at your church. When I come to your church, when you are preaching, I leave before the service is over to get away from them all."

I understood that, but I had to stand my ground. "The time will come when you can get away from people who are seeking your autograph or wanting to hold conversations with you about your writings. Perhaps they will simply accept you into the community of men and women. This community will remind you constantly that you are not alone and that you are a member of a communion, a company of both the living and the dead, all of whom are in the presence of a living God. In any event, are you aware of everything that baptism entails?" I asked, trying to give a little.

Camus shrugged. "My experience is limited to my early church training and the little bit that you have told me," he said, recalling that baptism is a religious rite performed by a priest or minister on a baby. "He puts water on the head of the child and blesses it. . . . It is a religious miracle of sorts, so that if the child should die, it would not go to hell." He said that beyond that, he knew very little.

"Yes," I said. The baptism is an outward and visible sign that an infant has been initiated into the fellowship of Christ's church.

The child not only becomes a participant, but also becomes an heir to eternal life. That is to say, physical death will not end the gift that is given through baptism.

I went into more detail. "In the case of an adult, he may approach alone. The person then stands before the priest or minister as he addresses not only him but the entire congregation."

I noticed a frown appear on Camus's face, but I continued. "The minister says that baptism is an outward and visible sign of a gift, the gift of the Spirit of God brought into the body and mind of the person being baptized."

I noticed Camus cringing again. He must have seen the questioning look on my face because he explained: "For me, baptism and confirmation would be a more personal thing, something between me and God."

"But baptism and confirmation are both a private and a public commitment to a life with Christ. They are a welcoming into the family of God, which is the church here on earth, both visible and invisible. At the end of the baptism, the minister confirms you as a full and responsible member not only of the family of God, which is personal, but also of the church, which is a community."

Camus shook his head, leaning back in his chair, obviously disappointed. "I cannot belong to any church," he said. "Is this not something that you could do? Something just between us?"

I cannot say that I blamed him for his hesitation. Camus was one of the most famous Frenchmen alive. His writings touched the disaffection the people of France were feeling after the war. Display of this sort would have all of France abuzz, and many of his fans would feel betrayed. But his trepidation was more than that.

By his very nature, Camus was a man who could never belong to an organized church. He was truly an independent thinker, and no matter how modified his feelings toward Christianity had become, he could never be an active member of any church.

"Perhaps you are not quite ready," I said. As pleased as I was, I could not fully commit myself to the idea. I would be leaving in a few more days, and he would have time to contemplate what he really wanted. This was a major decision for both of us, and I wanted to be sure that there were no doubts about his next step. With a few more months, we could both be certain that this was the right decision. I laid my hand on his and said, "Let's wait while you continue your studies."

SHELDON M. NOVICK

The Temptation of the Sublime

from *DoubleTake*

The novelist Cynthia Ozick and I were invited a few months ago to talk about Henry James—elevated gossip—on a radio program that fell flat, but there was a moment in it that had a certain drama for me. When I said that Henry James wrote novels with a message, and that the message was his often-quoted "Live! Live all you can!," Ozick silenced me by asking, "What do you mean by 'live'?"

Her question was meant, I think, to draw me out on James's sexual activities, which were being most oddly debated in the newspapers at the time, but I didn't take her point, and thought she was asking me to explain what a full life might be. I had no ready answer for her then, and don't know that I can answer briefly now. But it may help to examine a time in which James was living intensely, and see what light is there.

It is black, damp January in the south of England, in the year 1909. Henry James is sixty-five, living alone with his servants in a silent old brick house lit only by oil lamps and firelight. His work has not been going well; there are pains in his chest, warning of heart trouble. He has no friend near at hand. Anxious despair and the inertia of depression descend upon him without in the least diminishing the intensity of his pain. He all but ceases to eat, for food has become tangibly distasteful to him—he says that he suffers from "food-loathing." Twenty-five years earlier, as he well remembers, his father starved himself to death in a similar depression; now his own body seems to call for death. The village doctor, the good Skinner, tries to cheer him; he bundles James up and brings him along as he goes on his rounds. But the relief is momentary, and James retires to bed.

The young Theodora Bosanquet, James's newly hired stenographer, writes now to his family in the United States to tell them most tactfully that James is ill. Soon Harry, his nephew and godson, is on his way from Cambridge, Massachusetts, and James scribbles a grateful note to his brother William and his wife, thanking them for paying Harry's way:

Dearest Ones.

It is an unspeakable relief & blessing to have Harry with me, & I cling to him with almost frenetic intensity. But I am sorry to say I haven't been able to do justice to his advent by any continuous or valid improvement. My flares & flickers up are followed so damnably by relapses, & the drops seem so deep & disheartening that I am afraid I am rather demoralized & abject. Here is a wail for you—the voice of my present dejection—& of my infinite yearning. My sense of the matter is that I *can* get better & that I am worth saving for such magnificent work as I want still to do,—& oh so *can!*—& was never more full of the ardent dream of. But somehow I want more help than I can now—after these so many dismal weeks—pretty well ten—give myself in solitude. I shall repay you a thousand fold! oh I cling to Harry! Make it possible for him to stay on a while—& write some further tender healing, sustaining, reassuring word to your poor demoralized & baffled old Brother

Henry James

In April, William and his wife, Alice, arrive to provide cheering company, and Henry does revive somewhat. But in July comes news of the sudden death of their younger brother, Robertson, of heart disease, and the death knell tolls for William as well: his own heart trouble gravely worsens. Henry rouses himself to guide William home to an agonizing and protracted death.

Henry was then the last survivor of his family of origin. Over the course of twenty-five years he had returned to America for his parents' final illnesses; he had been at his sister's bedside during her long illness and death; now he had seen his older brother die. He described the scene to his friend Edith Wharton:

[William] grew rapidly worse from the start & suffered piteously & dreadfully (with the increase of his difficulty in breathing); he suffered so & only wanted, wanted more & more, to go. The sight of the rapidity of it at the last was an unutterable pang—my sense of what he had to give, of his beautiful genius & noble intellect at their very climax. I am inexpressibly glad to have been, & even to be, here now—I cling to my sister-in-law & my nephews & niece: they are all (wonderful to say) such admirable, loveable, able & interesting persons, & they cling to me in return.

Looking into this extended moment of time we can begin to see the intimate place that illness and death have in the lives of the old: they become the physical center and expression of family and friendship, the intense realization of shared hopes and fears. To live in the years when James was most strenuously pronouncing his motto "Live!" meant to live in the presence of death. What did James make of his deep acquaintance with death, which shadowed his last years and his last works? This is a question one approaches gingerly and with hesitation.

Let me linger for a moment on the letters just quoted, in which James describes his own illness and his brother's death. There is an admirable quality that shines through them, of emotional presence; James was living through his travails without stinting, as he always advised his friends to do, and plainly this is part of what he meant by "Live!" James was continually immersed in the particularity of the moment, a quality that gave his personality the force we call charisma.

We see also in these letters a suppressed sense of ecstatic contrasts: Henry's depression contrasts with the magnificence of the work he would otherwise be doing; William's death extinguished his genius at its climax. There is the tone of artistic composition, of contrasted light and dark. And, farther submerged, we sense Henry's devotion to duty, the belief that a life must, and can only, be justified by such contrasts—death summons us to be magnificent.

On his return to England, after his brother's death, Henry set aside plans for a new novel and undertook the pious duty of a surviving son: he began work on a memoir of his father and elder brother. This became a vast, sunlit account of their shared life in Albany and New York City, rendered in a new style freed from logic and linear sequence, a pure composition in light, like Monet's paintings. This recollection of his earliest memories was brought to life in his final friendship with his brother: the friendship of old men.

We all know Henry James as a novelist of refined sensibility, whose work sometimes seems to be spun out of gossamer, yet in this memoir he recalled, one might say, the facts of life: love, cash, death. Indeed, the material facts of his family's history fascinated him, and one sees the same absorption with material fact in his stories: he wrote of the narrow constraints on freedom imposed by poverty, by ignorance; of the irrationality of passion; of the beauty and injustices of history, all solidly persisting into the present; of history embodied in the stones of Rome and the fog of London.

Bear in mind, now, that facts, the central events of an embodied life—love, cash, death—come to one at particular times and places. Here, for instance, is Henry James receiving his first payment for a published work:

> I see before me, in the rich, the many-hued light of my room that overhung Ashburton Place, from our third floor, the very Greenbacks, to the total value of twelve dollars, into which I had changed the cheque representing my first earned wage. . . . Other guerdons, of the same queer, the same often rather greasy, complexion followed.

Here is cash as a physical object, payment in greasy bills. Such facts have moral qualities: the greasiness is not just physical; there is something a little dubious about this wartime paper money.

This attention to fact is not surprising, really, for James was an idealist by upbringing and conviction—an "idealist" in the metaphysical sense, that is. As he tells us in his memoir, he and William grew up in an essentially religious household, in a religious age. Aside from a brief period of lapse into what he called the "materialist fallacy," Henry (like William) believed in the objective reality of spirit and moral principle. For an idealist there is no mystery about the realm of spirit, which is the realm of simple truth. The puzzle is the intractability of historical fact, which must be accepted on faith. For Henry and William James, this was not an intellectual matter solely but a constantly recurring, sensuous wonder at the exuberant beauty of material life.

It was not so much the particular facts discovered by science but the intractability and seeming irrationality of fact itself that fascinated and disturbed the late, post-Darwinian Victorians. Here, for example, is one of Henry James's contemporaries, Alfred North Whitehead:

It is a great mistake to conceive this historical revolt [the scientific revolution] as an appeal to reason. On the contrary, it was through and through an anti-intellectualist movement. It was the return to the contemplation of brute fact.

The salvation of reality is its obstinate, irreducible, matter of fact entities.

The painter Titian, whose work James admired and to a degree emulated, often took for his subject the mysterious quality of embodied fact—the strange spirituality of gold, the power of naked flesh. In his great painting of the Pietà, intended for his own tomb, the foreground is dominated by a naked old man (a self-portrait) prostrate at the Virgin's feet and the luminous solidity of the Magdalene's outstretched hand.

This is the essentially religious sensibility in which both William and Henry James were raised, and so it is not surprising that it forms the common language in which they had their conversations and arguments. William was a scientist and Henry an artist, but both were in search of the deep meaning of the material world. William began as a physician, and his first important work is *The Principles of Psychology* (1890), the foundation work of empirical psychology in America; when he was completing this work he wrote to Henry that he had "to forge every sentence in the teeth of irreducible and stubborn facts." He introduced into the United States the experimental psychology, or "psychophysics," that he had encountered in German universities, and he was essentially a scientist of experiment and observation, from which he tried, late in life, to draw his philosophy. Here is a summation of his character from his friend and pupil George Santayana:

The William James who had been my master was . . . the puzzled but brilliant doctor, impatient of metaphysics, whom I had known in my undergraduate days . . . or it was the genial author of *The Principles of Psychology,* chapters of which he read from the manuscript and discussed with a small class of us in 1889. Even then what I learned from him was perhaps chiefly things which explicitly he never taught, but which I imbibed from the spirit and background of his teaching. . . . Chief of these, I should say, was a sense of the immediate: for the unadulterated, unexplained, instant fact of experience.

If Henry and William James lived in the same moral universe, spoke the same language, and, in their different ways, wrestled with the mysterious irrationality of fact, they were still very different personalities. Henry, I think, was interested in what is constant and universal in experience, while William always seemed drawn to its impermanence and flux. Henry believed and felt that duty, and the constraints imposed by historical fact, made it possible for life to be an art, to be sublime; these constraints created form and narrative structure. The contrast of moral light and dark made life not merely beautiful but magnificent.

"Live" for Henry was an active verb, and he was not modest in his ambitions. Life was or should be an art—the art of the performer, perforce. One *ought* to strive for the sublime; in a life constrained by facts, this meant an acceptance of the shadow as well as the light. A life was a composition, and Henry used the artists' word for the quality of composition: *tone.* At the conclusion of his satirical novel *The Sacred Fount* (1901), the protagonist—a man of theory and superficial existence, trapped in his ideas—is said fatally to lack tone.

This idea of life as a constructed whole, limited and framed by historical fact, underlay Henry's notions of art. He was a realist, and the subject he sought to portray was *character:* the highly particular manner in which lives were lived. Painters in his day had learned to use pure pigments to stimulate a perception as of light itself; so Henry James learned to use words to stimulate the nervous system of his readers in a way that evoked sensations and created memories in his readers that seemed to be their own. (I recall a first visit to Liverpool that James describes as if it were my own, admittedly distant, experience.) In his last, late style James used abstract nouns, intransitive verbs, and abstract adverbs a great deal, almost never merely naming a physical object; like the pure colors of the impressionists, his language produced in the viewer's eye a vivid, concrete sensory experience of sight, sound, and feeling, even of taste and odor.

One goes along without thinking of ultimate facts very much; then some intense experience penetrates the fog of drowsy thought and escapist imaginings in which we live our lives. Perhaps we have traveled to a new place, an unfamiliar climate. The air seems magically clear, colors more intense and somehow meaningful; we look with a child's eye, a beginner's innocence. Perhaps it is a face, inches away or pressed close; an embrace; all the odors and murmuring and light that were present then and only then. These are the moments that James evokes.

Such moments come with a special imprimatur of truth. They are fruitful of reflections: one thinks, afterward, and tries to give meaning and shape to the experience. Sometimes, unhappily, the experience itself is entirely submerged by our explanations and analyses. The moment is not altered; it is only the fog of thought that keeps one from seeing it clearly. James's characters are most successful in understanding their circumstances when they turn to experience itself, the moment that pierces like a needle. Isabel Archer sees her husband remain seated while Mme Merle stands beside his chair; there is something here that instantly penetrates her awareness but that must be patiently evoked and recovered.

James gives us such pearls of experience, in whose translucent depths we find whole landscapes. For James, it appears, the storyteller's art was to string these pearls into a narrative that embodied a comprehensible truth. There is simple factual truth (are the stories naturalistic, accurate as to facts?), but James said repeatedly that this sort of scientific accuracy, in which he thought the French naturalists excelled, was insufficient for realism. The story itself had to be true as well. Works of fiction may not be factually correct, but they are true—should be true—in the sense that fables are true, that Bible stories and Homeric myths are true: they embody timeless meanings. James's realism consisted of joining the timeless truths of myth to the solidly factual data of ordinary experience. As he once put it, the balloon of his fancy was tethered to the earth.

Late in his own life, William James arrived at a similar understanding. The pearls of momentary experience, he thought, could be strung in various ways; and each narrative, seen in retrospect, had its own meaning.

William approached the question of living from the opposite side as Henry. William was a champion of liberty, of the revolt against history and authority; a questioner, never willing merely to accept the constraints of material fact. "Existence was a perpetual re-birth," Santayana writes of William's philosophy, "a travelling light to which the past was lost and the future uncertain. The element of indetermination which James felt so strongly in this flood of existence was precisely the pulse of fresh unpredictable sensation, surrendering attention hither and thither to unexpected facts."

To William the fact of death, like any fact, was always to be questioned and doubted. He hoped for messages from beyond the grave, testifying to the survival of the spirit; when his sister, Alice, died he famously cabled to his brother Henry, who was at her side, to determine whether she was not dead but in a trance from which she might yet awaken.

At the time one sees death approaching, the mysterious irreducibility of fact, of embodied life, takes on particular importance. What does it mean that our personality, so richly subjective, is embodied in a mass of flesh? In Henry James's day one could speak of the Incarnation of the Word, a regular and explicit theme in James's stories, and of death as liberation from the flesh; in *The Tragic Muse* (1890), James's meditation on life as art, he described the portraits in the British Museum as successive embodiments of the Word. Today we are uneasy with such talk, however, even as a metaphor, and are obliged to search for other language.

Alice James can help us in this matter as few others can, speaking of her own approaching death from breast cancer:

> It is the most supremely interesting moment in life, the only one in fact, when living seems life, and I count it as the greatest good fortune to have these few months so full of interest & instruction in the knowledge of my approaching death. It is as simple in one's own person as any fact of nature, the fall of a leaf or the blooming of a rose, & I have a delicious consciousness, ever present, of wide spaces close at hand, & whisperings of release in the air.

Taken out of context this trembles on the edge of sentimentality—would be sentimental, in fact, if not written by a woman in pain and immersed in the sensations of bodily dissolution—but the letter as a whole, and the journal Alice kept to document the performance of her death, are as businesslike and objective as a newspaper report. Like her brothers, Alice was intensely interested in the stuff of ordinary experience and wrote about her discoveries with extraordinary brilliance. The journal she kept in her final months is a unique record of courage in the face of the intractable, ordinary experience of dying.

As Alice shows, dying—the act of surrendering oneself to death—can be a temptation; it is a surrender to materiality that brings with it a cessation of thought and of the yammering of conscience; duty is at an end, and the meager pinpoint of selfhood vanishes into the warm embrace of the universe. Henry revealed a similar view of death in a letter of consolation to his friend Margaret Brooke, whose daughter-in-law had died. Brooke's son had been devastated, but, James observed,

> life will still be there for him after a while—his youth has all to do yet—How one doesn't, no, absolutely doesn't, envy him for that; but in a manner pities him only the more. Oh, how I feel with you about soft-bosomed death—it's like the lap of my dear mother opening out for me again after all the torments of years for me to bury my head in it and cry. How we shall glide on the great, strange stream! But let us not anticipate.

There was always, too, a practical aspect to death and dying. Immediately after his brother William's funeral, Henry, knowing that he himself would not live many years longer, went into Boston with his nephew Harry, who was a lawyer, and made a new will, providing in it for William's widow and children, who were otherwise without substantial means. In each of the five family deaths that had preceded this one, the women of the family had gathered and made arrangements for the widows and children: now the task fell to Henry. In his new role as head of the family he visited New York City, the home he had shared with his brother. In addition to making family visits, he saw the new Rockefeller Institute for Medical Research, in New York City, the first such in the United States, which had been built on the old Schermerhorn plantation, far uptown.

The novelist was conducted on his tour of the hospital and research facility by Lawrence Godkin, the son of James's old friend and editor, E. L. Godkin, and by James D. Greene, the manager of the institute. They entered a laboratory, and Greene introduced in rather grand terms the young doctor (they were all quite young men and women there) who had charge of it. The doctor was Peyton Rowe, who recalled the encounter some years later:

> Mr. James laid a hand on my shoulder heavily and exclaimed, "How magnificent! To be young and have divine power!" It was perturbing, so much so that I answered, "Not so young as I look," tacitly acknowledging the power. The usual showing of mice with tumors took place, and Mr. Greene and Mr. Godkin shortly went out. But Mr. James lingered, hesitated, and then asked, with a wave of his hand at the cages of mice, "Has the individuality—I might say, the personality—of these little creatures impressed itself upon you?" Yes, he really said that; one could not forget or misplace any word.

As it happened, James Greene was soon to join John D. Rockefeller Jr.'s personal staff, and the institute was in need of a new manager. James knew that his nephew Harry was unhappy in his stultifying law practice. Within weeks of his uncle's visit to New York, Harry was offered the post of manager of the Rockefeller Institute. After protracted reflection and strong urging from his mother and his uncle, he accepted. Harry's immensely pleased uncle Henry, now back at home in England, wrote to him an affectionate note of congratulation:

> Your Rockefeller appointment fills me with joy and pride— pride that is for the Institute itself—and fills me almost beyond endurance with the conscious image of your father, and of the noble and exquisite pleasure it would have given to him. But he is now the dim and passing, yet all the more participating, presence in everything that for better or worse may happen to us, and a presence that fairly presses the scales to make the thing always happen for the better.

In the winter of 1915–16, James was bedridden and close to death. He had suffered a stroke that left him partly paralyzed. He told his friend Fanny Prothero, who sat at his bedside, that the stroke seemed to be narrated, as if dramatically, by a voice that said, while he was still falling, "So here it is at last, the distinguished thing!"

And then a second stroke, followed by pneumonia. Now very gravely ill, he began to dictate a new work. His stenographer and now devoted friend, Theodora Bosanquet, wrote to Edith Wharton:

> I can't bear to contemplate any dragging out of life for him under such conditions. As it is it's almost more than I can bear to go into his room (as he so often wants me to do) to take down from his dictation fragments of the book he imagines himself to be writing. At the same time that it is a heart-breaking thing to do, though, there is the extraordinary fact that his mind does retain the power to frame perfectly characteristic sentences—even whole pages of pure

"Henry James" prose composition. And the fragments he dictates do, in the queerest way, hang together—they seem to form part of a book he is writing in his mind about Bonaparte. He leaves huge gaps undictated, but everything somehow fits into the scheme. It's the most extraordinary thing to watch the bits falling together.

Bosanquet was soon removed from the sickroom and replaced by a nurse, who reported in the mornings that James seemed during the night to imagine that he was dictating a book; but no further record was made of his dictations, which continued until his final unconsciousness. From the fragments that Bosanquet recorded and kept, we can see that in this last work, for which he had been preparing for many years, he gathered up the relics of the past; in the person of Napoleon Bonaparte he stored them in the great museum of the Louvre Palace; he recalled and transmuted his final relations with his brother in America, and his efforts to make provisions for his family. Perhaps his making provisions in his will for William's widow and his helping Harry to find a place in New York were in the back of his mind. Among the fragments that Bosanquet recorded, for instance, is this letter, apparently part of the Napoleonic work. Although James is speaking in the diction of Napoleon, he leaps up onto the stage himself and shows how the lines ought to be spoken:

My dear Brother and Sister.

I offer you great opportunities, in exchange for the exercise of great zeal. Your position as residents of our young but so highly considered Republic at one of the most interesting minor capitals is a piece of luck which may be turned to account in the measure of your acuteness and experience. A brilliant fortune may come to crown it and your personal merit will not diminish that harmony. But you must rise to each occasion—the one I now offer is of no common cast, and please remember that any failure to push your advantage to the utmost will be severely judged. I have displayed you as persons of great taste and judgement. Don't leave me a sorry figure in consequence but present me rather as your fond but not infatuated relation, able and ready to back you up, your faithful Brother and Brother-in-Law,

Henry James.

And so we see James in his final moment, composing his life in memory, and recording its beauty and shadow in a novel.

The religious, philosophical idealism in which Henry, Alice, and William James lived and thought was the context in which death was given meaning. This is how we must understand Henry's continual insistence that art was life, that it made what was human in life. Mere beauty was not enough; one's duty was to compose a life imbued essentially with moral principle, one that was not merely aesthetically pleasing but also sublime. "Live!" was a command: the motto held within it a consciousness of the nearness of death, the deep shadow that made the highlights joyous; it was a command to do one's duty, to accept the terms on which life was given. In this sense we can understand the importance that James gave to final moments, the conclusion of the composition that gave life shape and meaning. We can honor him for a death that in his own terms was noble, one in which he completed his life as a sublime work. It ended with his effort to transmute the performance itself into a lasting work of fiction. That the effort was not entirely successful, that it was defeated indeed by the stubborn materiality of flesh and illness that he made his life's study, does not diminish the value of the attempt.

Henry James was a man of his time. I do not entirely share his beliefs, nor do I find his extraordinary ambition as congenial as Alice's matter-of-factness or William's rebellious questioning. There is something unnerving and grandiose in the search for perfection that was Henry James's Protestantism. But if we are to understand James and our own history, we must at least try to understand him on his own terms.

On reflection, then, I would say to Cynthia Ozick that what Henry James meant by his motto was this: "Live in such a way that you embody in memory and action the best of those who went before; live not just for beauty or pleasure but to be sublime!" This, I think, was the central strand on which he strung his pearls.

William, Alice said, was always catching up with his younger siblings, and only when they were old did he seem to understand her ambition to die well. I suppose it is the fate of the critic always to lag a little behind the performance, to write the review. Performers are often tyrannical and unpleasant; teachers may be more reflective, congenial, and tolerant. We can imagine Henry and Alice performing their works, and William, with his impatient curiosity, observing, explaining. Henry, William, and Alice, drawn together by old age and death, playing their different parts; in memory they have become a family, a collaboration in living. Which is also what Henry James meant.

Millennium Map of the Universe
(from the National Geographic Society)

from *The Gettysburg Review*

It's a beautiful heaven, shining aqua
arrangements on black, scattered
chips of pure turquoise, gold, sterling
white, ruby sand; dimmer clouds
of glowing stellar dust; beads
like snow, like irregular pearls.

Last week, I thought this heaven was
god's body burning, as in the burning
bush never consumed, sudden flarings
of the omnipresence, the coal tips
of god's open hand, the brilliance of god's
streaming hair, the essence of grace
in flames, the idea of creation illuminated.
I believed each form of light and darkness
in that combustion was the glorious
art of god's body on fire, the only
possible origin of such art. Maybe god's
body remains invisible until it ignites
into its beginning. I could almost detect
the incense rising from that transfiguration.

But yesterday I believed it to be music,
the circling and spiraling of sound

in a pattern of light, a pattern I might
begin to perceive, each note, each count
and measure of the concert in progress
being visible, constellations of chords,
geysers of scales, the bell-like lyricism
of overlapping revolutions and orbits, deep
silent pauses of vacancy, as we might
expect, among the swells and trills,
the cacophony of timpani, the zinking
of strings. Yesterday this seemed
a reasonable thought, a pleasing
thought. It seemed possible.

Today, I see it is all signal numbers,
static and spate: the sun, 25,000 light-
years from the center of "our galactic
realm," around which we travel once
every 200 million years, you understand.
I don't resist the calculated mass of "our
supercluster." I don't deny those 100
trillion suns of our suns among which
we pass, turning over and over day
after night after day. The last "outpost"
in our cluster, before a desert cosmic
void begins, is named Virgo. I stop there
for rest and provisions, to water the horses,
pour oats in their trough, to cradle my child.

I wish I could sing like electrons
on a wheel. I wish I could burn
like god.

FLOYD SKLOOT

The Yoga Exercise

from *The Hudson Review*

Within a rushing stream of morning light
she stands still as a heron with one sole
held flush against the other inner thigh
and her long arms like bony wings folded
back so that when the motion of a breeze
passes through her body there is a deep

repose at its root and in an eye's blink
she has become this gently swaying tree
stirring in the wind of its breath while linked
to ground by the slow flow of energy
that brings her limbs together now in prayer
and blessing for the peace she is finding there.

JOAN D. STAMM

The Way of Flowers

from *Tricycle*

Beyond the fringe of urban farmland, where radish and rice fields meet pine-forested hills, stands an ancient temple in northwestern Kyoto called Daikaku-ji, or Big Enlightenment Temple. This venerable site is the birthplace of the Shingon sect, founded in the ninth century by Kukai, the famous saint, scholar, and poet. Daikaku-ji is also the former summer place of Emperor Saga, a ruler of the same era who loved and preserved the arts. Together with Kukai, Emperor Saga is credited with ushering in the Heian Period, a golden era of artistic and cultural achievement lasting three hundred years. Today, eleven hundred years later, Daikaku-ji is not only a prominent historical temple, but also the international headquarters of the Saga Goryu School of Ikebana.

The word *ikebana,* commonly translated as "Japanese flower arranging," literally means "to preserve living flowers," or "to preserve the essence of nature in a vase." Through learning a complex system of rules, artistic principles, and symbolic meaning, and by observing the beauty and quietude of nature, the ikebana practitioner strives to incorporate Buddhist concepts of peace, harmony, and reverence into daily life. Pursuit of the spiritual through the art of flower arranging is the greater study of *kado,* the way of the flowers.

Although Japan has various schools of ikebana, the Saga Goryu school is said to be one of the oldest. The story goes that one day Emperor Saga picked a handful of chrysanthemums growing on one of the two islands in the middle of Osawa Pond (a tiny lake on the grounds of Daikaku-ji) and arranged the flowers in a three-tiered manner depicting heaven, earth, and man. Thus the Saga school was born.

Nestled among pagodas and stone statues of Buddha, Osawa Pond has changed little from days of yore. Depending on the season, sightseers come from all over Japan to view flowering cherry trees, famous screens and scrolls, or the reenactment of Heian Period customs when aristocrats—ladies wearing twelve silk kimonos in harmonious shades—languished in phoenix-prowed boats. In autumn the inner temple gardens are filled with giant chrysanthemums, the national flower and symbol of royalty. The towering plants, pruned into heaven, earth, man configuration, line the perimeters of white stone gardens and creaking, centuries-old verandas.

To view the inner sanctuaries, visitors enter the Daikaku-ji complex over stone bridges thick with moss and lichen. In November, crimson-red Japanese maples adorn paths leading to the mammoth wood door. Inside, winding walkways, enhanced with carved balustrades and gold hinges, zigzag across moss gardens and end at shrines, viewing verandas, or dark corners. The temple, connected to the school and student dormitories by stepping-stones or meandering and embellished corridors, presents a disorienting triangular layout where monks and laypeople work, study, and practice Shingon Buddhism, a sect that uses chanting, visualization, and special body postures to achieve enlightenment.

A typical day begins at 5:00 A.M. with a call to morning service. Worshipers gather in a large tatami-matted meditation hall and wait for the monks to arrive. When the *shoji* doors open, everyone bows their head to the mat while a parade of priests—each one wearing a black silk kimono, a white under-kimono, white *tabi* (opaque split-toed silk stockings), and a saffron cloth uniformly draped over the left shoulder—flies into the room. At the collar of these traditional robes, where layers of white, black, and saffron meet in a clean flat fold, a wooden fan sticks up like a carp fin.

The monks take their places within the inner sanctuary, a separate area cordoned off by a low black railing. Images of Dainichi Nyorai (the universal Buddha) *shogonkas* (formal flower arrangements common to Buddhist shrines) and glittering gold objects that symbolize the radiance of enlightenment adorn the altar. As the priests sit on their heels and arrange long billowy sleeves, the only sound is the rustle of silk falling in graceful folds. Simultaneously they arrive at correct and poised postures while a young monk performs a ritual of transporting a sacred text from the altar to the presiding monk. A novitiate begins chanting the *Hannya-haramita shingyo* and is joined by the full-throated warbling of the others. The deep melodic male voices, synchronized into rhythmical tones and cadences, heighten the sacred atmosphere in which the Three Mystic Practices of correct body posture, cultivation of faith through meditative concentration, and divine chanting are employed.

After morning service, visitors, lay students, and monks dine together in the temple cafeteria on a typical breakfast of rice, fish, pickled vegetables, and tea. The light and healthy cuisine complements the discipline of religious worship and the study of *kado,* a series of ikebana classes that begin by introducing the twenty-eight prohibitions for choosing and pruning plant material. Many of these rules can be interpreted symbolically and act as a guide for not only flower arranging but proper living.

- Don't arrange flowers without knowing their names. (This shows lack of respect for the plant.)
- Don't use entangled branches. (This reminds us of rebellion against one's parents and goes against the teachings of Confucius.)

- Don't use branches that point straight up to heaven, don't use branches that point to earth, our mother, and don't use flowers that point to each other. (Heaven, earth, and man are considered sacred and to point at them would be considered rude.)
- Don't use branches that are even, as they will be in conflict with each other. (One path gives clarity, but two will create confusion.)
- Don't use branches that have two outgrowths going in opposite directions. (This will create conflict, which goes against the principle of harmony.)
- Don't go against the plant's natural growth. (Be true to yourself.)

In a low black bowl the teacher places a corn plant leaf at a forty-five-degree angle and positions a dracaena leaf and freesia blossom next to the corn leaf, making sure there are no gaps between stems in order to achieve the illusion of oneness. To show variety, she dethorns and prunes a quince branch and replaces the corn plant leaf with this new material while explaining the principles of *sai no hana*—an ecological style of flower arrangement for the twenty-first century that uses fewer flowers to create simple, elegant lines. Her actions are confident; her movements easy and graceful. In a matter of minutes, she has achieved an asymmetrically balanced arrangement that conveys a feeling of serenity and inner harmony. In gazing at such an arrangement, the viewer is reminded of the Shingon teaching that artistic creations are Buddhas in their own right; that nature, art, and religion are one; and that all persons are intrinsically enlightened but live in a state of delusion until awakened.

The teacher continues to write the twenty-eight prohibitions on the board while the students take copious notes.

- Don't arrange flowers so that they cover each other. (Each flower, like each person, should shine with individual uniqueness.)
- Don't make an arrangement that looks like an arrow going toward your guest. (This suggests violence and goes against the principle of harmony.)
- Don't use stems having the same width; instead, think of them as strings of a *samisen* (Japanese balalaika). (Different widths produce a variety of tones, an aura of complexity.)
- Flowers should not face the viewer like a mirror. (This implies narcissism and lack of humility.)
- Don't have two leaves be directly opposite each other. Prune one or the other. (Avoid competition, as it can turn into a battle.)
- Don't place flowers as if they are holding each other. (Stand on your own, strong and independent.)

Once these rules are established the class turns to the task of *morimono,* one of the five variations under the *Bunjinka. Bunjin* means "cultured person" and comes from *Bunjinga,* a Chinese drawing school introduced to Japan in the eighteenth century. Bunjinka incorporates freedom of composition and playfulness of design while still maintaining the artistic principles of balance and harmony. Arrangements in this style are given titles taken either from the symbolic meaning of the flowers—pine as eternal youth, rose as everlasting spring—or from old Chinese folktales and poems. To create morimono arrangements, *dai* (wood or bamboo platforms) are fetched from an ancient storeroom built with wood beams as thick as tree trunks and lined with heavy shelves sagging with the weight of hand-built ceramic containers.

On the rectangle dai (square shapes are considered uninteresting—too symmetrical), students place a Japanese pumpkin off to one side, consider the color combinations, stack carrots, peppers, and mushrooms in asymmetrical configurations, and are reminded that groups of three and five are better than fours and sixes, although two is okay. Bitter is good with sweet; green is good with red—all part of achieving yin and yang, the balance of opposites that makes a harmonious whole.

The final ikebana lesson goes back to the religious roots of the Saga school and the six elements of Shingon Buddhism: earth, water, wind, fire, space, and knowledge. Symbolically, these six elements embody aspects of Buddha-nature, each one perfect unto itself but not existing apart from the whole. Earth depicts mountains and prairies but also bones and muscles; water represents oceans and rivers but also blood and tears; fire is at once sunshine and body heat; wind symbolizes breath.

Many kinds of materials can be used in the shogonka style, but for this lesson the teacher uses long sweeping willow branches for fire and water, a pruned azalea branch for wind, leathery ferns for earth, pink amaryllis for space, and yellow lilies with cedar for knowledge. The colors create harmony; the six elements work as a dynamic unit; the whole radiates oneness of body and mind. To engage in the creation of a shogonka arrangement is to contemplate the body of Buddha through the metaphor of nature.

Once the arrangements are complete, they are placed in viewing alcoves to be contemplated as spiritually inspired art by anyone passing by.

George Weigel

Holy Land Pilgrimage: A Diary

from *First Things*

Saturday/Sunday, March 18–19, 2000

It's not quite Egeria's *Diary of a Pilgrimage,* but Evelyn Waugh's *Helena* is terrific reading, or rereading, on an overnight flight to the Holy Land: a resolutely gritty, profoundly anti-Gnostic rendering of Constantine's mother and her search for the true Cross, which, on Waugh's telling of the tale, was driven by the simple, sturdy conviction that the truth of Christianity must be tied to a certain place, a defined time, and real lives. Helena went to the Holy Land, in a word, because of a *sacramental* conviction—that in the Christian scheme of things, salvation history is not merely an idea; rather, the stuff of creation is transformed by grace into the instruments of redemption, right before our eyes. (*Helena* is also, like every other Waugh novel, wickedly funny, which helps on a ten-and-a-half-hour flight.)

I don't know whether John Paul II has ever read *Helena;* I rather doubt it. But he's coming to the Holy Land for the same reason Constantine's mother did. As he put it in a June 1999 letter to all those preparing to celebrate the Great Jubilee of 2000, "To go in a spirit of prayer from one place to another, from one city to another, in the area marked especially by God's intervention, helps us not only to live our life as a journey, but also gives us a vivid sense of a God who has gone before us and leads us on, who Himself set out on man's path, a God who does not look down on us from on high, but who became our travel-ing companion."

That is what the jubilee year is about, and like the dowager empress Helena, John Paul II, the evangelical pilgrim, is determined to remind the world of it—to make the world look, hard, at the stuff of its redemption.

On the drive into Jerusalem from the airport, I was struck by the flags on the lampposts: Vatican and Israeli flags, side by side, a sight that many here (and elsewhere) never expected to see. Something epic is afoot.

I haven't been in Jerusalem in nine years and the city has changed, in some cases dramatically. The massive new Mamilla development near the Jaffa Gate, the last of former Mayor Teddy Kollek's great building projects, seems about half-done, and not altogether successful, architecturally or commercially. I walked through it into the Old City, wondering whether I would remember how to get to the Church of the Holy Sepulcher. I did, and here, too, there were changes, notably the new interior dome over the edicule that holds the sepulcher itself. It's a bit garish, in the modern Italian style, but one comes to the Church of the Holy Sepulcher not for the aesthetics, but to pray. And amidst the cacophony of Sunday afternoon tourists and pilgrims it remains perhaps the easiest place in the world to pray: not so much formally, but as a matter of practicing the presence.

Back at the Jerusalem Hilton, overlooking the Old City, my new colleagues of NBC, MSNBC, and New York's WNBC have been transforming the tenth-floor presidential suite into a combination newsroom-and-outdoor studio, and chaos prevails. The local journalistic chatter, two days before the Pope's arrival, is about security. Israel is mounting the largest security operation in its history for the papal pilgrim, dubbed "Operation Old Friend," and the word is that seventy pounds of explosives were found last week in a house controlled by Hamas extremists. Friday's *Jerusalem Post* has a huge picture of a Pope float being made for a Purim parade this week, and I'm told that Pope costumes are a hot item among some young Purim celebrants. Semtex and Pope floats, ancient shrines and modern flags: welcome to Jerusalem in the year of Our Lord, 2000.

Monday, March 20

Further explorations in the Israeli press and a few phone calls to friends and colleagues suggest that an incredible number of personal, ethnic, religious, ecumenical, interreligious, organizational, and, of course, political agendas are at play in the last twenty-four hours before John Paul arrives. Spin is everywhere. Some upstart local religious leaders are competing for market share in what they assume will be a growing interreligious dialogue after the visit. The established figures—Jewish, Christian, Muslim—are busy trying to frame the papal visit according to their respective organizational and political agendas. The politicians, by contrast, seem relatively restrained thus far. In one sense, this entire hermeneutical rumble—trying to define what it all means before the Pope even lands—is a tribute to John Paul II, the man whose blessing everyone, or almost everyone, seems to crave. On the other hand, the struggle for interreligious turf, ecumenical precedence, and political advantage misses the essential point of the Pope's visit.

That's what I tried to stress in my first segment on MSNBC today: this is a *pilgrimage,* and like everything else John Paul II does, it has an evangelical purpose. John Paul is not coming to the Holy Land to say to the world, "Look at me"; he's coming to say, "Look at Jesus Christ." I also underlined the deeply personal meaning of this pilgrimage for the Pope. In the first weeks of his pontificate, he had had a bright idea: he should spend his first Christmas as Pope in Bethlehem. Mass consternation ensued among the traditional managers of popes—Bethlehem was in disputed territory; the Holy See didn't have diplomatic relations with any state in the area; the logistics would be impossible on such short notice; popes simply didn't *do* this sort of thing. For one of the few times in twenty-one years, John Paul let his evangelical instincts be trumped by the ingrained cautiousness of his diplomats.

But for years afterward, he would ask them, whenever the subject turned to the Middle East, *Quando mi permetterete di andare?*—"When will you let me go?" In the 1994 apostolic letter, *Tertio Millennio Adveniente,* he floated the idea of a pilgrimage to the great sites of biblical history: Ur, home of Abraham, father of believers; Mt. Sinai, site of the Covenant and the Ten Commandments; the Holy Land; Damascus, to mark the conversion of St. Paul; Athens and the Areopagus, to recall Paul's sermon on the "unknown God," which John Paul has long thought an apt metaphor for the Church's situation in the modern world. And still those in the Vatican whose professional responsibility it is to fret continued to, well, fret: how could it be arranged, how would he navigate the minefields of Mideast politics, who could make sense of the logistical nightmares? Finally, in that June 1999 letter, the Pope signaled that he had waited long enough, and simply announced that he was going.

The Iraqis blocked the Ur pilgrimage, demanding that the Pope defy the UN's no-fly zones; the Pope settled for a day of "spiritual pilgrimage" at the Vatican, visually centered on Rublev's icon of the angelic visitation to Abraham. Sinai, however, went off beautifully in February, despite some chippiness by the Greek Orthodox leaders at St. Catherine's Monastery, who declined to pray with the Bishop of Rome. Now, tomorrow, John Paul II will be a pilgrim in the Holy Land. And despite my media colleagues' mantra about the "frail and failing pontiff"—I've been arguing that the real story is how much he does at seventy-nine years old with a form of Parkinson's disease and a leg that doesn't work too well—I think it's fitting that he's coming as an old man. Because what will happen here is the existential confirmation of things the Pope has said and written for decades: with obvious effort, he is going to bear witness to what he believes is true, and what he has taught as the truth, about Christianity, its relationship to Judaism, its respect for other world religions, its commitment to human rights, peace, and justice.

I was impressed by my MSNBC colleagues during our first segments working together. They are smart, friendly, and maintain an amazing professional calm amidst what seems to my amateur eye nothing short of bedlam. Chris Jansing, the anchor, is also willing to let her "anchor buddy" (as I'm known in the argot) spin things out for a decent length of time. She understands that this isn't an event whose truth is readily captured in sound-bites—and after months on the road covering presidential politics in Iowa, New Hampshire, South Carolina, Michigan, and elsewhere, I daresay she finds that a relief.

In Amman, where John Paul stopped for a day en route to the Holy Land, the papal Mass was well-attended. The Pope's subsequent meeting with the Jordanian Catholic hierarchy was a reminder of what the term *universal pastor* means. Some bishops in the West may resent the primacy of the Bishop of Rome; for bishops here, trying to keep small churches afloat in a Muslim sea, the universal pastoral responsibility of the Pope is a lifesaver. On a slightly different plane, the Jordanians and the Palestinians in what is now Israeli-occupied territory on the West Bank are embroiled in a public controversy over the precise site of Jesus' baptism; one doesn't risk a charge of impiousness by suggesting that the argument has more to do with future tourist dollars than with the fine points of biblical archaeology.

In between MSNBC segments I had dinner with Father Michael McGarry, a graduate school classmate and the director of the Tantur Theological Institute. We went to a Palestinian restaurant, Philadelphia, in East Jerusalem, and while the food was superb, I was reminded during the drive that beyond the Damascus Gate lies a different world—at 7:30 at night it was largely lifeless and virtually empty. A poster in the restaurant displayed a photo of John Paul II and Yasser Arafat superimposed on a photo of Jerusalem, with the headline in English, "Welcome to the Palestinian Holy Land." It was a harbinger of another form of spin and a rather expansive reading of the Oslo peace accords.

TUESDAY, MARCH 21

At breakfast this morning I met an immensely learned and kindly rabbi, the friend of an NBC colleague. The rabbi admired John Paul II greatly and asked what I thought the Pope had in mind for the future of Catholic-Jewish relations. I replied that the Pope, while welcoming the achievements of the thirty-five years since Vatican II, now wanted to move the dialogue to a new, theological level. The rabbi became obviously uncomfortable. When I asked whether I had just heard alarm bells going off in his mind, he smiled and said that indeed I had. When I asked why, he said he thought that the kind of theologically enriched, religiously focused dialogue John Paul II envisioned was simply impossible. When I asked why that was the case he replied, simply and without rancor, "Because your sacred text is anti-Semitic."

The obvious next question was what *that* meant, and my interlocutor cited the Gospel of John and its multiple references to "the Jews" in their confrontation with Jesus. I replied that two hundred years of New Testament scholarship had demonstrated that many of the Gospel accounts were written in the polemical context of a bitter family feud, one that eventually led to the parting of the ways between what became Christianity and what became rabbinic Judaism. Moreover, I suggested, the phrase "the Jews" in John's Gospel simply couldn't be read as if this were the minutes of a blackballing at a 1928 meeting in an upscale New York men's club. The rabbi seemed struck by this formulation, but then said that, while he accepted what I had just reported, surely this was not the way the majority of Catholics read the New Testament. I assured him that, when the people of my suburban Washington parish heard "the Jews" during the Good Friday liturgy, they were not hearing what he feared they heard.

This conversation gave personal texture to some polling data I had been reading before and after my arrival in Jerusalem. Fifty-six percent of Israelis, one poll reported, have no idea that the Catholic Church publicly condemns anti-Semitism and works against it. Very few understand the change in the Catholic relationship to Judaism since Vatican II. Several local Jewish leaders have suggested that Jewish ignorance about Christianity is a scandal and an impediment to interfaith relations that can no longer go unaddressed. This, I suspect, has been a problem for years, but it's a side benefit of the papal visit that these things can now be said publicly. The Anti-Defamation League, to its great credit, took out two-page ads in several Israeli papers yesterday, letting the Pope speak for himself in a series of quotable quotes on Jews, Judaism, the abiding covenant with the Jewish people, the State of Israel, and the Holocaust. These citations are a welcome addition to the mix, but that it had to be done tells us something about the imperatives of the immediate future—and not just in Israel.

When the Pope's Royal Jordanian Airbus landed at Ben Gurion Airport this afternoon, the arrival ceremony confirmed what those flags on the Jerusalem lampposts had suggested: this will be a week of icons. The Pope waving a hand in salute at the Israeli flag; the Pope listening attentively as "Hatikvah," Israel's national anthem, is played; the Pope being welcomed to the Jewish state as an honored guest by its president and prime minister; the Pope reviewing an Israeli Defense Force honor guard—these are very powerful signals for John Paul's Jewish interlocutors that things have changed, dramatically, in Catholic-Jewish relations. What the Pope and Israeli president Ezer Weizmann said was fine (although there will certainly be discussion in the future about Weizmann's blunt political reference to Jerusalem as Israel's eternal capital). But the iconography was crucial. The Pope has been saying things about Jews and Catholics for two decades. These images are confirming that what was said was what was meant.

WEDNESDAY, MARCH 22

John Paul spent the entire day in Bethlehem, now under the control of the Palestinian Authority (the "PA," as everyone here calls it), and at the Dehaishe refugee camp. In an interview yesterday with Tom Brokaw, Arafat had insisted, again, that St. Peter was a "Palestinian." I remarked to a colleague that that was true, in the sense that Rabbi Gamaliel and Rabbi Akiba were "Palestinians," but I didn't think that this was the point Arafat was trying to make.

It was, however, the first episode in what became a day-long effort to use the Pope's presence in the PA for the PLO's political purposes. John Paul's measured (and Vatican-standard) remarks about the importance of a Palestinian "homeland" were immediately translated by Suha Arafat, wife of the PLO chairman, into a "clear message for an independent Palestinian state" (although the word *state* did not appear in the Pope's text—deliberately, as I later learned). The papal call for justice for the refugees at the Dehaishe camp was quickly spun by Palestinian commentators into a Vatican demand for a "right of return" for all those displaced by the first Arab-Israeli War in 1948 (although the phrase *right of return* was not used, again deliberately). Arafat himself got the day off to a politicized start by welcoming the Pope to Palestine "and to holy Jerusalem, the eternal capital of Palestine." The tangled question of Jerusalem's international legal status and future notwithstanding, this claim for a city that has never been the capital of an Islamic state was of a piece with Arafat's overreach on the "Palestinian St. Peter" and his 1995 Christmas reference to Bethlehem as the city of the "Palestinian Jesus."

It's difficult for reporters accustomed to covering political stories to understand that, when the Pope speaks of justice and human rights, he's speaking as a pastor, not as a politician or negotiator. Then there was a mild flap over the Pope's kissing a bowl of Palestinian soil on his arrival in Bethlehem: did this mean he was recognizing a Palestinian state (as the PA spin machine quickly insisted)? Joaquín Navarro-Valls, the Pope's able press spokesman, ended that line of speculation with a simple statement: "It would have been very strange of the Pope not to have kissed the earth at the place where Christ was born."

Moreover, the Pope's words about justice for a Palestinian people whose "torment is before the eyes of the world" and had "gone on too long" were just as plausibly aimed at the leadership of the Palestinian Authority as well as at other states in the region. The PA is a mess. The economy is a shambles and corruption is rampant; one of our camera crews, in order to shoot film in Bethlehem, had to get ten different press passes, meaning that ten different PA officials or offices had to be paid off. Christians can't buy land or other forms of property in the PA—not by law, but because it's simply not done, and it's well understood that any attempt to do so will bring retribution. So the economic pressure on Palestinian Christians increases steadily, leading to further Christian migration from the Holy Land, a major Vatican concern. The large-scale corruption in the PA was also, I suspect, on the Pope's mind when he spoke at Dehaishe: corruption is not simply lining the pockets of PA officials, it's blocking any serious economic development efforts for these refugees. Whatever signals it may have sent politically, however, the papal visit to the camp was an enormous success in human terms. One relief official told a visiting American bishop that the Pope's presence had given the refugees a measure of hope for the first time in decades.

One has to feel terribly sorry for ordinary Palestinians. Pawns of other Arab states' anti-Israeli politics for years, but now on the verge of achieving a state of their own (which everyone I talked to expects to be declared this year), they are saddled with a mendacious, corrupt, and inept political leadership. The day-long PA spin control operation sat poorly with a lot of the press and with Holy See officials who have been insisting that this is a *pilgrimage*. The condition of Christians in the PA also puts the recent Vatican/Palestinian agreement in the proper perspective: by insisting on a religious freedom provision in the agreement (a clause the PA first resisted, but on which the Vatican dug in its heels), the Holy See has created a legal situation in which it can be of some assistance to Palestinian Catholics when the Palestinian state, which will likely be unfriendly to them in various ways, is a fact.

In the midst of the Palestinian spin, Israeli counterspin, and Vatican aggravation at PA hamhandedness, John Paul's wonderful homily in Bethlehem got little attention. "The joy announced by the angel" to the shepherds of Bethlehem "is not a thing of the past," the Pope said. "It is a joy of today—the eternal today of God's salvation which embraces all time, past, present, and future. At the dawn of the new millennium, we are called to see more clearly that time has meaning because here Eternity entered history and remains with us forever. . . . Because it is always Christmas in Bethlehem, every day is Christmas in the hearts of Christians."

This afternoon, a WNBC reporter told me that the Israeli government had confirmed that its security people had asked the Pope to wear a bulletproof vest in Nazareth and he had refused. What did I make of this? I said that something similar had been proposed after the assassination attempt in 1981 and had met with the same response. This was not, I told the New York audience, papal chutzpah; it was religious conviction. Karol Wojtyla has believed for more than six decades that he is not in charge of his own life. To wear a bulletproof vest would be to deny the conviction that makes him who and what he is—the conviction that God is in charge of his life, which is the source of John Paul's fearlessness and freedom. The Pope is, of course, heavily protected by police and other security forces. What local authorities do to avoid having a wounded or dead Pope on their hands is beyond his control.

Thursday, March 23

This was a day of solemn drama and wrenching emotion. It began with a private Mass for the papal party in the Cenacle, the "Upper Room"—the successor of Peter and his collaborators concelebrating at the traditional site of the institution of the Eucharist and the priesthood, the place where the Church was born on Pentecost. Then, after a meeting with the chief Ashkenazic rabbi, Yisrael Meir Lau, and the chief Sephardic rabbi, Eliahu

Bakshi-Doron, the Pope went to the Israeli presidential residence for a conversation with President Weizmann. And from there, John Paul II was driven to the Holocaust memorial at Yad Vashem.

This unforgettable visit was preceded by weeks of speculation and agitation: "How far would the Pope go?" Attempts to explain that this was not a zero-sum negotiation in which one side's gain was another's loss got little traction amidst the rhetorical grenades being freely tossed about. A few weeks before the papal pilgrimage, Rabbi Arthur Hertzberg had told an Israeli audience that Karol Wojtyla had been passively acquiescent during the wartime slaughter of Polish Jewry. A little later, James Carroll had lectured at David Hartman's Jerusalem institute, arguing that the real issue here was to jettison the "theology" that had "made the Holocaust possible"—presumably a reference to Carroll's bizarre notion, first floated in *The New Yorker,* that Vatican I's definition of papal infallibility had caused the Shoah. More sober souls, among them the ADL's David Rosen, have been quietly explaining in recent days that a papal "apology" for Pius XII is simply not in the cards. But what has gone largely unexamined is the question of how a playwright's undocumented speculation—Pius XII's alleged in-difference to the Holocaust as portrayed by Rolf Hochhuth in *The Deputy*—has become, in many minds, a *given*.

It was not an atmosphere that seemed appropriate to the seri-ousness of the papal pilgrimage or the gravity of what Yad Vashem represents, and concerns were expressed yesterday and this morn-ing that the entire visit could self-destruct today. In the event, however, John Paul took all of this to an entirely different level in a simple ceremony of awesome solemnity that reduced to ashes the endless "how far" chatter.

Joaquín Navarro-Valls once asked John Paul whether he ever cried. "Not outside," the Pope replied. No one who knows him could doubt that the Pope was crying inside as he walked slowly toward the eternal flame in Yad Vashem's Hall of Remembrance and then bent his head in silent prayer. No one could doubt that, in his mind's eye, he was seeing the boyhood friends from Wadowice who had perished in the death camps. No one who knows how the experience of the Nazi occupation had shaped Karol Wojtyla's determination to defend human dignity could doubt that he was hearing the jackboots on the streets of Kraków again.

The Pope, a shared history etched in his face, bent in prayer over the eternal flame at Yad Vashem—here was the second icon indelibly imprinted on the memory of the modern world and on the consciousness of Catholics and Jews. Here was another indication that things could never be the same again.

John Paul began his brief address with Psalm 131 ("I have become like a broken vessel. . . . But I trust in you, O Lord") and then said what ought to have been said to so many of those trying to spin the papal visit to Yad Vashem before the Pope had even arrived: "In this place of memories, the mind and heart and soul feel an extreme need for silence. Silence in which to remember. Silence in which to try to make some sense of the memories which come flooding back. Silence because there are no words strong enough to deplore the terrible tragedy of the Shoah."

Then, after reminding everyone that remembrance was *"for a purpose,* namely, to ensure that never again will evil prevail, as it did for the millions of innocent victims of Nazism," John Paul, knowing that too many Christians had become ensnared in that web of evil, offered an act of repentance from the heart: "As Bishop of Rome and Successor of the Apostle Peter, I assure the Jewish people that the Catholic Church, motivated by the gospel law of love and by no political considerations, is deeply saddened by the hatred, acts of persecution, and displays of anti-Semitism directed against the Jews by Christians at any time and in any place." Most especially including, it was clear, the times and places memorialized at Yad Vashem. Prime Minister Ehud Barak replied with a moving statement that neither ignored nor pursued the arguments about relative responsibilities for the Shoah; like the Pope, the prime minister understood that this was too solemn a moment for anything other than remembrance and a mutual commitment to a different future.

The weight of history became almost unbearable when the Pope walked slowly across the Hall of Remembrance to greet seven Holocaust survivors. But here, too, it seemed, was another icon: the Pope was not receiving the survivors, he was honoring their experience and their memories by walking, with difficulty, to meet them. It was a gesture of respect that did not go un-noticed or unremarked. Our NBC/MSNBC newsroom and studio, which was usually a bedlam eighteen hours a day, fell completely silent.

A few days later, an Israeli friend, a soldier-intellectual who has seen a lot in his life, called late at night. "I just had to tell you," he said, "that my wife and I cried throughout the Pope's visit to Yad Vashem. This was wisdom, humaneness, and integrity personi-fied. Nothing was missing; nothing more needed to be said."

Later that afternoon, a tripartite interreligious meeting, on which John Paul had insisted, illustrated just how difficult "the dialogue" is, in and around Jerusalem. The Grand Mufti of Jerusalem had refused to participate; Chairman Arafat had dele-gated Sheik Taysir Tamimi, an Islamic judge from the PA, to be the Muslim spokesman. Tamimi and Rabbi Lau flanked the Pope on a dais at the Pontifical Notre Dame Institute. Lau began by speaking of the need for peace and dialogue in everyday life; then, as *The New York Times's* Alessandra Stanley wrote, he "put an abrupt end to both by thanking John Paul for 'your recognition of

Jerusalem as [Israel's] united, eternal capital city.'" The Pope had not done that—the Holy See, which takes no position on the question of sovereignty in Jerusalem, nevertheless insists that access to the city's holy places and their integrity be secured by an "international statute"—and someone in the audience shouted, "The Pope did not recognize Jerusalem." Things got more volatile when Tamimi welcomed the Pope, in Arabic, as "the guest of the Palestinian people on the land of Palestine, in the city of holy Jerusalem, eternal capital of Palestine," and was met by loud applause by the audience. He went on to insist, in a rather frenzied rhetorical style, that there could be no peace in the region until all of "Palestine" was united under "President Yasser Arafat"; more applause followed. The moderator, Rabbi Alon Goshen-Gottstein, tried to save the meeting by reminding those present that they were supposed to have come "as religious people who can put aside our politics." John Paul spoke briefly and pointedly of religion as "the enemy of exclusion and discrimination, of hatred and rivalry, of violence and conflict," but shortly after he finished, Sheik Tamimi abruptly got up and left the meeting. It was later explained by a Vatican official that the sheik had leaned over to the Pope before departing and explained that he had a "previous engagement." One had to wonder precisely what engagement trumped the Pope in the sheik's mind.

FRIDAY, MARCH 24

I managed to get away for a couple of hours of pilgrim-time this morning: the Cenacle, the Dormition Abbey, the Holy Sepulcher again. Walking through the Old City from Zion Gate through the Jewish Quarter to the Christian Quarter, I couldn't help noticing the ubiquitous cell phones and the refreshing number of black faces, the result of the ingathering of Ethiopian Jews.

The papal Mass at Korazim today, on the Mount of Beatitudes, was the largest gathering in the history of the State of Israel: over 100,000 young people, from all over the world, in a kind of mini-World Youth Day. A local news agency reported that a bulletproof screen had been erected around the altar platform, noting that this was the first time this had been done at a papal Mass "since Detroit in 1987"—which is no compliment, I suppose, to Korazim. The Pope was in fine form, voice strong and clear, as he so often is with teenagers. Why, WNBC asked, did they find him so attractive? Because, I suggested, he didn't pander to them but challenged them to moral heroism. John Paul's own "sermon on the mount" also asked the youngsters to be "joyful witnesses and convinced apostles," the evangelists of the twenty-first century. A television producer for a network that will go unnamed asked me, "How long has the Catholic Church been into evangelism?" "About nineteen hundred and sixty-five years," I replied.

After the Mass, John Paul went to Tabgha, to pray at the site of the multiplication of loaves and fishes, and then to Peter's house at Capernaum, which has been excavated in recent years. One could sense the wonder in John Paul's face: here was Peter's 263rd successor, praying at Peter's house. One also got the distinct impression here, as at Bethlehem (where the Pope managed to be by himself for a few minutes in the Grotto of the Nativity), that the best moments of this trip for John Paul are the moments when he can be a pilgrim and simply pray. They are, necessarily, fewer than he would like. But they are unmistakably intense.

SATURDAY, MARCH 25

John Paul II celebrated the Solemnity of the Annunciation today at the traditional site of the angel Gabriel's appearance to

Mary of Nazareth. This part of the pilgrimage had been preceded by high tension. An incomprehensible decision by the Israeli government to grant a permit for the building of a mosque in the plaza outside the Basilica of the Annunciation had led to riots and festering ill will. The mosque decision—which, as one Vatican official put it privately, would lay the basilica under "permanent siege"—remains under review, and the Holy See is determined to reverse it. For today, however, this controversy was not the center of local attention. John Paul was almost crushed by the exultant congregation as he walked into the basilica; his secretary, the ever-calm Bishop Stanislaw Dziwisz, fended off hands trying to touch the Pope from left and right by a judicious distribution of rosaries. Once again, the beauty of the liturgy and its location notwithstanding, John Paul was clearly most at home when he managed some time for private prayer in the Grotto of the Annunciation, doubtless repeating the *Fiat voluntas tua* that has characterized his own life and Marian spirituality.

Later today, on MSNBC, Rabbi James Rudin of the American Jewish Committee took on the question of whether the Pope should wear his pectoral cross when he visits the Western Wall tomorrow—the latest local controversy, it seems. Rudin was perfect. In "real interreligious dialogue," he said, "we respect the other for what he is and we begin the conversation from there." Off camera, Rudin told me that the same issue had come up when plans were being finalized for John Paul's historic visit to the Synagogue of Rome in 1986. There, it seemed, the proscription on crosses is so severe that ushers would walk through the congregation and rap the knees of anyone caught crossing their legs. Chief Rabbi Elio Toaff was beseeched by some of his congregates to explain the situation to the Pope and ask him not to wear his pectoral cross. Toaff agreed and went to see the Pope. John Paul said, in so many words, "Look, if I were coming to the Synagogue of Rome as a tourist I'd be happy to wear jeans. But I'm coming as the Bishop of Rome and the universal pastor of the Catholic Church, and to make that and all it means unmistakably clear I have to dress as I always do." Toaff came out of the meeting and told his startled followers that he had indeed raised the point with the Pope and they had both agreed: the Pope should wear his pectoral cross.

While the Pope was lost in prayer this evening at the Church of the Nations in the Garden of Gethsemane, Father Mike McGarry celebrated Mass for the MSNBC Catholics in our own "upper room"—in this instance, my quarters at the Jerusalem Hilton. Leaving Gethsemane, John Paul called on the Greek Orthodox patriarch, Diodoros I, at his residence. What could have resulted in another unpleasant ecumenical scene was transformed when the Pope embraced and kissed the ailing patriarch, who remained seated. John Paul insisted that "only by being reconciled among themselves can Christians play their role in making Jerusalem a city of peace for all people." The Pope then spontaneously proposed that all those present say the Lord's Prayer together, each in his own language. By coming to Diodoros, John Paul lived out the truth of what he had suggested in *Ut Unum Sint* and elsewhere: that he really burns to pray with the Orthodox, and that he doesn't imagine the Bishop of Rome playing the jurisdictional role in the East that he currently does in the West.

SUNDAY, MARCH 26

John Paul II, walking eighty-six slow steps to the Western Wall this morning, praying there, and, like millions of pious Jews, leaving behind a prayer-petition: here was the third great icon for the future of the Catholic-Jewish dialogue. The letter the Pope left repeated what had been said at the liturgical "cleansing of the

Church's conscience" in Rome on the First Sunday of Lent: "God of our fathers, you chose Abraham and his descendants to bring your name to the nations. We are deeply saddened by the behavior of those who in the course of history have caused these children of yours to suffer. And asking your forgiveness, we wish to commit ourselves to genuine brotherhood with the people of the covenant." But now it was being said *here,* in this singular place, by a man whose reverence for that place could be read in his whole demeanor. It was another image driving home the point that something fundamental had changed, irreversibly, in the relationship between Catholicism and living Judaism.

Prior to this, John Paul had visited the Haram al-Sharif, the Temple Mount, where he met a delegation of Muslim leaders. The Grand Mufti, Sheik Ikrima Sabri, read the Pope a lecture and told him bluntly that Jerusalem is "eternally bonded to Islam." According to papal spokesman Navarro-Valls, the Pope was unaware that the Mufti had been engaging in Holocaust denial and Jew-baiting in a series of interviews during the weekend. John Paul's response to the Mufti's lecture, that he considered Jerusalem the "holy city par excellence" and "a part of the common patrimony" of Judaism, Christianity, and Islam, did not seem to make much impression on the Mufti's politicized supersessionism.

From the Pope's point of view, the Mass at the Holy Sepulcher, which he celebrated after his visit to the Western Wall, was the climax of the entire pilgrimage. Here, he had written in his June 1999 letter, "I intend to immerse myself in prayer bearing in my heart the whole Church." As it happened, John Paul was not satisfied with one immersion in prayer during that Eucharist at the tomb of Christ. Later in the day, he asked to be permitted to come back, privately, and after the security people had recovered from the shock, the Pope spent another half-hour as a pilgrim, not only at the tomb, but climbing up the difficult stone steps to the eleventh and twelfth Stations of the Cross, in order to be able to pray at Calvary. It was another icon, the Pope living out the truth to which he had committed himself decades before: Jesus Christ as the answer to the question that is every human life.

As John Paul's El Al 747 took off from Ben-Gurion Airport this evening, I couldn't help recall what one Jerusalem inter-religious leader had called, a week ago, "the growing unease about the chances of [the Pope's] success." Yet John Paul had done it again. By being what he had said all along he intended to be—a pilgrim—he lifted the entire week above the quarrels, conflicts, hatreds, and pettiness that are the daily bread of affliction in the Holy Land. What a remarkable thing it was, one television col-league said, to see an adult among the squabbling children of the Middle East. But more than maturity has been on display here for the past seven days. The Pope drew the response he did because of his transparent faith.

The effects of this pilgrimage will likely be enduring, perhaps even epic. The sea change in Catholic-Jewish relations has been registered by people who may have heard something about it pre-viously, but have now seen it embodied. One can only hope that the Palestinian people, seeing what mature leadership looks like, will be able to demand it of their own leaders. As for the impact on the Catholic Church, I'd venture the guess that this pilgrimage will, one day, loom large in the deliberations of the conclave that chooses John Paul's successor—many years from now, I devoutly hope. Even as the Pope was walking in the footsteps of Christ in Galilee and Judea, middle-level curial bureaucrats and disgruntled liberal Catholic intellectuals were putting out the word to the press that the next Pope would be an elderly Italian. But surely, after this week, something else has been decisively clarified. The overriding question in the next conclave will not be. "Where was so-and-so born?" It will have to be, "Who can offer the world the kind of leadership we saw in Jerusalem in March 2000?"

LAWRENCE WESCHLER

The Novelist and the Nun

from *The New Yorker*

Last week, Mark Salzman, the forty-year-old author of four often luminous volumes (a pair of memoirs and a pair of novels), released his most accomplished work to date, a fictional narrative entitled *Lying Awake.* The book, a lean (its typescript came in at under a hundred pages), seemingly effortless tour de force, was, according to its author, the product of nearly six years of agonized blockage, doubt, and misgiving.

"Sister John of the Cross pushed her blanket aside, dropped to her knees on the floor of her cell, and offered the day to God"— thus begins Salzman's improbably absorbing tale of a cloistered Carmelite nun in the midst of a spiritual crisis. *Every moment a beginning,* she thinks, *every moment an end.* Presently, she gets up, dons her robe and wimple, and goes over to her desk to review a sheaf of poems, the writing of which had kept her up till well past midnight the night before. They are the latest evidence of an outpouring of grace that mysteriously began three years earlier, slaking what had degenerated into a dry and cramped midlife vocation.

She rises, tidies her room, and silently carries her washbasin down the hall to the dormitory bathroom. She empties its contents into the sink: "The motion of the water as it spiraled toward the drain triggered a spell of vertigo. It was a welcome sensation." Instead of going to the choir to wait for the others, she returns to her cell, kneels down once again, and unfocuses her eyes:

Pure awareness stripped her of everything. She became an ember carried upward by the heat of an invisible flame. Higher and higher she rose, away from all she knew. Powerless to save herself, she drifted up toward infinity until the vacuum sucked the feeble light out of her. A darkness so pure it glistened, then out of that darkness, nova.

In the radiance, Salzman records, Sister John "could see forever, and everywhere she looked, she saw God's love." At length, thoroughly ravished, she returns to herself and, as soon as she can move again, opens her notebook and begins once more to write.

End of the first brief chapter. During the next few chapters, it becomes evident that Sister John's visitations have been arriving at an increasingly harrowing physical price, that they are preceded by ever more debilitating headaches, and that in fact something is decidedly wrong. Eventually, she breaches the walls of the convent community to go to an appointment with a neurologist, who gives her a battery of tests, including a CT scan.

These tests uncover a small tumor in the temporal lobe, just above Sister John's right ear. Such tumors elsewhere in the brain have been known to occasion convulsions and seizures. Although they manifest themselves epileptically in the temporal lobe, too, as the neurologist now tries to explain, here the seizures tend to be more psychological, or even spiritual, in character—fever spikes of transcendent well-being. Dostoyevsky was said to have suffered from such visitations; and so, apparently, did St. Teresa of Avila, the founder of the Carmelite Order.

Sister John is devastated by the diagnosis (*"Please, God, take anything, take my life . . . but don't take Yourself away from me, don't tell me I haven't known You at all"*), and unconsoled by assurances that the tumor is eminently operable. Returning to the convent, she is racked with misgiving: Had this entire passion merely been some kind of vast illusion, or, rather, was it God's manner of making himself felt in her life? What is she to make of her ongoing (and more and more wrenching) transports? Then again, perhaps she is expected to think of the operation itself as a test of her faith. But the prospect of returning to the aridity of her prior monastic existence is almost more than she can bear. After such knowledge, what forgiveness—and what grace?

This, then, is the vocational crisis, the existential crux, to which Salzman's narrative brings his protagonist, the shadings of which he only now starts to draw out at length—heartrendingly—like a master cellist.

A master cellist, as it happens, is what Salzman himself once seemed on the way to becoming. We were talking about that alternative life one morning recently as we sat out on the yucca-shaded back porch of a wood-and-stucco bungalow he shares with his wife, the documentary filmmaker Jessica Yu, in the chaparral foothills of the San Gabriel Mountains, on the outskirts of Los Angeles. Salzman is unlike anything you would have expected if *Lying Awake* were the only one of his books you ever read. (On the other hand, he's exactly like what you would have expected had you encountered only his two books of memoir, *Iron & Silk* and *Lost in Place.*) He's neither Catholic nor particularly religious in any conventional sense—and he isn't a bit dour. He's spry and mischievous: a human gleam. He's powerfully built (if somewhat on the slight side), with a mime's bearing. He shambles about with a sort of lope and is subject to explosions of glee. Yet, at heart, he's a mournful fatalist, which is to say that he is truly the son of the father to whom he dedicated his second book, *Lost in*

Place, a memoir of *Growing Up Absurd in Suburbia,* in the following terms:

> For Joseph Arthur Salzman,
> artist, astronomer, social worker, beloved father and good natured pessimist, whose reaction to this book was to say that he enjoyed it, but felt that my portrayal of him was inaccurate. I put him, he complained, in an excessively positive light.

Salzman's mother, Martha, on the other hand, has a sunny disposition. Formerly both a concert pianist and a concert oboist, she later became a harpsichordist and teacher. It was from her side that Mark's love of music flowed, though not, as it happens, immediately. "I started with the violin, and then piano, but neither of them really took," he now recalled. "Then, one evening, my parents dragged me to a cello recital—I was about seven at the time—and from the moment the young player walked onto the stage with that instrument I was captivated, I was enthralled. I mean, the shape of it, the color, the varnish like the glaze on a caramel custard. And for a second, as the guy was setting up, I got a peek at the far side of the instrument, and it was like a tiger's back, all gloriously striated; and the way he then held the thing, as if he were riding a tiger, holding it by the neck and drawing the music out of it—and the sound! My God, I was completely hooked."

For the next ten years, Salzman devoted himself to the cello— well, not entirely. It turned out that he, too, was torn between two passions. Only, in his case, as readers of *Lost in Place* know, the other consuming enthusiasm of his adolescence was kung fu: he established an incense-reeking shrine in his parents' basement, in Ridgefield, Connecticut; and, swathed in tie-dyed pajamas and a

Surprise Bald Head Wig (his parents wouldn't permit the thirteen-year-old to shave his head), he practiced kicks and lunges for hours at a time. After that, he practiced his cello.

And he wasn't half bad at it; at sixteen, he was accepted at Yale, having applied as a potential music major. Two weeks before starting Yale, however, Salzman ventured up to Tanglewood, in Lenox, Massachusetts, to attend a recital by Yo-Yo Ma. "And that was absolutely one of the transformative experiences of my life," he said. "I'll never forget how Yo-Yo walked out onto the stage. I mean, most performers walk out completely stiff, like this, and you can sense the sobriety, the utter focus, the intense concentration—the barely concealed terror. And I don't even mean that as a criticism: the technical level expected of performers nowadays is so insanely high that you'd be crazy if you weren't terrified. Yo-Yo, by contrast, came out like this—totally relaxed, guffawing, almost slap-happy, casually waving to friends in the audience, you know, 'Oh wow, great, what are you doing here?' Completely, but completely, unfazed.

"And then he started to play. Bach—the fifth suite for unaccompanied cello. And his playing was so beautiful, so original, so intelligent, so effortless that by the end of the first movement I knew my cello career was over. I kid you not. People talk about Yo-Yo Ma's superhuman technique. Let me tell you: superhuman technique is only the tip of the Yo-Yo iceberg. What really sank my ship was how much he was obviously enjoying himself: he was lost in the music, freed by it, speaking through it, in love with it. He was enjoying himself as much playing as most of the rest of us do when we're listening, and as I myself never did when playing, not to speak of practicing.

"When I heard Yo-Yo play, I suddenly realized that I wasn't just inadequate—I wasn't even making music. I was training to be a showoff, that's all. My playing was to true music what a résumé is to a piece of real writing. My true calling, I realized, was not the cello, never had been. My true calling was to teach kung fu. So I put the cello into deep storage, and, reporting to Yale, I majored in Chinese."

Salzman excelled at Chinese. In 1982, just out of college, he traveled to Changsha, the remote capital of Hunan Province—an unusual undertaking for an American in those early days of the Communist thaw—to teach English at a medical college and, more to the point, to study Chinese martial arts at their very headwaters. Returning to New Haven two years later, he set about composing a memoir of the experience, the narrative that became *Iron & Silk,* his first book. (During this period, he met Jessica Yu, a beautiful and self-assured Yale sophomore, who was the daughter of a Shanghai-born oncologist. Somehow, their early relationship survived both her relative obliviousness of her Chinese origins and his disconcerting habit of smashing his bare fist into a steel plate a thousand times a day as part of a conditioning ritual.)

Iron & Silk, which was published in 1986, proved to be a considerable success, and, indeed, had something of a Holden Caulfieldesque popularity on college campuses. It was later the basis for an ill-conceived movie, starring Salzman himself, filmed in mainland China. (The shoot ended on June 3, 1989, the eve of the Tiananmen Square massacre.) One would have no conceivable reason to look for that film nowadays except that it allows one to witness Salzman in full martial ecstasy: a startling vision.

Once Jessica had graduated from Yale, the couple moved to her home haunts, in the San Francisco Bay area, where Salzman wrote a novel, *The Laughing Sutra,* a magic-realist picaresque that traces the adventures of a Chinese orphan and his sidekick, a mysterious two-thousand-year-old knightly warrior. The Salzmans presently transplanted themselves to Los Angeles, and Jessica started making independent documentary films. A few years later, she won an Academy Award for a short-subject documentary, *Breathing Lessons,* about a writer who spent most of his life in an iron lung. (At that year's televised ceremonies, Jessica, sheathed in a borrowed strapless gold-embroidered black Mary McFadden dress and draped in Harry Winston jewels, began her acceptance speech with the observation "You know you've entered new territory when your outfit costs more than your film.") Mark, meanwhile, had begun work on his second novel, *The Soloist.*

"So here I was," Salzman resumed. "This was maybe fifteen years since I'd more or less abandoned the cello, and I was finding myself writing this novel about an embittered failed wunderkind, a cello prodigy whose career had suddenly and mysteriously come undone at the age of seventeen"—Salzman interrupted himself, laughing. "I love it when people come up and ask, 'Where do you get your ideas for your novels?' Anyway, suddenly it was as if this character had become hypersensitive to pitch, or his sense of tonal confidence had broken up, and he was unable to continue concretizing. He'd fallen away into an empty, deracinated life of teaching, and now he was middle-aged, and, what with one plot turn and another, he finds himself given charge of this little Korean boy, a phenomenal cello prodigy, and all these feelings start welling up in him.

"As I was coming to the end of the book, I realized how badly I wanted this cellist to be able to enjoy playing once again—not as a concert soloist but just as someone who loves playing for the sake of the music, who strives for the ideal that music represents but isn't destroyed by failure to reach that ideal. And as I was writing that scene I had the stereo playing in the background, and on came Bach's Fifth Suite, the one that Yo-Yo Ma had been playing the day he tore through the hull of my ship and sent me to the bottom of the ocean. I was describing this moment when the cellist, alone, drags the bow across the strings, just to hear the music come alive, and how it does come alive for him, and how now when he makes mistakes he no longer cares, he doesn't think of them as a crime against music but, rather, as an act of nature, like the random cracks that show up in those Oriental teacups everybody's always raving about.

"After I'd completed that scene, I remember thinking, If I can do that for him, why not for me? So I rented a cello—my own was still back in Connecticut in deep storage—and I tried acting out the scene I'd just written, and it was wonderful. That was ten years ago, and I've been playing every day since, and I can honestly say that nowadays, playing, I feel the way Yo-Yo looked. How I sound is an entirely different matter."

I'd come out to L.A. because I'd heard that Salzman had recently started offering a performance piece—cello and narrative— that relayed the saga of the composition of his new novel, set to a score by Bach. There was to be a performance that very afternoon in the Mark Taper Auditorium of the L.A. Central Library.

I hurried downtown and was comfortably in place when Salzman came onto the stage, cello in tow, wearing a gray T-shirt and casual black pants, relaxed, guffawing at the audience's friendly reception, waving to longtime pals scattered in the seats. Laying the cello on its side, for the moment, but declining as yet to take his seat beside it, he launched into his talk.

"Bach wrote six suites for unaccompanied cello," he began. "They were nearly lost—in fact, the autograph manuscript was never found, and only a few copies, handwritten by his wife, managed to make it through. Once rediscovered, for the longest time they were simply ignored, mistaken for exercise études. The story goes that at the age of thirteen the prodigy Pablo Casals was rummaging around in a secondhand shop in Barcelona, and he found a dusty copy of these pieces he'd never heard of; he bought them, took them home, studied them, and was later to describe the experience as the greatest revelation of his life. He worked at them every day for twelve years until he had the courage to play them publicly, and then he seemed to never stop performing them, and with absolutely intimidating authority. These pieces have become to cellists what Shakespeare's plays are to actors, or Rembrandt's painting to painters: the foundation of the repertoire, the music we can forever return to and never exhaust." (In *The Soloist,* the boyhood mentor of Salzman's protagonist asserts "that Bach's musical inspiration was divine in origin, and that to play Bach properly was an act of religious devotion.")

Salzman went on to suggest that he had developed a theory as to why these pieces become so meaningful to cellists. "Because, you see," he said, "I believe these pieces function as stories—not specific stories. I don't mean, for instance, that the Second Suite is about the birth of Bach's twenty-third son, or anything like that. No, I think that when we play them our emotions take a journey that so closely resembles a narrative journey that I believe there's got to be a relationship between the two. And I want to illustrate this point by taking you on two parallel journeys—the musical one, of course, but then another as well, the narrative of the genesis of my most recent novel, from its original conception to the final version." He'd be performing Bach's Third Suite, he explained, which, like the others, consisted of six movements; similarly, the story of his novel's evolution broke into six segments.

Before proceeding, Salzman assured his audience that he wasn't going to be making any great claims for his musical competence. He went through some of the same points he'd gone over with me about the history of his vocation as a cellist, invoking George Bernard Shaw's observation that "Hell is full of musical amateurs: music is the brandy of the damned." He then recounted how he'd been reading a tale by the neurologist Oliver Sacks about an Italian immigrant whose temporal-lobe epilepsy had resulted in visions of his boyhood village so vivid that he'd felt compelled to render them as paintings. Sacks had pointed out that such epilepsies are sometimes characterized by an intensification of emotional life and a general sense of illumination and faith. "And I found myself thinking, Imagine if someone already committed to religious life were to develop such a disorder. Wouldn't she interpret its symptoms as a confirmation of her vocation? And let's up the stakes: Let's say that under the spell of such seizures she starts writing poems, and they start getting published, and they start selling, so much that the royalties save her convent from bankruptcy. A lot of these convents are hanging by their fingernails. Only there are problems, of course, not the least of which is the jealousy of her fellow-nuns. Furthermore, if the condition goes untreated, it could get worse. On the other hand, if these are valid mystical experiences and she gets an operation to have the disorder treated, she might be giving up graces of God just in order to improve her health. How would she experience this news? And what would she do?"

Salzman picked up his cello and sat down. Taking the bow, he smiled broadly and announced, "The Prelude!" He momentarily pulled the bow aside, and added, exultantly, "Isn't that a great idea for a novel?" before launching into the piece with robust self-confidence. As he played, I was reminded of a scene in *The Soloist* in which the protagonist recalls hearing of a scuba diver who grabs a passing whale by its fin and finds being pulled along by such a creature to be the most incredible experience of his life. Salzman's protagonist adds that it can't have been that different from playing onstage.

After the Prelude, Salzman said that the next movement was called an allemande and was more tentative, reflective, and searching in tone. "Questions stumbling toward answers" was how he put it—"not unlike what I myself was going through in the months after my first inspiration. For example, what sort of person was this nun? How old was she? What made her first decide to join the order? And how early had her disorder kicked in? And then, as well, other sorts of questions, like: Why had my last three books sold so few copies? Why was I so conspicuously absent from *The New Yorker's* 'twenty best young fiction writers in America' issue last year? What was that all about? I mean, really, was I just a 'nichey' writer, as mediocre a writer as I was a cellist? And, more to the point, my last protagonist had been impotent and this one was celibate: why didn't my characters *ever have sex?*. . . But seriously, I took to wondering, how could I make this book more interesting, more . . . you know . . . more *commercial?*" He gazed out at the audience for two beats, longingly, searchingly, before picking up his bow once again and announcing, "The Allemande."

When that movement ended, Salzman declared, "Now comes the Courante, which is confident, pleased with itself, reckless even, but you get the sense that it's headed for danger, like those bubbly teenagers in all those horror movies. Because the thing is, then I had an idea: What if my nun falls in love with her neurologist? Let's say he's one of those cold doctors who don't relate well to patients. Maybe he's mourning the loss of the identical twin brother with whom he'd shared such a close identity; she is mourning the imminent loss of her sense of the presence of God. They have something in common. Sparks fly. This attraction develops and they have to decide what to do. In the end, they decide to go their separate ways, but both are changed for the better by the experience.

"What a great idea! It'll be like a cross between the movie *Witness* and the movie *Awakenings,* my people will get in touch with

Robin Williams's people, we'll package it all with Winona Ryder as the nun, I'll make so much money that I'll have medical benefits, a pension plan, an investment portfolio. I'll throw a party for the twenty best young writers in America, and it'll be like the prom scene in *Carrie!*" He was beside himself. He marshaled his bow once again: "The Courante."

Setting aside his bow at the end of that movement, which he had indeed raced through with almost reckless gusto, Salzman said gravely, "And now comes the slow movement, the Sarabande, the center of emotional gravity of the entire piece. If I had to give it a title, I'd call it 'Facing the Consequences of Hubris.' But still in C major, and C major is an optimistic key, so it's not about complete defeat, at least not yet." He took a deep breath. "I spent the next five years writing my surefire best-seller. Five years, and it was the most terrible experience of my life. I could not get my characters to act like real people. I couldn't get them to talk like real people. Hell, I couldn't even get them through doors: 'Her hand reached toward the handle of the door.' . . . 'Her hand extended toward the oaken knob of her' . . . No no. Jeesh. By the third year, my concentration was so shot that any sound distracted me and just drove me crazy, so I took to wearing a huge towel wrapped around my head and stereo earphones on top of the towel, and that worked except that I have two cats, and they liked to sit on my lap when I worked, which distracted me. And so I made a tinfoil skirt, because cats don't like tinfoil. I wore that outfit every day, until one day I saw the gas-meter reader hiding behind a tree outside, staring in at me, and that distracted me even more. So I finally moved to the one place where I felt so trapped that the only way I could get out was through writing, and that was the passenger seat of my car, out in the driveway, in which I proceeded to pretty much ensconce myself for a whole year. Now, I drive an old station wagon with a moon roof, and one of the cats was still so angry

about the tinfoil skirt—and now, on top of that, the move outside—that every day she would walk out, clamber up the hood
and up the windshield, and plant herself squat squarely in the
middle of the moon roof. And I tell you that the view from where I
sat was the perfect metaphor for what I was going through: writing
that novel, I was just staring up a cat's ass.

"Anyway, finally I finished, and all I felt was exhaustion, there
was no joy. But I thought that maybe others, reading my manuscript and not knowing what had happened, would say, 'It's beautiful, it was worth it.' So I sent it out, and the response came back,
well, mixed. My friends said they liked it, but they more or less
knew that was a requirement of the job. My editor back in New
York sent me thirty pages of notes, and they were severe criti-
cisms. I remember one sentence in particular: 'Mark, we need to
talk about main characters.' My agent said, 'I think this belonged
in the oven a little longer.' People looked at me with *pity.*

"I was like the literary equivalent of a beached whale. I couldn't
even look at a sentence without my eyes crossing. I thought about
abandoning the project. But what was I going to do if I just
scuttled it? Who was to say that I wouldn't just hit the same wall
with my next effort? And what if it was *that* close to working and
I just needed to push myself a little further? Hell, the Unabomber
had published more than I had over the past five years. At least he
was getting something out there. I decided I had to go on somehow, and all I could think of was throwing it all out and starting
from scratch." Salzman seemed to tremble palpably at the memory of the experience as he reached once more for his bow: "The
Sarabande."

The music was indeed lugubrious, almost harrowing. "So," he
resumed, when it was over. "On to the fifth movement, the Bourrée, which is in effect two short pieces, the first in C major, the
second a dark shift into C minor, and then the first played all over

again, C major, but transformed by the experience of having passed through the other.

"The problem was obvious: the love story never belonged there. I had to return to my first impulse and focus entirely on the nun's question: had hers been an authentic relationship with God, or was it, rather, solely with her own longing to be holy? And the next year was a good year: no tinfoil skirt, no car. And, when it was done, I felt vindicated. I had passed my own test; I myself had stuck it out; I was an artist after all. I completed a manuscript, and last summer, when I performed a first version of this talk at a writers' conference in Sun Valley, I was able to report that I'd learned what writing's all about. The book was done, and it was good. Meanwhile, I'd sent the manuscript off to my editor, and a few weeks later I called her up and I asked her, all expectant, how she liked it, and she said, 'I missed the doctor.' But then I reread the book myself, and I fell completely apart: because the thing was, it did suck. I had written a bad book. And I was destroyed.

"Anyway, that October I'd been scheduled to spend five weeks at one of those New England artists' retreats where you get your own cabin and everything is geared toward fertile solitude—you know, you don't even report for lunch, they tiptoe up and leave a picnic basket on your porch so you don't have a second of distraction. I'd been imagining that, finished with my nun book, I'd be starting a new project: I had no idea what I was going to do. But now I was afraid I'd become like Jack Nicholson in *The Shining*. There'd be all those happy artists prancing through the forests with their picnic baskets, and they were all going to have to die, one by one.

"But my wife, my wise, wise wife—and can you imagine what I'd been putting her through all those years?—she told me that a change of scenery would be good. And so I went, though without any particular intention of writing: that book had hurt me enough. I just wanted to exist as if in a kind of Zen retreat.

"And you know what? It was like waking from a bad dream. All of a sudden, everything was like a gift: the fall colors, the sounds, the little homemade cookies in the picnic baskets. But mainly the removal of all the reminders of art as a profession, as a way of making money or gaining a reputation and the like. Rather, here I was in a community of people who seemed dedicated to art almost like a sacred pursuit. And the irony was not lost on me that I was now living essentially like a Carmelite nun."

He smiled, and reached for his bow. "The Bourrée." After he completed that passage, he hardly paused before declaring, "Which brings us to the last movement, the Gigue, which in effect proclaims, 'Eureka! We're done!' I had my cello with me there in the cabin, which was a perfect place to be playing Bach: those reverberant wood walls. And I took to playing it every day, and it was while playing that suddenly I had this truly astonishing insight.

"The thing is, I'm agnostic. I was raised in a nonreligious family. Before I started the book, pretty much all I knew about Christianity was what I'd learned from Linus on *A Charlie Brown Christmas*. My character had dedicated her life to living by faith, not reason. Whereas, of course, I live by reason. I'd assumed that such a character would be quite a stretch for me, but that was all right: a good writer welcomes that kind of gulf."

But it turned out that it wasn't that much of a stretch after all, he went on. The artistic wager—the commitment to devote ever-lengthening years of one's life, say, to the production of a novel; the conviction that such a commitment will make any sort of difference to anyone else—is manifestly unreasonable. "I take it on faith that art is worthwhile. I go on because I believe it's the right thing to do, not because I know it is.

"Suddenly, sitting there in my cabin, I realized that all along I'd been living my nun's life myself. And, once I saw that, the book wrote itself in five weeks, with me in a state that I can only describe as euphoric. *I* was the one the other artists wanted to kill. The words were coming to me with labels attached: 'Put me next to him.' And, when it was done, the way I felt about that book made everything that had come before worthwhile: they were no longer six years of sorry-ass bungling but, rather, now I could see them all as a purposeful journey toward . . . toward . . . well, I don't know, I suppose toward a new level of obscurity and financial crisis, but toward a new level of understanding as well.

"For me, art and music are alike in that they are about creating dissonance and then feeling compelled from within to resolve it. Bach literally could not stand leaving a dissonant harmony unresolved. In ordinary life, we face dissonances every day which we can't resolve—there's not enough time, we don't have the authority or the influence or the knowledge. But when we write or listen or read or play we relive the experience of making the journey from chaos to order, and that feeds us, reminds us, heartens us, gives us courage to face all the journeys where there is no such promise. And that's why Bach's suites are stories." Salzman smiled. "And so, to the Gigue!"

In the days after Salzman's performance at the L.A. library, I reread *The Soloist,* and I was struck by its first lines:

This morning I read an article suggesting that Saint Theresa of Avila, a sixteenth-century Spanish mystic noted for her ecstatic visions, suffered from a neurological disorder known to cause hallucinations.

It turns out that Salzman was being haunted by the idea behind *Lying Awake* long before he started it. And, more confounding, the insights that Salzman's cellist protagonist manages to struggle his way toward—the saving epiphanies that rain down like grace upon him at the novel's end—were the very sort that Salzman himself could have benefited from, if only he'd been able to recall them and to marshal them:

> On that day I began to have a different idea about why I couldn't play onstage anymore. I'd always assumed it had to do with my sense of pitch, because that was certainly what I'd noticed had changed. I couldn't hold onto the dead center of notes anymore because my pitch had become too sensitive; my fingers couldn't keep the notes pure enough. It felt like trying to split hairs with a butter knife.

But now the aging wunderkind starts to think that maybe the problem never had anything to do with his ear; that, rather, it had to do with his very ambition toward perfection.

> For all practical purposes [I] forgot that absolute intonation does not exist. As my mind focused on the impossible goal of achieving pure intonation, I became unable to feel the music.

He starts to understand that "you cannot make great music happen; you can only *prepare* yourself for it to happen." And that, in a sense, is the saving insight that finally descended like grace upon Salzman at that writer's colony—and descends in the end on the protagonist of the book he created there, although it descends on the two of them in opposite ways. The paradox is that succeeding to write is the grace that falls on Salzman, even as what he writes *about* is the seeming evaporation of that capacity in Sister John:

A group had formed at the Blessed Virgin's shrine to pay respects. Mother Emmanuel left to join them, but Sister John stayed behind to finish clearing the fountain. When she got the water flowing properly, she stepped back, took her bell out of her pocket, and rang it. The sound cheered her, then vanished into the deep blue air, which seemed to go on forever.

The key word in that passage, which concludes the book, is *seemed*. The deep-blue air *seems* to go on forever, in contrast to the blinding certainty that consumed Sister John in the midst of those fever spikes of transcendence with which the book began: She *could* see forever, and everywhere she looked she saw God's love.

It may just be that seeming is the human portion—the transcendent grace, a knowledge that is damnably difficult to attain and even more difficult to sustain. It is something that artists—and not only artists—seem to learn and forget all over again as they struggle to return to where they started. The irony here is that the moment Salzman (and his protagonist, Sister John) realized the futility and the vanity of seeking perfection was the moment that Salzman was at last able to achieve something approaching a perfect little novel.

Santa Teresa

from *Portland Magazine*

On the train to Avila, tamarisks are in bloom. Pines. Junipers. Arid shrub country pocketed with boulders. Magpies. Poppies. The *meseta* or plateau country of central Spain looks much like my home in the American southwest. Little excess. Nothing wasted.

The medieval walls surrounding the *ciudad antigua,* the old city, of Avila are the threshold to the world of Santa Teresa in the early sixteenth century. Even though the walls were built miraculously five hundred years earlier by 1,900 men in nine years after the town had been reclaimed from the Moors, it is her presence that lingers.

Hundreds of swifts circle her city; pink, white, and yellow roses flourish against the stone wall. Bouquets of wildflowers are left in her honor. Overhead three storks fly toward the bell tower of Carmen, where they nest. Did Santa Teresa know these birds, these mediators between heaven and earth? These swifts and storks must have swayed her thinking. Surely the Holy Spirit appears in more incarnations than doves.

To whom do I pray?

A Spanish woman sits in the row across from me in the Iglesia de Santa Teresa, reciting her prayers in whispers as she rotates each bead of her rosary through her fingers. Her hands are folded beneath her chin. She alternates her prayers with the reading of scriptures.

To whom do I pray?

I kneel before the statue of Santa Teresa, gilded and animated by the soft light in this small dark alcove. Her right hand is outstretched as though she were about to touch Spirit, her left hand covers her heart.

I close my eyes and listen.

After many minutes of silence, what comes into my mind is the phrase, "wet not dry."

I close my eyes tighter and concentrate more deeply, let these words simply pass through as one does with distractions in meditation. Again, the words, "wet not dry." The woman across the aisle from me is weeping. Her private utterings, *para ti,* for you, for you, are audible. I open my eyes feeling little emotion and look down at the worn tiles beneath my feet. The Spanish woman faces the saint, bows, crosses herself, and leaves.

Wondering if I should be here at all, I try once again to pray. In the stillness, the phrase returns.

All I can hear in the sanctity of this chapel is what sounds at best like a cheap antiperspirant jingle. I do not feel my heart. Filled with shame, I look up at Santa Teresa's face.

Later that afternoon, I steady myself by sitting beneath an old cottonwood tree, similar to the ones I have sat under a hundred times in the desert. I open Santa Teresa's autobiography, *The Life of Saint Teresa of Avila by Herself* and randomly turn to a page: ". . . and God converted the dryness of my soul into a great tenderness."

I turn another page: "Only once in my life do I remember asking Him for consolation and that was when I was very dry. . . . "

And another: "It is my opinion that though a soul may seem to be deriving some immediate benefit when it does anything to further itself in this prayer of union, it will in fact very quickly fall again, like buildings without foundations. . . . Remain calm in times of dryness."

Santa Teresa's book articulates "the Four Waters of Prayer." She says simply that wetness brings us "to a recollected state." A well. A spring. A fountain. To drink deeply from the Spirit and quench the aridity of the soul to retrieve, revive, and renew our relationship with God.

Where are my tears? Where is the rain? I ask myself. "I am now speaking of that rain that comes down abundantly from heaven to soak and saturate the whole garden."

The leaves of the cottonwood tree shield me from the heat as I read her *Confessions* slowly: "Who is this whom all my faculties thus obey? Who is it that in a moment sheds light amidst such great darkness, who softens a heart that seemed to be of stone and sheds the water of gentle tears where for so long it had seemed to be dry? Who gives these desires? Who gives this courage? What have I been thinking of? What am I afraid of?"

The smells of lavender and rosemary collide in the garden. Something breaks open in me. My soul is brittle, my body a desert. What might it mean to honor thirst before hunger and joy before obligation?

Un botella de agua. Necesito un botella de agua. These are the first words out of my mouth this morning as I awaken from a dream.

The Monasterio de Encarnación, a dignified granite fortress north of the wall, is not far from the *parador* where I am staying. In 1534, Santa Teresa walked through these doors when she was twenty years old. It is closed. I sit on the stone steps outside the corridor. *Hace calor.* I settle in the shade and read more of Santa Teresa's words: "All its joys came in little sips."

The mystic writes about women and the importance of discretion in speaking of one's spiritual experiences, the need to share with others of like mind for solace and safety, reflection and inspiration.

Joseph Smith believed so fully in Santa Teresa's visions that he had himself sealed to the Carmelite nun in "the everlasting covenant of marriage," not uncommon to the "spiritual wife doctrine" he initiated through the revelation and practice of polygamy. He recognized her as a spiritual soulmate, trusting that revelations from God have been and will be continuous through time, that the truth is soul-wrenching, having said himself that he shared only a hundredth of what he saw when the heavens opened up to him. Schooled in the hermetic traditions of Santa Teresa's time, he might have felt as though they were contemporaries, sympathetic to her roving states of being.

I am weak, light-headed, perhaps because of the heat, perhaps because of the intensity of Santa Teresa's story: a child who at the age of ten vowed to be a nun but at age fourteen blossomed into a vibrant young woman enraptured by the sensory pleasures of the world, gifted in poetry and literature.

She fell tumultuously in love and was so frightened by her own sexuality that she confessed to her father, who immediately sent her to the convent; there, struggling with the disciplined life set by the nuns against her own instinctive nature, she succumbed to violent seizures and bouts of hysteria that eventually left her paralyzed for years, seized by the darkest of visions. Unable to move, her pain barely tolerable, she renounced all medical treatments and relied solely on prayer, never giving up hope of being healed. At one point, when she was deep in a coma mistaken for death, the nuns dug a grave for her. And then the miraculous day arrived.

In 1540, she awoke to find her arms and legs no longer paralyzed. She had successfully passed through her journey through hell. Teresa de Avila stood up and walked. It was proclaimed a miracle, a cure that reached the masses, whereupon people from surrounding villages came to see the nun whom God had healed.

Her life from that point forward was a testament of austere devotion and simplicity, but she never gave up her pen.

Inside the *monasterio,* there are relics: a wooden log that Santa Teresa used as a pillow; a small statue of Christ "covered with wounds," which is said to have been very important to her spiritual awakening of great compassion and sorrow; a statue of Saint Joseph, who taught her how to pray. The nuns have passed down the story that this statue used to talk to Santa Teresa. When she left on her travels she would leave him on the prioress's chair. Upon her return, he would tell her everything that had gone on in her absence.

The key to her cell where she lived for twenty-seven years begs to be turned. Turn the key. Santa Teresa's hand opens the door.

Stillness.

Downstairs, there is a tiny revolving door made of oak. It was the only access the nuns had to the outside world, sending messages out with one turn and receiving them with another in silence.

I descend further into the stark parlor where San Juan de la Cruz and Santa Teresa were *suspendidos en éxtasis,* lifted in ecstasy. Once again, I sit quietly. The word *casado* comes into my mind— married, a prayer of union, a state of oneness with God and with whom we confide our bodies. The Divine Lover. In these moments of pure union, body, soul, and spirit are fused.

Ecstasy. Elevation. Suspension.

The bells of the Monasterio de la Encarnación begin ringing. In the courtyard, two young girls are singing; one is playing the guitar, the other is clapping with her eyes closed. I walk down the road to the plaza, where there is a fountain bubbling up from a stone basin, and sit down.

Teenagers play in the pool below the fountain. They flirt and splash each other, then the young men and women, soaked, hoist each other up and over the stone wall and disappear. A man interrupts their frolicking to fill two jugs tied together by a rope that he swings over his neck.

The small plaza is quiet. I walk to the fountain and wash my face and hands and arms. The water is cold and invigorating.

An old man in a black beret comes to the fountain carrying a plastic sack with two one-gallon water jugs. He is wearing blue canvas slippers.

I learn he is from one of the outlying *pueblos* in the mountains, that he makes this journey once a week to collect water for his wife from this particular fountain. His wife is especially devoted to Santa Teresa de Avila. She believes this water restores the spirit and all manner of ailments. He invites me to drink the water with him.

I watch him walk carefully over the uneven cobbles and cannot guess his age. He is a small and handsomely weathered man. He lifts his weary legs over the steps of the fountain, stoops down, and then with great deliberation begins to fill each bottle. He fills one with about an inch of water, shakes the bottle, then pours it out, filling it the second time as he sits down on the stone ledge above the spout. The old man enjoys several sips, wipes his mouth with the back of his hand, and fills it again.

Joining him from below, I cup my hands below the running water and drink.

The old man gestures to one of the two bottles he has just painstakingly filled. It rests on the ledge like a prism separating light as the sun shines through.

At first, I do not understand. Perhaps he is offering me another drink?

Gracias, pero no.

He persists.

Para mí?

He nods. He hands me one of his bottles. I hardly know what to do. The old man had walked so far for this water. What will his wife say when he returns home to the mountains with only one bottle? How to receive this gift? What can I give him in return? I hold the jug of water close and feel its refreshment even against my skin.

Gracias, señor, para tu regalo.

De nada

The old man nods and smiles and slowly shifts his weight on his right hand to ease himself up. He bends down and puts the other bottle in his bag.

After he is gone, I look back toward the fountain. "For tears gain everything; and one kind of water attracts another. . . . "

A True Daltonic Dandy

from *DoubleTake*

It was a rainy February afternoon, and I was waiting, shivering, on the platform of the Dartmouth railway station in far southwest England, more deeply disappointed than any seventeen-year-old schoolboy ever needed to be. The skies were slate gray, and although it is nearly forty years since the moment when my entire life changed utterly, and forever, I remember vividly thinking there was much more than the usual somber portent in the grayness of the clouds—for gray, in a sense, was what that entire day had really been about.

I had gone down to Dartmouth, in the county of Devon, to interview for a place as a midshipman-student in the Britannia Royal Naval College—Britain's equivalent, though an older one, of Annapolis. Much rested on this interview. All of my schoolboy life, I had just one cherished ambition—to be an officer in Her Majesty's Navy. I was destined, I supposed, to be so supreme a success that at the culmination of a distinguished career at sea I would, by the age of fifty-five (the age I am now, as it happens), be commander of an aircraft carrier, the *Ark Royal,* maybe, or the *Illustrious.* I saw myself in crisp tropical whites, my cap heavy with gold braid, my manner calm and reassuring, issuing quiet orders for the mighty vessel to turn this way and that through the crowded seaways of some faraway tropic strait. I would personify the goodness and assurance of Empire (we had one, back then); I would bring order and style to troubled, distant waters; and I would fully expect to made admiral, even a sea lord, before my day was done.

It was half an hour earlier, before I had even become aware of the cold February rain, that this reverie had come to an abrupt end. It had done so in an entirely unexpected way—with the loud thwack of a suddenly-slammed-shut spiral-bound book and an evil laugh from a cruelly amused naval doctor. I had been sent up to see him after it became clear that all my other examinations—my written papers, my psychological profile, my interview, a generally perceived soundness in wind and limb—had certified me as a near-ideal candidate. This ghoul, as I unfairly saw him for years after, was to conduct the last, perfunctory series of tests—one of which, the like of which I had never seen before, involved my looking at a number of disks, petri-sized, that were covered with a sort of *pointilliste* pattern of colored, but mostly grayish, dots.

He pointed to one of the disks and asked a single question: "What number do you see?"

For a second, I fancied it might be some diabolical trick, some psychological mumbo jumbo, a kind of numerical Rorschach test. But such suspicion prompted only a moment of hesitation before I blurted out the answer. Some of the dots were a definite lighter gray than those around them. "Forty-three," I said. "Forty-three."

His manner changed quickly. He peered at me over his half-moon spectacles, intrigued. "You're certain?" he asked. Maybe there really *was* some kind of trickery at hand. I looked once more. But no, there was no doubt. "Forty-three," I said.

And then—this being a scene that was to be played out later, again and again, in a sort of cinematic mental slo-mo, while the Devon rain sheeted down—he stood and held out his hand.

"Thank you for coming in, young man," he said. "But I don't think we need detain you any further."

I blinked, quite failing to understand. He coughed, had the decency to look a little uncomfortable. And then delivered the coup de grace.

"Her Majesty's Navy will not, I regret to say, be able to make use of what I am sure are your otherwise admirable talents. You will never stand in any official capacity on the bridge of a ship. You suffer from, or are afflicted by, the condition that is known as Daltonism. You are, I am sorry to say, and at the very least, red-green colorblind. You should have seen another number. You should have seen twenty-nine." He must have seen how crestfallen I was, for he held my hand a moment longer than was proper and added, "I am so very sorry."

Daltonism. As I trudged wretchedly back to the station that afternoon, I cursed and recursed what had once been a hallowed name. John Dalton, heroic Cumbrian polymath, the great physicist and chemist and mathematician who had come up with the ideas of the dewpoint, the aurora, and the hygrometer, and who had revived the atomic theory of matter, had become, in one terrible instant, my nemesis. And since he had become so via the word that was now typed on my rejection form in a bright eighteen-point vermilion (and which wasn't at all gray, and which I could see all too well), he had become an eponymous Nemesis, too. Not that he had ever wanted the eponym. It had been given to him, posthumously, by an excitable Frenchman. In 1794, John Dalton had written a paper, "Extraordinary Facts Relating to the Visions of Colours," in which he had suggested that because he had blue eyes, so the lens-liquids in his eyeball were tinged with blue, and he was as a result unable to see the colors of flowers exactly as others did (his brother Joseph was similarly cursed). Although his theory of cause turned out to be entirely wrong—his autopsy fifty years later showed his eyes to be filled with exactly the same colorless, vitreous humor as everyone else's—his observations were entirely correct: some people, for some reason, were to various degrees blind to the colors around them, and to them the world was a very different place.

Some years after Dalton's death, an overenthusiastic Parisian ophthalmologist named Prevost decided that it would honor the late physicist to have the well-recognized affliction named after him. And the name has since stuck, despite a long and bitter campaign among Dalton's English supporters, who still whine about it being monstrous to have their hero memorialized in the language only for the name of a kind of physical deficiency. I suppose if I had thought about it on that gray winter's day, when to me color blindness was a deeply wretched curse that had snatched an entire intended life from my grasp, I would have readily agreed: Why name so sorry and pathetic a condition after so splendid and distinguished a man? And yet, more recently, as I have considered the accumulation of evidence relating to my own condition, and just how it has affected—or left unaffected—my subsequent life, I have begun to wonder whether old John Dalton would really have minded.

Perhaps, just perhaps, color blindness is not in fact a deficiency at all, any more, say, than is left-handedness. Perhaps it is truer to say that we have become persuaded to believe that not being able to tell some shades of red from some shades of green is a sad departure from the norm—"Oh, poor fellow, it must be too awful"—when in fact those who have the gene on their X chromosome that results in this inability are actually, and in a curious way, rather privileged. Perhaps in truth we Daltonics are differently abled—only in saying so I am not using the phrase to comfort or to hide. I don't mean the humbug that is offered to cheer up someone who is confined to a wheelchair or an iron lung, for the abilities of such an unfortunate really are, by their very nature, more limited than different. But the abilities of a confirmed

Daltonic, as I have known myself to be for the better part of forty years, are truly and blessedly different. In many senses they are not limited at all, and the rather few actual shortcomings seem to trigger or to prompt an equal number of compensatory advantages.

People who are not color-blind are enormously intrigued when they meet a man who is (which is twenty times more likely than meeting a woman who is: the relentless arithmetic of the gene pool sees to that, confining most women to carrying the gene while not being affected by it). "How do you cope with traffic lights?" the curious nearly always ask first, followed by the inevitable "What color is this, then?" as they offer up some object—a tie, a sweater, the jacket of a book, the evening sky—for amused examination. But then, equally invariably—after a brief conversational diversion into pseudophilosophy and the what-really-is-color-anyway-it's-all-down-to-individual-perception set of arguments, they ask a third question. It has been my weary answering of this one, time and again, that has led me to wonder if there are in fact signal advantages to being a victim of Daltonism. For they generally ask something along the lines of: "How do you know what clothes to put on every day?" And I tell them, to their surprise, that I never have a problem at all. I tell them that I make choices from the wardrobe every morning based on my assumptions about color, not on my knowledge of it. They then reply—and not just to be polite, I know—by saying such things as "Amazing, you do pretty well," or more simply, "I just love your tie" (or "your shirt" or "your jumper"). And what they are surprised by is the bald fact that though I have a rod-and-cone-inhibited, recessive-gene-related, X-linked limitation on my absolute knowledge and understanding of color, I have some inexplicable set of compensatory skills that enable me to dress, every day, in a far more dazzling and spectrum-selective way than almost all of my friends and colleagues. And I make this boast—less trivial than it sounds—because I am indeed known for making pretty good choices yet for wearing clothes that seem to match, only just, and for choosing ties and shirts and jackets that work, still only just, and that take the range of chromatic possibilities and use them in ways that others might not dare to try. I have, in short, none of the inhibitions that afflict "normal" people, the polychromatically unimaginative: I have instead the bio of a true Daltonic dandy.

And it was this idea—that color blindness might in fact present an advantage on at least one level of my life, and not be very much of a problem—that prompted me to try to remember other things, to build a body of evidence, anecdotal and otherwise, that might prove the theory that color blindness is, as Martha Stewart might one day concede, a Good Thing. I remembered first that at Oxford, for example, where I studied geology, I became uncannily good and quick at identifying the mineral samples that were given to us as tests, cut into thin sections ready for the microscope. Others in my class would be presented with a thin section of Shap granite, say, and they would be promptly thrown by the fact that the crystals of quartz and orthoclase and plagioclase feldspars they saw in the eyepiece appeared, at least in some specimens, to be subtly and similarly colored. But I wouldn't care one whit for the colors, and I would put the crystals on the microscope table under a polarizing light and then twist them this way and that and would immediately see through their various hues without being distracted at all by their prettiness or drama, would notice the characteristic structures that lay underneath the colors, as plain as the nose on your face. Up would shoot my hand—"Please, sir, please, sir, I've identified them." I was quite obnoxious and for a raft of other reasons was never destined to be other than a rotten geologist. But I could identify minerals, big-time, and in large measure I could do so because I could see, in an instant, their texture and their structure and not have that masked by the superficial irrelevance of their surface colors.

Then again, friends would ask to take me hunting—for unlike all the rest of the people in the average shooting party, my unusual visual arrangement would allow me to see a deer hiding in the woods no matter how hard it had tried to blend in, with all its natural advantages of camouflage. The others looked at the forest and saw colors—seeing essentially nothing other than an immense collage of browns and greens and reds without end or interruption. I, on the other hand, looked into the woods and saw texture—and my eye would pan slowly over the unmistakable textures of leaves, branches, leaves, and more leaves—until, all of a sudden, there was the texture, equally unmistakable, of fur and flesh and eye and horn—in short, a deer. (I might add that I was rarely eager to stay and see a kill, though: more than once I was told to be careful walking up to the carcass because I could not see, or discern, the trickle of fresh red blood running across the browns and greens of the forest floor. I was good at finding the deer when it wanted to hide; but once it was done for and had no chance of hiding, there were parts of it I could never see.)

The Royal Air Force, I was later told, hired color-blind servicemen to act as spotters: from aircraft flying at great heights, such men could see right through the camouflage with which an enemy on the ground might try to hide artillery pieces or trenches or headquarters buildings: texture, once again, was all. A recruiting officer, amused at my lack of a military record, pointed out that had I tried in 1962 to enter the RAF instead of the navy (which clings to a somewhat humorless insistence that deck officers ought be able to tell red and green navigation lights apart), I would most certainly have been offered a job. I might not have been able to fly an RAF plane (in America, the FAA has recently made it slightly difficult for me to get a private pilot's license too), but I would have been, as he put it, made use of.

And since then, tales have collected by the scores. Color-blind people are unusually proficient at solving mazes, seeing journey-ways through them at a speed that seems to elude those "normal" people who must process spectrum-related as well as spatially re-lated information whenever they first see the puzzle. The color-blind are very good at all aspects of maps, at map reading and mapmaking, and at strange sports like orienteering that involve the rapid reading of complex pieces of cartography and the mak-ing of rapid decisions based on the readings. Color-blind people have a penchant for choosing things—wallpaper, flowers, clothes, vases—far more rapidly, far more impetuously, and yet far less capriciously than those for whom color is just an additional way of complicating an already complicated choice. That is not to say the color-blind person ignores color—but rather he will make his selection based on a range of other factors. Structure, texture, shape, feel are to him the most important. Color, being in many cases a matter confined merely to the surface, has, unlike the other aspects, little to do with the quiddity of the thing and, as a device for choosing, comes last.

So when I look back on a color-blind life, what do I see? I see, at the very least, the entirely welcome fact that I avoided the navy—a profession which, after all, as Winston Churchill once said, was based on the traditions of rum, sodomy, prayers, and the lash, and which I am now heartily glad never to have joined. I see also that I had a brief but interesting career as a geologist, as one who was peculiarly able to identify his rocks and minerals. Then again I see, rather more trivially, that I have, over the years, dressed quite well and have worn a large number of very notice-able ties—which, if nothing else, has allowed me to interview quite well and to get invited, perhaps, to one or two decent dinner tables. I look back on a writing life in which I have been reluctant, for obvious reasons, to describe the colors of things—I have shied away from obviously purple prose, if I may be allowed the pun—and have instead concentrated on the less obvious aspects. This technique, if I can so dignify it, has prompted a few very generous critics to offer praise for work they say is more incisive, or more shrewd, or more carefully observed—which is all well and good, except that I know it is writing based on a kind of observation that stems from my rod-and-cone-starved inability to look at things exactly as others do. And that, it seems to me, is the kindest feature of this shortcoming; that just as left-handers act in all ways differently, and just as the obsessively fastidious make choices that others never would, so the color-blind, compensating and covering up by turn, fix an eye on the world that is interesting in a way that is very different.

Not all the compensations have been of benefit to me, of course. I have had no invitation yet to become a spotter with the RAF. Nor (since in fact I do not hunt) have I been asked to set off for Mongolia in search of camouflage-loving big-horned sheep. But in all other respects, mine has been a life of delighted Daltonism, in which I have not once worried that I cannot see—as people endlessly point out to me each December—the bright red berries on the bright green holly bush, nor that I fail to tell apart immediately the traffic lights on streets in Beijing (where the lights are arrayed horizontally), nor that I am banned from navigating my boat at dead of night between the buoys leading into my local harbor in western Scotland. Nor does it unduly bother me that a friend I've known for years told me recently she had a head of flaming red hair. I had always supposed it to be gray. And I had liked it that way, since gray has come to be a color for which I have a real affection. I have had a fondness for it ever since that rain-drenched walk, from Britannia College to Dartmouth station, during which I had my sudden monochromatic epiphany and which turned out to be so much less melancholy and devastating an event than I had first imagined.

Clear Night

from *Shenandoah*

Clear night, thumb-top of a moon, a back-lit sky.
Moon-fingers lay down their same routine
On the side deck and the threshold, the white keys and the
     black keys.
Bird hush and bird song. A cassia flower falls.

I want to be bruised by God.
I want to be strung up in a strong light and singled out.
I want to be stretched, like music wrung from a dropped seed.
I want to be entered and picked clean.

And the wind says "What?" to me.
And the castor beans, with their little earrings of death, say
     "What?" to me.
And the stars start out on their cold slide through the dark.
And the gears notch and the engines wheel.

Biographical Notes

Lorenzo Albacete, a Roman Catholic priest, is a professor of theology at St. Joseph's Seminary in Yonkers.

Marc Barasch is the author of *Healing Dreams, The Healing Path,* and (with Caryle Hirshberg), *Remarkable Recovery.* He was previously an editor at *Psychology Today* and *Natural Health* magazines and is the former editor-in-chief of *New Age Journal* (which won a National Magazine Award under his tenure). Twice a finalist for a P.E.N. award, he also works as a film and television producer.

Wendell Berry is the author of more than thirty books of poetry, essays, and fiction, including *Entries, Another Turn of the Crank,* and *A World Lost.* He lives in Henry County, Kentucky, with his wife.

Ben Birnbaum, a native of Brooklyn, New York, is executive director of marketing communications at Boston College, editor of *Boston College Magazine,* and special assistant to the president of Boston College. His published works include essays, poems, and short fiction.

Robert Cording teaches English at Holy Cross University. He has published three collections of poems: *Life-list,* which won the Ohio State University Press/Journal award in 1987; *What Binds Us to the World* (1991); and *Heavy Grace* (1996). He has received fellowships from the National Endowment of the Arts, the Connecticut Commission of the Arts, and Bread Loaf. In 1992 he was poet-in-residence at the Frost Place in Franconia, New Hampshire. He lives in Woodstock, Connecticut, with his wife and three children.

Mark Doty is the author of three books of poems and two memoirs, *Heaven's Coast* and *Firebird.* A Guggenheim, Ingram-Merrill, and Whiting Fellow, he has also received the National Book Critics Circle Award and the PEN/Martha Albrand Prize for Nonfiction. He teaches at the University of Houston, and divides his time between Houston, Texas and Provincetown, Massachusetts. His next collection, *Source,* is forthcoming.

Brian Doyle is the editor of *Portland Magazine* at the University of Portland. He is the author of *Credo,* a collection of essays about faith, and coauthor, with his father, Jim Doyle, of *Two Voices,* a collection of their essays. His essays have appeared in *The American Scholar, The Atlantic Monthly, Orion, Commonweal,* and *Yankee,* among other publications. His essays have been reprinted in *The Best*

American Essays 1998 and *1999,* in *The Best Spiritual Writing 1999,* and in the anthologies *Thoughts of Home, Family,* and *In Brief.*

Andre Dubus III's books include *House of Sand and Fog* and *Bluesman.*

David James Duncan is the author of the novels *The River Why* and *The Brothers K.,* a collection of stories and memoir, *River Teeth,* and a new book of "freeform nonfiction," *My Story as Told by Water.* He lives with sculptor Adrian Arleo and their daughters on a Montana trout stream, where he is at work on a comedy about reincarnation and human folly called *Nijinsky Hosts Saturday Night Live.*

John Landretti is an essayist who lives with his wife and son in Roseville, Minnesota. He works as an adult education instructor. He enjoys hiking and reading, especially works that address the natural sciences, myth, and religion. In recent years, several of his essays have appeared in *Orion.*

Leah Koncelik Lebec received a Ph.D. in French literature and literary criticism from New York University. After the birth of her third child, she left teaching. When two of her children faced serious developmental challenges, she researched current theories about the etiology of developmental disorders as well as the standard intervention models proposed for such difficulties. Her experience led her to publish several books and articles on these topics. To protect her children's privacy, these works were published under a pseudonym. Today she lives in Connecticut with her husband, Alain Lebec, serves on the board of directors of several nonprofit organizations concerned with disabled or at-risk children, and is blessed to be a mother to three healthy young teens, Gabriel, Christina, and Xavier.

Bret Lott is the author of five novels, two story collections, and a memoir, *Fathers, Sons, and Brothers.* He lives in Mt. Pleasant, South Carolina, and teaches at the College of Charleston and at Vermont College.

Valerie Martin's latest book is *Salvation: Scenes from the Life of St. Francis.* She is the author of two collections of short stories and six novels, including *Italian Fever* (1999).

Alane Salierno Mason is a senior editor at W. W. Norton & Company. Her writing has appeared in *Vanity Fair, The Baltimore Sun, Context, Commonweal,* and various anthologies, and her new translation of *Conversations in Sicily* by Elio Vittorini was recently published by New Directions.

Daphne Merkin, a native New Yorker, attended Barnard College and Columbia University. Before devoting herself full-time to writing, she worked as a senior editor for Harcourt Brace Jovanovich. Her autobiographical novel, *Enchantment* (1986), won the Edward Lewis Wallant award for best new work of fiction based on a Jewish theme. In 1997, she published *Dreaming of Hitler: Passions and Provocations,* a collection of essays that includes the wide range of writing she has done for *The New Yorker, The New York Times, Film Comment,* and *Premiere.* She is currently a staff writer for *The New Yorker* and is at work on a new book, *Melancholy Baby: A Personal and Cultural History of Depression.*

Thomas Moore is the author of the best-selling *Care of the Soul, SoulMates, The Reenchantment of Everyday Life, The Soul of Sex, On the Monk Who Lives in Daily Life,* and many other books. He has also produced several audiotapes, videotapes, and the compact discs *Music for the Soul* and *The Soul of Christmas.* He lives in New England with his wife, Joan Hanley, his daughter, Siobhan, and his stepson, Abraham.

Howard Mumma was born in Springfield, Ohio, in 1909. He was educated in four universities and holds three earned degrees from Yale University and Yale Divinity School. He was ordained into the Methodist ministry in 1940 and served pastorates in Columbus and Cuyahoga Falls, Ohio. He was appointed district superintendent of the Akron District, Northeast Ohio Conference, the United Methodist Church, and chairman of the cabinet for the bishop of Ohio. Dr. Mumma served as a guest preacher at a number of churches in England, Germany, Switzerland, Denmark, and Norway. He currently lives in Tucson, Arizona.

Sheldon M. Novick is director of the Community Development Law Center and a scholar-in-residence at Vermont Law School, where he teaches American legal history. He is the author of prize-winning biographies of Justice Oliver Wendell Holmes and novelist Henry James. He lives in South Strafford, Vermont.

Pattiann Rogers is the author most recently of *Song of the World Becoming, Collected and New Poems, 1981–2001.* Her other books include *The Dream of the Marsh Wren, Writing as Reciprocal Creation,* and *A Covenant of Seasons* (with artist Joellyn Duesberry). Her poems have been awarded the Frederick Bock Prize from *Poetry* and five Pushcart Prizes. In 2000 she was awarded a residence at the Rockefeller Foundation's Study and Conference Center in Bellagio, Italy.

Floyd Skloot is the author of numerous books, including *The Evening Light, The Fiddler's Trance, The Night-Side,* and *Summer Blue.*

Joan D. Stamm is a freelance writer with an M.F.A. in writing and literature from Bennington College. During two years in Japan, she edited speeches, books, and articles on the peace potential of the *yakumo-goto,* a sacred Shinto musical instrument. Currently she lives in the Pacific Northwest, where she works with Southeast Asian and East African refugees and studies ikebana and Kadampa Buddhism.

George Weigel is a senior fellow of the Ethics and Public Policy Center, where he holds the John M. Olin Chair in Religion and American Democracy. His biography of Pope John Paul II, *Witness to Hope,* is an international best-seller published in eight languages.

Lawrence Weschler has been a staff writer at *The New Yorker* since 1981, where his work has shuttled between political tragedies and cultural comedies. His books range from *A Miracle, A Universe: Settling Accounts with Torturers* and *Calamities of Exile* to *Mr. Wilson's Cabinet of Wonders* and *A Wanderer in the Perfect City.* He is a contributing editor at *McSweeney's* and *Threepenny Review* and the new director of the New York Institute for the Humanities at New York University.

Terry Tempest Williams is the author of many books, including *Leap: A Traveler in the Garden of Earthly Delights* and *Refuge.*

Simon Winchester is the author of fourteen books, including the bestselling *The Professor and the Madman.* He has written for *The Atlantic Monthly, Harper's, Smithsonian, National Geographic,* and many other periodicals over an award-winning thirty-year newspaper career. His newest book is *The Map That Changed the World.* He lives in upstate New York and in the western isles of Scotland.

Charles Wright is the author of numerous books of poetry, which have been gathered into three major collections: *Country Music* (1982), *The World of the Ten Thousand Things* (1990), and *Negative Blue* (2000). *Black Zodiac* was awarded the 1998 Pulitzer Prize and National Book Critics Circle Award. Wright lives in Charlottesville, Virginia, and teaches at the University of Virginia.

Philip Zaleski is the editor of *The Best Spiritual Writing* series. His other books include *The Recollected Heart* (1995) and *Gifts of the Spirit* (with Paul Kaufman, 1997). He and his wife Carol Zaleski coedited *The Book of Heaven* and are now cowriting *The Language of Paradise: Prayer in Human Life and Culture.* A senior editor of *Parabola* and a lecturer in religion at Smith College, he lives in western Massachusetts with his wife and two sons.

Notable Spiritual Writing of 2000

Wendell Berry
"Life Is a Miracle," *Whole Earth,* Fall

Sandy Boucher
"Thirteen Hours," *Tricycle,* Spring

Rene Daumal
"The Great Magician," *Parabola,* May

David Duncan James
"Khawaja Khadir," *Orion,* Autumn

Sri Eknath Easwaran
"Discovering the Gita," *Yoga International,* April/May

Erik Erikson
"Erikson on His Own Identity," *DoubleTake,* Fall

Natalie Goldberg
"The Midwest Zen Summer of 1983," *Shambhala Sun,* July

Mary Gordon
"Desperately Seeking Joan," *Commonweal,* March 10

Francine du Plessix Gray
"The Work of Mourning," *The American Scholar,* Summer

Kathy Green
"Sailing in Kansas: A Berlin Memoir," *Tikkun,* March/April

Robert Hirschfield
"In the Land of the First Noble Truth," *Tricycle,* Summer

Timothy Jones
"The Uncensored Merton," *Books & Culture,* November/December

W. Paul Jones
"Beyond the Mercy of God?" *Weavings,* September/October

Johanna Kaplan
"Tales of My Great-Grandfathers," *Commentary,* July

Garrison Keillor
"He Was in the Arts, You Know," *Books & Culture,* March/April

Tracy Kidder
"The Good Doctor," *The New Yorker,* July 10

Phillip Lopate
"The Countess's Tutor," *DoubleTake,* Summer

Kobutsu Zenji Malone
"A Roshi on 'The Row,'" *Shambhala Sun,* January

Erin McGraw
"True Believer," *The Gettysburg Review,* Autumn

Rebecca Mead
"The Yoga Bums," *The New Yorker,* August 14

Seyyed Hossein Nasr
"God: The Reality to Serve, Love, and Know," *Sophia,* Winter

Richard John Neuhaus
"Father, Forgive Them," *First Things,* March

Mary Odden
"The Sound of a Meadowlark," *The Georgia Review,* Spring

Virginia Stem Owens
"The Hour of Our Death," *Image,* Spring

Scott Savage
"Identity Quest," *Utne Reader,* March/April

Philip Simmons
"Living at the Edge," *UUWorld,* September/October

John Jeremiah Sullivan
"Diaries of a Country Priest," *Oxford American,* May

Douglas Thorpe
"A Bow for One's Students," *Parabola,* August

Ptolemy Tompkins
"Recovering a Visionary Geography," *Lapis* 11

David Updike
"A Word with the Boy," *DoubleTake,* Spring

Allison Wallace
"The Honeybee's Incredible Edible Metaphor," *Orion,* Summer

Walter Wangerin Jr.
"From Paul: A Novel," *Image,* Summer

Alan Wolfe
"The Opening of the Evangelical Mind," *The Atlantic Monthly,* October

Philip Yancey
"Seeing the Invisible God," *Books & Culture,* May/June, June/July

A List of Former Contributors

Luci Shaw
Huston Smith
David Steindl-Rast
Ptolemy Tompkins
Janwillem van de Wetering
Terry Tempest Williams

THE BEST SPIRITUAL WRITING 1999

Introduction by Kathleen Norris
Virginia Hamilton Adair
Max Apple
Marvin Barrett
Wendell Berry
S. Paul Burholt
Douglas Burton-Christie
Léonie Caldecott
Tracy Cochran
Robert Cording
Annie Dillard
Brian Doyle
Andre Dubus III
Alma Roberts Giordan
Bernie Glassman
Mary Gordon
Ron Hansen
Seamus Heaney
Edward Hirsch
Pico Iyer
Tom Junod
Philip Levine
Barry Lopez
Anita Mathias
Walt McDonald
Thomas Moore
Louise Rafkin
Pattiann Rogers
Jonathan Rosen
David Rothenberg
Luci Shaw

Eliezer Shore
Louis Simpson
Jack Stewart
Barbara Brown Taylor
Ptolemy Tompkins
Janwillem van de Wetering
Michael Ventura
Paul Willis
Larry Woiwode

THE BEST SPIRITUAL WRITING 2000

Introduction by Thomas Moore
Christopher Bamford
Lionel Basney
Wendell Berry
Scott Cairns
Jimmy Carter & Miller Williams
David Chadwick
Robert Cording
Alfred Corn
Harvey Cox
Annie Dillard
Gretel Ehrlich
Frank X. Gaspar
William H. Gass
Natalie Goldberg
Mary Gordon
Deborah Gorlin
Jeanine Hathaway
Linda Hogan
Ann Hood
Andrew Hudgins
Pico Iyer
Philip Levine
Jacques Lusseyran
Anita Mathias
William Maxwell
Bill McKibben
Robert Morgan

Richard John Neuhaus
John Price
Robert Reese
David Rensberger
Pattiann Rogers
Marjorie Sandor
Jim Schley
Roger Shattuck
Kimberly Snow
Anne Stevenson
John Updike
James Van Tholen
Loretta Watts

Reader's Directory

For more information about or subscriptions to the periodicals represented in *The Best Spiritual Writing 2001,* please contact:

The Atlantic Monthly
77 N. Washington Street, Suite 5
Boston, MA 02114–1908

Christian Century
104 S. Michigan Avenue, Suite 700
Chicago, IL 60603-5901

DoubleTake
55 Davis Square
Somerville, MA 02144

First Things
The Institute on Religion and Public Life
156 Fifth Avenue, Suite 400
New York, NY 10010

Fourth Genre
Michigan State University Press
1405 S. Harrison Road
25 Manly Miles Building
East Lansing, MI 48823

The Gettysburg Review
Gettysburg College
Gettysburg, PA 17325-1491

The Hudson Review
684 Park Avenue
New York, NY 10012

Image
Center for Religious Humanism
3307 Third Avenue West
Seattle, WA 98119

The New York Times Magazine
229 West 43rd Street
New York, NY 10036

The New Yorker
20 West 43rd Street
New York, NY 10036

Notre Dame Magazine
583 Grace Hall
Notre Dame, IN 46556-5612

Orion
Orion Society
195 Main Street
Great Barrington, MA 01230

Parabola
656 Broadway
New York, NY 10012

The Paris Review
541 E. 72nd Street
New York, NY 10021

Portland Magazine
Waldschmidt Hall
University of Portland
5000 N. Willamette Boulevard
Portland, OR 97203–5798

Shenandoah
Washington and Lee University
Troubadour Theater, Second Floor, Box W
Lexington, VA 24450-0303

Tricycle
92 Vandam Street
New York, NY 10013

Utne Reader
LENS Publishing Co., Inc.
1624 Harmon Place
Minneapolis, MN 55403

Credits